ROUTLEDGE LIBRARY EDITIONS:
THE ECONOMICS AND BUSINESS OF TECHNOLOGY

Volume 40

# MANAGEMENT INFORMATION SYSTEMS

# MANAGEMENT INFORMATION SYSTEMS

## The Technology Challenge

Edited by
NIGEL F. PIERCY

Routledge
Taylor & Francis Group
LONDON AND NEW YORK

First published in 1987 by Croom Helm

This edition first published in 2018
by Routledge
4 Park Square, Milton Park, Abingdon, Oxon OX14 4RN
605 Third Avenue, New York, NY 10017

*Routledge is an imprint of the Taylor & Francis Group, an informa business*



*British Library Cataloguing in Publication Data*
A catalogue record for this book is available from the British Library

ISBN: 978-1-138-50336-6 (Set)
ISBN: 978-1-351-06690-7 (Set) (ebk)
ISBN: 978-0-8153-5401-7 (Volume 40) (hbk)
ISBN: 978-1-351-13187-2 (Volume 40) (ebk)

**Publisher's Note**
The publisher has gone to great lengths to ensure the quality of this reprint but points out that some imperfections in the original copies may be apparent.

**Disclaimer**
The publisher has made every effort to trace copyright holders and would welcome correspondence from those they have been unable to trace.

# MANAGEMENT INFORMATION SYSTEMS: THE TECHNOLOGY CHALLENGE

Edited by
NIGEL PIERCY

CROOM HELM
London & Sydney
NICHOLS PUBLISHING COMPANY
New York

Croom Helm Ltd, Provident House, Burrell Row,
Beckenham, Kent, BR3 1AT
Croom Helm Australia Pty Ltd, Suite 4, 6th Floor,
64-76 Kippax Street, Surry Hills, NSW 2010, Australia

British Library Cataloguing in Publication Data
Management information systems: the
technology challenge.
1. Management information systems
I. Piercy, Nigel
658.4'038 T58.6

ISBN 0-7099-4030-0

First published in the United States of America by
Nichols Publishing Company, Post Office Box 96
New York, NY 10024

**Library of Congress Cataloging-in-Publication Data**

Management information systems.

Includes index.
1. Management information systems. I. Piercy,
Nigel.
T58.6.M352 1986 658.4'038 86-18112
ISBN 0-89397-260-6

Printed and bound in Great Britain

# CONTENTS

## LIST OF FIGURES

# LIST OF TABLES

## PREFACE

This volume attacks what is perhaps one of the most fundamental and pervasive aspects of new information technology - the basic change in the groundrules concerning the flows of information within and between organisations. This implies far more than simply making existing information systems more efficient and we are faced with a massive change in the operation, and even existence, of organisations in the sense that we know them.

This present exercise grew out of the first volume in the UWIST/Croom Helm Series on Management and New Information Technology, which was entitled The Management Implications of New Information Technology (editor Nigel Piercy). In that first volume we took a general view of the impact of new information technology on production systems, on employment and labour relations, and on the design, control and structure of organisations, leading to the identification of a major gap in strategic thinking and the practical need in industry to give urgent attention to the formulation of strategies to cope with and exploit new technology.

The concept underpinning this present collection of contributions has its source in that last part of the first volume.

The approach in constructing this book was to ask a group of people drawn internationally, from industry as well as the universities, to turn their attention to the impact of new information technology on the management information system and to track the implications for management. It was quite explicit in this that we would have to expect and accept conflicts in opinion between the contributors. Inevitably this has produced a relatively disparate group of papers reflecting different viewpoints and points of focus, and indeed also reflecting the ambiguity inherent in the terms of reference provided.

Nonetheless, the disparate nature of the collection is presented as a source of richness rather than a weakness. The technological revolution with which we are concerned continues to unfold and it is unlikely that any of the contributors - and certainly not the editor - would claim to have the 'right' answers for management.

Our audience is the postgraduate student of management, but above all the practitioner in the field of management information systems, and it is our hope that we have provided a relatively rich source of ideas and proposals.

Gratitude is owed to the contributors to this volume and the anonymous secretaries, research assistants, and so on, who made those contributions possible. More specifically thanks are owed to Miss Carol Andrewartha for producing the manuscript and to Miss Tracey Dinnick, both at UWIST, for producing the artwork, and to Deborah Martell and Nicholas Alexander, my Research Assistants, for producing the index.

Nigel Piercy
UWIST, October 1986

# 1. Technology and Information

by Nigel Piercy

It is relatively clear that at the present time there are widely diverging opinions on the real impact of new information technology (NIT) on and in business organisations. At the one extreme there are those who focus on the technical potential of NIT in its many operational applications in the factory and in administrative systems. At the other extreme there are those of us (e.g. Burges and Piercy, 1985; Piercy and Burges, 1986) who have expressed reservations about the extent to which such a technical potential can sensibly be realised in the practical content of business organisations - and indeed have been pilloried by technological enthusiasts for such 'Luddism'. In spite of the protests, however, in this writer's view there remains an enormous gulf between the technological potential offered by engineers and systems specialists, and the technological reality experienced and coped with by managers. There seems considerable value in focusing on the nature of that gulf.

This volume, in common with the others in the Series, is really concerned with three significant managerial issues. The first is, indeed, to make explicit the frequently obscured potential of NIT in business. While many works have emphasised the overt technical applications in automating factory operations, in replacing and supplementing human efforts in the office, and in up-grading business information systems, rather less attention has been given to the impact on inter-organisational relationships, competitive structures, the fundamental nature of organisations and the employment they offer, and other pervasive issues of strategic importance. While these latter issues are pervasive, they are also frequently covert - at least initially, and their significance is underestimated in practice.

The second goal is thus to make explicit the NIT issues facing strategic management. The urgency of this function is illustrated by recent evidence that firms, in the UK at least, are largely ignoring any effect of NIT other than the operational. For example, a 1984 PA Technology study found that 45% of companies reported that new technology had made little or no impact on their activities in the previous five years and 39% had no defined strategy for innovation or the application of NIT in the following five years (Pattie, 1986).

The third goal of these works is also focused on the gulf between technological potentials and realities and is concerned with the constraints which exist in the implementation of NIT, and the managerial policies which are demanded to cope with them.

In the context of this general brief, this present book has attempted to analyse one of the more obvious and immediate impacts of NIT - that on the management information system (MIS).

An initial problem in this task was that there is no universally accepted understanding of what is meant by the MIS. Approaches taken here represent views of the MIS varying from the MIS as all forms of information, to the MIS as specific, normally financial, control systems for top management. No attempt is made here to resolve this dilemma, and each of the chapters must be taken in the context of its author's concept of the MIS.

While the contributions to the book are diverse in their approaches to considering the impact of NIT on MIS, they have been grouped into three broad categories: those concerned with the social and organisational impact of NIT; those focusing on the potential impact of NIT in different business contexts; those providing insights into the NIT impact in practice; and finally those where the concern is not with the operational impacts of NIT, but the broader strategic implications of the NIT/MIS interface.

## The Social and Organisational Impact of New Technology

In this area the point of departure was the more general study of the managerial and organisational implications of new information technology (Piercy, 1984), leading to four very different approaches.

First, Frank Land provides the viewpoint of the systems analyst or manager, which starts with the organisation's information requirements and the complex issue of how information is used by managers together with the 'social policy' aspects of NIT in the MIS, to identify essential preconditions for the implementation of technology-based information systems and the need to consider not merely systems design but social design and user participation in design processes. With this complex foundation established, Land turns to consider the tools and techniques which are available to support his approach to systems design.

A somewhat different perspective is adopted by Roger Mansfield in his chapter. Rather than the problems of design and implementation of NIT in MIS, Mansfield is concerned with the impact of the NIT-driven MIS on the general management task, and particularly the changing nature of the information available for decision making and control. Mansfield's conclusion is that the major impact of the NIT innovation is to revolutionise the tasks of strategic management and to more this key organisational role steadily towards the automation of many policy decisions. This question is taken further in the concluding part of the book.

Finally in this section, Annette Davies focuses on the behavioural and organisational reactions to systems change, and the link between systems design and work design leading to support for the notion of participative systems design introduced earlier by Land. She concludes that the design and implementation of sophisticated information systems is not simply a technological problem, but is an organisational and political issue.

The major theme emerging from this section is that although the impact of NIT may be approached from different disciplines and viewpoints, there is convergence on the critical human issue as the key to implementing NIT in an effective way. This is demonstrated in the context of technical systems design, the definition of the top management function, and in work design lower in the organisation.

## NIT Applications in Theory

Attention turns next to the application of NIT to the MIS in a number of specialised areas: in small business, in management accounting and in marketing.

First, Roger Groves examines the adoption of new technology-based budgetary systems in small companies, outlining the diffusion of NIT in this sector and the potential applications, but stressing the behavioural and organisational changes implicit in this diffusion, and the particular importance of change agents. He concludes that the critical underlying success factor is improved understanding of the changes in systems and for personnel which are required by NIT.

Secondly in this part of the book, Christopher Cowton reviews the impact of NIT on management accounting, emphasising the opportunities offered, in terms of the application of techniques, and then focusing on the implied change in the organisational relationship between management accountants and other information specialists. He identifies a particular threat to the traditional management accounting role from the manager himself acting as information processor, using NIT, suggesting the need for a more responsive advisory role to be adopted by the management accountant.

The remaining chapters in this section both deal with the impact of NIT on marketing. Deborah Martell reviews what is known about the impact of NIT on internal and external information functions in marketing. Barrett, on the other hand, is concerned with the potential for upgrading the organisation's marketing accounting system. Although such advances are not necessarily based in the concept of NIT, they are unlikely to be implemented in the absence of technological capacity. For this reason Barrett's chapter is included as a demonstration of one direction in which the technology may allow the marketing information system to develop. Specifically, Barrett is concerned with the evaluation of marketing activities in financial terms, and the design of systems which match the organisation's environment, its marketing strategy, and the organisation structure of the marketing department.

## NIT Applications in Practice

This part of the book turns to the somewhat limited available evidence about the implementation of NIT in the business context.

First, Stephen Hill discusses the results of a survey of engineering firms, focusing on the underlying reasons for the lack of acceptance of advanced information systems in business.

Secondly, Richard Ingram provides a detailed account of the development of NIT-based MIS in the UK motor industry, drawing on his extensive practical experience in that field. His account concerns itself firstly with MIS in production control in the context of computer integrated manufacturing at Jaguar Cars, and then with MIS and office automation at Austin-Rover.

Ingram's chapter is rooted in practical experience rather than academic research and offers many novel and compelling insights into the practical use of NIT.

Indeed, perhaps the major theme of this section of the book is to offer some illumination of the void which remains between the potential of NIT and experience of the reality of its implementation. This provides a salutary note of caution for these of us who are optimistic about the progress of the technology, as well as suggesting a number of important areas which are likely to be susceptible to empirical research.

## The Strategic Implications of NIT

Finally we turn to an examination of the strategic implications of NIT in the MIS context, from three leading international authorities in the field - William R. King of the University of Pittsburgh, William E. Halal of the George Washington University, and Michael Earl of Templeton College, Oxford.

The present writer has argued (Piercy 1984, 1985) that it is the strategic implications of NIT which are the most underrated and ignored by managers, and the three chapters in this part of the book provide both illumination and guidance in just this area.

First, William King focuses on the issue of the development of strategic business advantage from NIT. He argues and illustrates the case that the role of information in business has dramatically changed, leading to the notion of information-based comparative advantage in developing business strategy. He then provides us with a conceptual framework for operationalising this concept of information as a strategic resource.

This chapter poses a challenge to managers and analysts to identify and exploit the changing role of information in their businesses, in an original and insightful way.

Secondly, William Halal turns to the question of organisational networks as overturning many of the prevailing assumptions regarding organisational structure and institutional relationships. He illustrates the intellectual disruption provided by NIT and the complexity created, which leads, he suggests, to 'confederations of entrepreneurs' in a multi-dimensional matrix and eventually a decentralised network rather than a traditional hierarchical form. His optimism about this type of change is encapsulated in his description of an 'entrepreneurial boom' and the role of the 'intrapreneur' in the organisation. Halal provides a perspective too on interorganisational networks and the 'global suprasystem' leading to the 'flowering of enterprise'.

Halal's contribution is both challenging and original and serves to lead us away from the concept of NIT as simply computerising the MIS towards the impact on the nature of organisation and their relationships and the roles that people play in them.

With this foundation describing the impact of NIT on business strategy and the strategic business unit, we turn finally to Michael Earl's chapter to focus our attention on the critical process of actually formulating information technology strategies.

Earl seeks to provide us with a framework which captures awareness, opportunity and positioning with regard to NIT, as a vehicle for the identification of NIT strategies, through multiple methodologies.

It is to be hoped that this chapter closes the loop in a particularly exciting way - we started with the proposition that there was a gap in strategic thinking relating to NIT, we then delineated why that gap was of growing importance, and finally we demonstrated the strategic nature of that gap. Earl's contribution provides us with practical and intellectual guidance in what to do about this gap.

In total, with the reservations expressed earlier, this book is presented as a novel approach to one of the most critical issues facing management in the remaining years of this century.

## REFERENCES

Burges, S. and Piercy, N. (1985) 'Question of Hit or a Myth', Times Higher Education Supplement, 20 September, 16

Pattie, G. (1986) 'Can-Do V. the Timid Lions', Sunday Times, 2 March, 18

Piercy, N. (1984) The Management Implications of New Information Technology, Croom Helm/Nichols, Beckenham

Piercy, N. (1985) 'How to Manage IT', Management Today, March, 72-5

Piercy, N. and Burges, S. (1986) 'Managers and Word Processors', Director, forthcoming

# I THE SOCIAL AND ORGANISATIONAL IMPACT OF NEW TECHNOLOGY

# 2. Social Aspects of Information Systems

by Frank Land

## INTRODUCTION

All organisations need information systems in order to function effectively. Every information system, whether for a one-man business, a parish council, a multinational corporation or the government offices of a large industrial nation, is made up of a number of components. Some of the components are artefacts - pencils and paper, word processors, computers and communication networks, operating systems and procedure manuals, but all information systems require people to construct, to work and to operate the artefacts. Even a completely automated information system still requires people, and in practice, information systems rely on people using and interacting with the artefacts.

Information systems vary enormously in the extent to which they rely on formal standardised and structured information-handling techniques as against informal, and often ad hoc and subjective techniques. All information systems utilise some elements of both. A model of an information system (Figure 2.1) illustrates the relationship between the different components of an information system and shows the formal and informal aspects. The information system exists in a real world which consists of objects (some concrete, such as machines, stock and buildings; some abstract, such as budgets, accounts and sales forecasts). The system uses people (customers, suppliers, managers, clerks, etc.), rules (embodied in legislation, in established procedures, in rule books and codes of practice), norms (often deeply engrained ways of doing things and modes of thinking and practice) and commands (such as standing orders, call-off lists, etc.).

A person - the information user in Figure 2.1 - has to perform some task in relation to the real world. He may be a manager making a decision or a clerk carrying out a task. Whichever he is, to carry out his task he needs information about the real world, which can often be obtained directly. The manager could, for example, walk into a steel store to

**Figure 2.1: Information Systems Model**

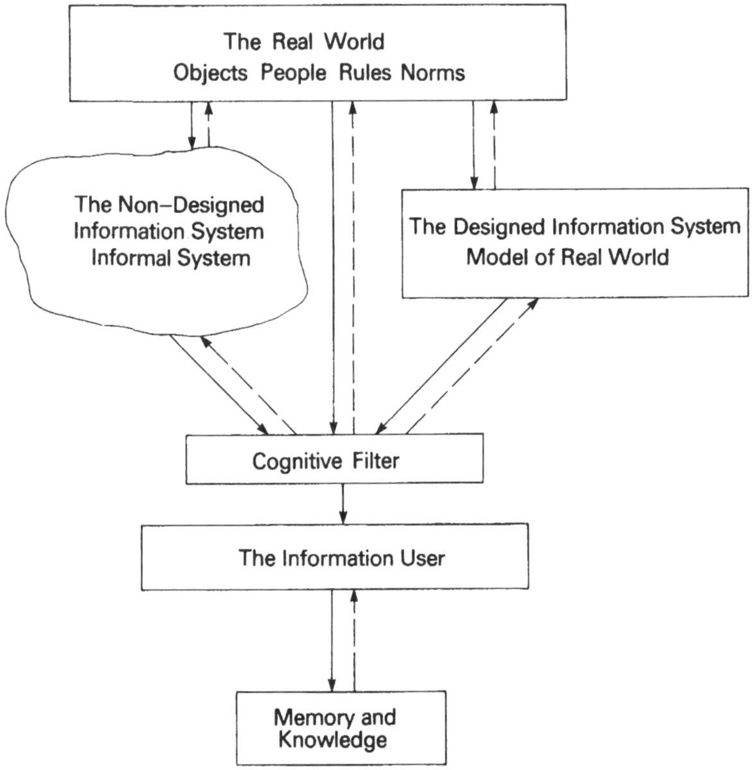

check for himself how much steel bar was left in stock, or he could use the formal, designed information system. This might consist of a stock ledger card on which a stock control clerk had entered receipts and issues of steel bars, or alternatively, it might consist of a computer stock control system, which the manager could interrogate to discover the level of stock by using a terminal. But the manager could also call up his stock room supervisor and ask him how much steel bar was in stock, thus using an informal, undesigned information system.

Most information systems have three principal information sources: the real world which may be inspected or observed; the designed information system which may be programmed to draw attention to some real world event or problem, or whose database or files may be interrogated; and the informal (undesigned) system which is often used to provide qualitative or evaluative information about the real world, and which substitutes for the designed system if, for any reason, its intended users cease to place their trust in its veracity.

## TYPES OF INFORMATION

A useful starting-point for the analysis of our model of an information system is to classify information according to basic type: descriptive, probabilistic and qualitative (Land and Kennedy-McGregor, 1981).

### Descriptive Information

In order to operate an enterprise it is necessary to make use of a vast amount of data which describe the real world - data which attempt to provide a picture or map of the real world which is of sufficient accuracy and resolution to enable a planner or decision-maker to take actions even if he is at some distance from the 'world' in question. It is possible to distinguish three different sorts of descriptive information.

(a) Description of the rules that govern or constrain the affairs of the real world. These are of two kinds: the first consists of unchanging inviolate rules such as the laws of nature, as well as some of the practices which become so ingrained in a culture it is practically impossible to change them. A good example is the rule which forbids devout Muslims from eating pork, or that which insists an accountant posts a journal entry as a debit to one account and a credit to another.

The second consists of rules which are subject to change or interpretation: many legislative rules fall into this category. The common denominator of this class of descriptive information is that it is very often highly formalised and therefore lends itself to application by computer.

The embodiment of the rules which govern or constrain action takes the form of the commands and instructions which cause action to be taken. These can be a part of the designed system. A good example is the rule-book of an industrial enterprise which sets out in considerable detail, in the form of instructions, the operating procedures to be followed by the workforce. Standing orders used in banking systems are another example: these are instructions for the bank to make specific payments, at a specified time, to a named payee. In many administrative systems, the legal statutes which the system exists to apply - for example, the payment of social security benefits - are translated into instructions by means of a code of practice set out in a manual. A computer program too, is the embodiment of a set of rules in the form of instructions, and provides a part of the designed system. Expert systems are computer systems which replicate the knowledge of a specialist (for example, a medical specialist) in the form of rules which enable the computer system to make judgements such as medical diagnosis (Bramer, 1981; Feigenbaum and McCorduck, 1983). Commands also exist, however, in the undesigned informal system. They arise out of situations, often unplanned or unforeseen, where immediate decisions are needed.

Instructions which are expressed in a form which suggests there is no room for discretion may nevertheless be interpreted in the real world in entirely different ways. The rule-book referred to above is a good example. In practice, operating procedures are widely divergent from those laid down in the rule-book. Indeed, 'working to rule' is a form of industrial action designed to cripple the effective working of the enterprise.

(b) Description of the state of the real world. Much of the information held in files and data bases records the apparent state of the real world at some point in time. A stock record shows the amount of stock held in a material store at the time the stock record was last up-dated. In a real-time system the stock shown at time t should correspond to the actual stock in the store at time t. While descriptions can refer to physical objects in the real world, as in the stock example, they can also refer to abstractions such as 'the budget', or concepts such as 'net present value'.

In practice, the picture of the real world provided by the information system, by means of files and data bases, may not correspond to the actual situation in the real world because the system may be incapable of providing a totally accurate view of the real world. There may be many reasons for this. In general, a formal system is based on the recognition of 'legitimate' transactions, but many systems are subject to interferences from unrecognised or non-legitimate sources. For example, an inventory control system may be subject to petty pilfering of which the formal system has no knowledge; informal practices may exist which go unreported, such as the storekeeper's habit, in one enterprise, of issuing 35-inch stockings as 36-inch when he ran out of stock of the latter. Information users have to be aware of the extent to which the description of the real world is valid. One of the most common problems with computer-based information systems is that if the picture of the real world provided by the computer ceases to be trusted, those expected to use it develop alternative sources of information (informal, unofficial systems), or attempt to sample the real world itself (take a look at the bin to see how much is available).

(c) Description of changes in the state of the real world. Most of the changes referred to are the result of explicit events or activities which are reported by means of messages or transactions: something happened and it is recorded. In other situations the changes to the state of the real world may be implicit: a message or transaction may be generated only if an expected event does not occur.

All three types of descriptive information form a major part of formal information systems. Descriptive data are often most useful if they are formalised, standardised and structured. Frequently the structure is deeply embedded in fundamental concepts relating to a particular information system. To an accountant, the basic structure of the profit and loss account is axiomatic and not subject to question. But even at a more trivial level, descriptive information about the real world is best presented in a standardised structured form, and the more widely and frequently such information is used the more important it is that it should fall into an understood and accepted pattern. This is illustrated by the outcry whenever it is proposed, for example, to change the design of a telephone directory.

## Probabilistic Information

Descriptive information attempts to replace the real world of objects, of rules, and of events by a set of symbols which map the real world on a one-to-one basis. This is not always possible. Sometimes the real world has to be inferred from a description of only a sample of that real world, or by making guesses based on assumptions about the statistical behaviour of the real world. Information systems include large amounts of information which is inferred on the basis of assumptions (sometimes untested) of statistical distributions and behaviour. There are several different kinds of probabilistic information.

(a) Predictive information. This attempts, on the basis of statistical regularities and knowledge (or guesses) about the future, to provide a model of some aspect of the real world in the future. All planning activities rely on predictive information. To the extent that real world activity behaves in a regular way, it is possible to predict future activity by the use of statistical forecasting techniques. In that sense, predictive information becomes part of the formal information system. The calculation of insurance risks for life assurance can be defined precisely by the use of mortality tables. At least in the long run, the insurance company can depend on getting that side of its premium calculation right. But the other side of the equation - the money earned by the insurance company on premium income invested in the stock market - is subject to much less regularity and is affected by a large range of influences, some of which are very difficult to define. As a result, those who have to decide how to invest the premium income need the support of a formal information system which helps to assess the effect of alternative investment policies on the basis of statistical and economic assumptions. Beyond the formal system they have to use their judgement, which may be influenced by a variety of pieces of information which may be received from a number of quite informal sources. A recent study (Lawrence et al, 1984) compared the reliability of statistical forecasts with forecasts, of the same situations, carried out by human experts. The study showed that over the test period the human forecasts proved to be somewhat more reliable than the forecasts produced with a number of different statistical techniques.

(b) Information which attempts to describe the real world by means of inferences from a limited set of observations or measurements of the real world. This type of information is used, for example, when important marketing decisions are taken on the basis of share of the market statistics obtained by interviewing a sample of consumers, and when a civil engineering contractor bases assumptions about the quality of steel beams in the construction of a bridge on a quality check on a sample of the beams received from each supplier.

(c) Information derived from a model of the real world. Many real world situations are so complex that it is not possible to observe and measure all the relevant variables, or even to know which of the many variables are relevant. In such cases it may be possible to construct a model of the real world situation and to simulate the behaviour of the real world. For example, it is possible to make a mathematical model of a machine shop and to use the model to simulate the effect on production of various shop loading strategies. Because the model is usually based on simplifying assumptions about the real world, it can provide only an approximate guide to the real world behaviour. Models make use of statistical techniques based on assumptions about distributions, and may also use data derived from samples. Models can be explicit mathematical models or they may exist in the form of implicit concepts in the minds of planners or decision-makers. For example, systems designers, in designing an information system, base their design on their own perception (model) of human behaviour rather than on observed behaviour. Informal implied models play a major part in all human activities. These models are often dependent not on facts, but on assumptions derived from the designer's own preconceptions and personality.

## Qualitative Information

Both descriptive and probabilistic information represent the objective real world as it is or as it might be expected to be. But those who have to plan future action or take decisions need to know not only the 'facts' about the real world, but also explanations of what gave rise to the facts, and a variety of qualitative elements relating to the real world. The descriptive part of the information system can tell a civil engineering contractor, by means of a standard variance report, that there has been excessive use of steel in one project. To take action to prevent further excessive use of steel, the contractor needs an explanation of the variance - to an extent, this can be provided by the formal information system, but for this to be possible a range of possible explanations have to be foreseen and a form devised which enables the responsible official to encode the explanation. However, such systems cannot normally provide the richness of explanation which a less formal system could invoke. The tone of voice and the phrases in a spoken reply can give the questioner a much better insight into the real cause of the variance than any number of formal written reports. Hence, a great deal of information of this type is provided by a blend of formal reports and informal discourse. Again we can distinguish between a number of different types of information in this category.

(a) <u>Explanatory information</u>. Information explaining why a real world situation arose, of which the material variance described above is an example.

(b) <u>Qualifying and qualitative information</u> used to moderate descriptive information from the formal system. Such information may be derived from many sources, some of them outside the official designed information systems. If for example, the designed system reports that a salesman's performance is down on budget, the formal explanation may suggest unexpected difficulties in contacting customers. The informal system via a chance remark may suggest that the salesman in question has a drinking problem. Most effective systems work because they succeed in permitting the formal and the informal components to co-exist. Many less effective systems fail because the designers of the systems have succeeded in stripping away the informal elements of the information.

(c) Patterns and norms. These form part of the memory of how things should be done and are often used in a completely subjective and informal way to evaluate and judge. Such information is rarely made explicit but exists in the mind of the decision maker or planner. Indeed, the use of norms may take the form of action almost reflex in their application. Some of the norms are associated with values: A civil engineering contractor operating in the United Kingdom would expect to be very concerned and demand an investigation if an unexpected debit were shown on a sub-contractor's account; The same discrepancy might well be regarded as acceptable or normal if he were operating in a country where bribery was the rule.

(d) Judgemental information. Judgemental information tends to be based on a subjective or intuitive appreciation of a situation. A senior manager may supplement the formal information system by asking a trusted subordinate for his feelings about the matter. The senior manager may act on the basis of that judgement even if the formal system suggests an alternative course of action. In other situations a manager may only act on the basis of the formal system if a knowledgeable subordinate supports the prediction of the formal system. Evidence from empirical studies suggests that the more successful organisations are those that retain a significant level of informality in their organisational structure and the way they handle information (Earl and Hopwood, 1979).

(e) Information about values, attitudes and power. Some of the mainsprings of action in organisations and some of the most powerful motivating forces are the result of people's values and their attitudes towards particular issues. The efficiency with which a job is carried out may depend in part upon the technical apparatus available to do the job, but crucially on the attitude the employee has to the job, and the extent to which the job gives him satisfaction. Some of these factors may be assessed by the use of formal techniques during the design stage of an information system but, in the main, information relating to values, attitudes and power is derived from the informal system.

## Other Types of Information

Most designed information systems deal in objective, verifiable data which are used to support the operational, planning and decision-making functions of the organisation. Sometimes the information system is used for the purpose of shaping attitudes, beliefs and behaviour. In all organisations political processes are at work, and the raw material for these processes is information. Information is selected, manipulated, and presented (or concealed), in such a way as to gain the maximum impact, as, for example, in persuading others a certain course of action is to be preferred, or a course of action proposed by someone else is not feasible. The formal information system may be used selectively in negotiations with trade unions, or with a bank when applying for an extra line of credit, and in the daily bargaining which goes on between different departments in most organisations. To individual managers (and others, such as shop stewards) the availability of information represents power in the bargaining process, and they may hoard information for use in negotiations. As a result, it may prove very difficult to persuade information hoarders to release certain kinds of information for incorporation in the organisation's database.

One of the most common complaints from computer professionals is that users cannot make up their minds what information they need, but when the system is subsequently implemented users demand different information. Studies have also indicated that what managers <u>say</u> they do in order to make a decision varies considerably from what they actually <u>do</u> when faced with a decision-making situation (Argyris and Schon, 1974). One reason for this discrepancy, and for the difficulties faced by systems analysts trying to assess the information needs of managers, is the frequency with which the cue to take a particular action is given by information from an unexpected source, or by information which was not anticipated as being relevant when the system was first discussed. Because the source is unexpected, or the information was not deemed relevant at the time the formal system was designed, this information cannot form a part of the formal system. A comprehensive data-base with powerful query languages can help to overcome this difficulty, but often the unexpected information is of a kind which does not lend itself to formalisation. For example a civil engineering contractor rescheduled the construction of a bridge when the steel industry went on prolonged strike. His original plan was to import steel beams from a Dutch supplier, but he had to make a further change in plans when he discovered his work force would not handle 'blacked' steel.

## INFORMATION IN SPACE AND TIME

All classes of information have a context which can be defined in terms of space and time (Stamper, 1979). A contractor has to build a bridge using safety margins for stress calculations derived from rules set out by the professional institute of civil engineering and applicable in the United Kingdom. The rules have been in existence for many years, but are due to be replaced by new rules which are intended to harmonise engineering standards in the European Community at a specified date. On the other hand, when the contractor tenders for the construction of a bridge to be built in Algeria, he has to apply a set of rules originally established in France, but in use now in Algeria.

Space conditions may be designated as - map references or coordinates on a map grid; addresses; place names or geographical locations.

The time coordinates may be expressed as: instants of time, as when a particular event took place; duration, commencing with a start date or time and finishing with the present, or a completion time or date; time relative to another event, e.g. 'must take place not more than two days after a specified event'; a direct reading from an instrument such as a clock or calendar; or indirectly by reference to a specifed event, e.g. 'the condition applies until the next delivery is received'.

In the same way that all classes of information have time and space coordinates, reports and output from the information system also have space and time requirements. An order for steel beams is relevant only if it reaches the supplier, at a designated location, by a certain date. A report on the over-spending of the budget is useful only if it arrives on the relevant manager's desk in time for him to take corrective action. In order to design an effective information system, the time and space coordinates of the system's outputs have to be defined.

## HOW INFORMATION IS USED

How a person uses the different types of information depends on a number of factors. Some of these are generic and some are related to the particular environment or situation in which the information is received. Some of the most important factors are the following.

(a) <u>The cognitive style and preference of the user (Kilmann and Mitroff, 1976; Kerola and Taggart, 1982).</u> Some people prefer and understand information presented in the form of pictures or graphs - others prefer narrative text. Some prefer information presented formally, or even in symbolic form - others prefer a more informal, freer style. One school of psychological research distinguishes between those who prefer to take in information in a strictly serial mode, who need to capture each element of a message, and those who prefer to see the 'shape' of a message and are able to grasp its content without the serial sensing of the other type. What determines cognitive style is not well understood: what is clear is that it differs considerably between different individuals. Each individual receiving a message will perceive the content of the message through a cognitive filter, which may select, amplify, reject, attenuate or distort portions of the message. As a consequence even quite simple messages may be interpreted differently by different individuals. Complex messages, such as those involving the description of a complicated sequence of events, or the rules embodied in a contract, will almost certainly receive many interpretations.

(b) Remembered knowledge. Again the working of memory is not well understood, and we have no ways of measuring what is in a person's memory, or how that information is accessed, or of discovering what knowledge the person possesses. Nevertheless, it is the association of information received through the senses, with knowledge stored in a person's memory, which determines the actions and responses to the received message and the resulting action. Hence two people may respond differently to the same message and interpret the same instruction in different ways.

(c) Language (Stamper, 1979). All information is conveyed to the person in the form of signals or messages. To be meaningful they must be embodied in a code or language. Different languages have different properties with respect to the interpretation of the codes. Natural languages are very rich in the range of information they can accommodate but they are inherently ambiguous. Formal languages, such as mathematical notation or programming languages, can be very precise, but may lack the capacity to cope with a wide range of concepts. A concept such as 'good' cannot be expressed by a programming language. Language, cognitive style and memory operate interdependently. Their operation is often rooted in the individual's culture, education and experience and an understanding of the importance of these factors suggests some approaches to the designing systems are to be preferred to others. It is interesting to note that the Human-Factor Research Group in Sweden (Kall, 1984) defines an information system as a 'social linguistic system technically implemented'.

(d) Environmental factors. In addition to the generic factors described above, a number of environmental factors influence the way a person will respond to information and which type of information source may be preferred. These environmental factors include: understanding of, and trust in, the designed system; the trust which is placed in the judgement of peers and subordinates; the time available to respond or take action, the pressure of work; the convenience or inconvenience of looking at the real world; and many others. Indeed, as the phrase 'working to rule' implies, few actual procedures follow the rule-book precisely, and much more use is made of the informal, unspecified system than laid-down procedures suggest.

An information system is thus a social system which uses information technology. The extent to which information technology plays a part is increasing rapidly. It is, however, impossible to design a robust and effective information system, incorporating significant amounts of the technology, without treating it as a social system. It is not enough to design a technical system, and then attempt to make it user-friendly, or to tell the designer to remember to take account of human factors.

## THE SOCIAL POLICY ISSUES

We can examine the relevance of social factors at a number of levels. At the macro-level - the level of public policy and the nation - a number of issues have received a great deal of attention in recent years, and will no doubt be the subject of debate for many years to come. While these issues are of concern to the practising systems analyst and designer, and may indeed have direct relevance to the nature of the system he is working on, they can only be dealt with by this paper in summary form. Perhaps the most important issues are the following.

(a) The impact of the increasing use of information technology. One of the major motivating factors in redesigning information systems is to displace labour, or to enable an increase in activity to take place without increasing the labour force. Critics of the technology argue that the primary effect of the implementation of new systems is to destroy jobs, and there is considerable evidence such job destruction can take place. On the other side it is argued that the technology releases resources for more productive work elsewhere, enabling new industries and new employment to be created (Cooley, 1980). Evidence is cited of previous technological revolutions, which resulted ultimately in more jobs and greater prosperity. The optimists regard technological unemployment as a strictly transitory phenomenon (Marchetti, 1981).

(b) The national role and standing of the information technology industry. The argument has been advanced in all the major industrial nations that a country that does not establish a strong and leading information technology industry, and which does not take steps to remain in the forefront by heavy investment in research and development, puts its economy at risk, and is doomed to second class status and inevitable decline. In a number of countries policies have been proposed and implemented which are based on these assertions (Land, 1984).

(c) The role of government. This includes the provision of funds for investment, research, development, education and training. A debate on the relationship and role of private versus public enterprise is in progress in many countries. In some the emphasis is on the need for collaboration between the private and the public sectors to achieve the leading position postulated as necessary for economic success (Alvey, 1982).

(d) Rights of employees. In addition to the problem of labour displacement, it is argued that the new information systems can degrade and 'deskill' work, so reducing the quality of working life. Individuals should have the right to defend themselves against such uses of the technology, to reject schemes which have an adverse effect on job satisfaction, and to be involved in the design of the systems in which they work (Mumford, 1981). In Norway a law passed in 1974 gave workers (represented by their union) the right to be consulted about changes in technology leading to changes in work practices. The law established a new position in Norwegian industry - that of the data steward whose role is to lead the negotiations on behalf of the work force on issues arising out of the proposed implementation of new systems (Hoyer, 1979). In other countries unions and management are required by law to come to co-determination agreements regarding the introduction of new systems. In the UK some unions (in practice mainly white-collar unions) have been able to insist on management signing Technology Agreements before they permit new systems to be introduced (Williams and Moseley, 1982). The detailed provisions of a Technology Agreement reflect the relative power of management and the unions, but all Technology Agreements aim to ensure that the implementation of a new system will not result in enforced redundancy. Other clauses usually insist that management shares information (future plans) with the union, that benefits are shared, that the workers have the right to be consulted about the design of the system, and that strict environmental and health conditions laid down by the union should be met. Systems analysts will be working in situations where the systems they design will be subject to scrutiny and even rejected by the people who will be expected to work with and use them.

(e) Rights of citizens with regard to privacy (Hirschheim, 1983). It is argued that the power of computer systems to store, link and collate information relating to an individual can prove a threat to that individual's privacy. Many countries have recognised the possibility of abuse, and have enacted, or will shortly enact, legislation which regulates the contents of data banks and proscribes certain types of data linking. The legislation prescribes the nature of public access to data banks, and the method by which an abused individual can obtain redress (Lindop, 1978). Elsewhere voluntary codes of conduct have been established in an attempt to prevent practices which could abuse the privacy rights of the citizen. Rules for the flow of information across national borders are also being drawn up, so that it becomes difficult to evade privacy regulations in one country, by setting up data banks in other countries which have looser, or no, regulations. However, the concept of the 'data haven' analagous to the 'tax haven' is already being discussed. The designer of new systems has to be aware of the conditions laid down in codes of practice and legislation to ensure that the system he designs is both legitimate and ethical.

## IMPLEMENTING INFORMATION SYSTEMS: THE ESSENTIAL PRECONDITIONS

At the level of practical systems design it is possible to take into account social as well as technical factors in the implementation of information systems. For a designed information system to be truly effective and to provide the organisation with cost/effective benefits, the system must normally fulfil a number of important preconditions.

(a) It must obtain the approval and esteem of those who work with the system and those who use it.

If a system fails to obtain approval before implementation, it will be resisted, probably resulting in delays and the subsequent misuse of the system. If it fails to satisfy the users once it becomes operational, it may be misused, supplanted by unofficial procedures, or even sabotaged. At the very least the electronic data/processing (EDP) department will be put under constant pressure to make changes to the system, resulting in high maintenance costs and poor utilisation. The fact that a new system succeeds in obtaining approval before it is implemented (prior approval) does not necessarily imply that it will also be approved once it is brought into operational use (operating approval).

(b) It must be capable of adapting (or being adapted) to meet changing conditions and changing requirements. A designed information system which cannot be adapted quickly may affect the ability of the organisation to continue in business, or may cause its decline and eventual failure. However, since information systems are social systems, and most social systems are robust, the informal, human component often finds a way of overcoming the failure of the designed system, though at the cost of some inefficiency. Hence the failure of the designed system to adapt to change may result in its losing the approval of its users, who devise alternative unofficial procedures to cope with the new conditions. The designed system is by-passed and falls into disuse.

(c) The various components of the information system - the designed and undesigned, the official and unofficial, the formal and the informal - need to operate in harmony and to be used to provide mutual support to the users of the system. A number of studies emphasise the importance of this point (Mintzberg, 1974; Earl and Hopwood, 1979). They show that organisations which maintain a blend of formal and informal systems perform better than organisations in which the formal system becomes dominant.

Analysis, design and implementation methods are needed, therefore, which recognise the three preconditions and attempt to ensure that they are met. There are three steps to be considered. The first is concerned with the organisation of the tasks of creating a new system. Questions relating to the respective roles of the professional systems analyst and designer and users have to be answered, as well as the best organisational structure to enable these roles to be filled. The second is concerned with the process of implementing change, and with the tools and techniques available to assist in carrying out the process efficiently and effectively. The third is concerned with the process of designing the system so as to fit with the capabilities, skills and cognitive preferences of those who will work with, and use, the system - this aspect of systems design is often called 'human factors engineering' or 'ergonomics', and is frequently described as making a system 'user-friendly'. Here we shall concentrate on the first two and merely summarise aspects of 'user-friendliness'.

## ORGANISING FOR GOOD SOCIAL DESIGN

### The Traditional Approach

If we begin with a very conventional view of how activities are organised for the design and implementation of a computer-based system we can develop a model like that shown in Figure 2.2. The process starts with the setting up of a computer team to carry out the analysis and design for a new system. This model shows very clearly the risks inherent in a traditional computer-department-driven approach.

## Figure 2.2: Systems Planning and Design - The Risks of the Traditional Approach

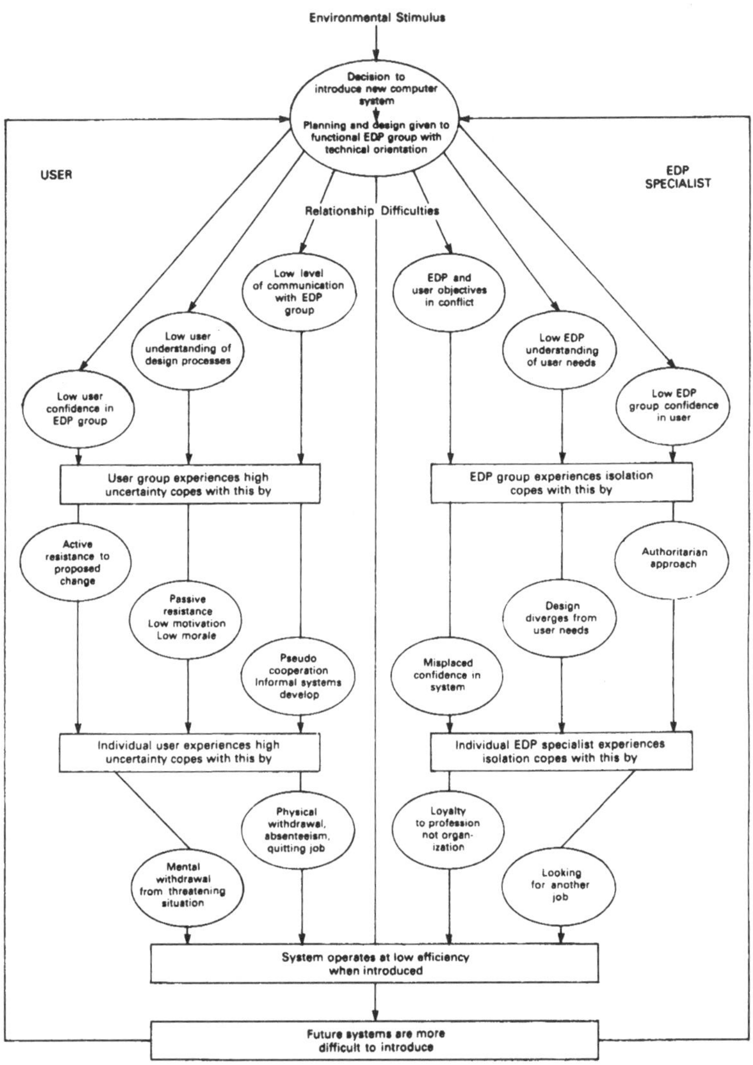

## Relationship difficulties

For the users this arrangement gives rise to the following difficulties. First, there may be a low level of communication with the data processing (DP) group. There are a number of reasons for this:

(a) The user and the DP specialist each have a very different 'image' of the organisation they serve. Their understanding of each other's need is restricted and this leads to inaccurate communications.

(b) The user is reluctant to reveal to the DP specialist the extent to which he is breaking company rules in the way he organises his daily work.

(c) The user may be afraid information given to the DP specialist will be used against him later.

(d) Because the user has little understanding of the design process, he does not realise what information is important and what is not.

(e) The user's principal interest centres on his substantive tasks and not on the information system he incidentally services. The DP specialist tends not to be interested in the user's job, but only in that part of the job concerned with information flows.

(f) The user is unable to visualise his behaviour within the proposed system. The DP professional is sometimes exasperated by the apparent unwillingness of the user to decide on the suitability of some new system component as, for example, a new report.

(g) Users tend to explain their actions in terms of rational behaviour, whereas their actual performance may be governed by intuition rather than by rational analysis. Studies of managers at work have shown that there is a discrepancy between how managers claim to take decisions and their actual observed decision-making behaviour (Argyris and Schon, 1974).

Second, there may be low user understanding of the design process. Computers are still widely regarded as esoteric and mysterious objects. This view of computers is reinforced by the way the media describe functions performed by computers. The phrase 'the computer tells us' for example, occurs in otherwise quite sophisticated talks or scientific articles. The DP professional stands out from an organisation as a person apart, endowed perhaps with a special understanding which enables him to communicate with computers. To some extent these difficulties are being broken down by the growth of personal computing and the spread of computer education in schools, but the user still has little real concept of what is involved in designing and implementing computer systems.

Third, there may be low user confidence in the DP group. The DP group is seen as responsible for the disturbance and irritation which is a consequence of the development of new systems. Any failure in the system once it is in operation is assumed to be the responsibility of the DP specialists. The DP specialists appear to disregard many of the facts about procedures which the users carefully explained to them. Above all, the DP group seems to have little interest in the problems of the individual user. Many identify the DP group as tools of management sent in to create redundancy, or to increase the control management already have over the work situation. Hence, the common observation that users have low confidence in the DP group.

Fourth, for the DP professional a parallel situation can develop, in which DP and user objectives are in conflict (Land et al, 1979). The DP specialist tends to design systems to make efficient use of computers and pays rather less attention to designing systems that provide for human values and needs. DP personnel have most often been trained to place a high value on rationality and the scientific approach, discounting factors which cannot easily be quantified or treated technically (Hedberg and Mumford, 1975). Many computer science educational programmes regard organisational or 'human factor' studies as outside their terms of reference. Additionally, the DP specialist is not rewarded on the basis of user job satisfaction with the system, rather he is rewarded for the technical elegance of the system.

Fifth, there may be low understanding of user needs. The DP professional is handicapped in understanding user needs in a number of ways:

(a) He cannot be an expert in all business functions. His tools of analysis are confined to the examination of formal business procedures. Nearly all the methods (such as methods of data analysis) which have been developed for systems analysis focus on a description of the information flow within an organisation and on the structure of the messages. Comparatively little work has been done on methods of analysing the essential systems which underlie present procedures.

(b) His system of values tends to make him neglect organisational and social needs.

(c) The differences in linguistic styles between user and DP professionals easily lead to mistakes and misconceptions, even where parties cooperate with the maximum of good will.

Finally, there may be low DP confidence in users. The DP professional faced by users with different sets of values, half hearted cooperation, reluctance to commit themselves to innovative and (in his eyes) progressive ideas, loses confidence in the users, and tending to undervalue their intelligence, perception, and the possibility they can play a greater role in analysis and design.

## The response to relationship difficulties

For the user group, the consequence of the relationship difficulties with the EDP specialist is a high degree of uncertainty and a fear of a loss of control over the work situation. Users tend to react in ways which attempt to maintain or restore their control and reduce the uncertainty with which they are faced. A number of behavioural options are available to them, and one or more of these may be used:

(a) Active resistance to proposed change. The user group through its trade union, or by means of more informal ad hoc groupings, refuses cooperation with the systems design team. Where the user group is powerful it can abort all proposed changes. Where the user group is weak, sanctions may be employed to force the group into a more cooperative or accepting stance. However, few systems proposals which meet active resistance can be implemented successfully.

(b) Passive resistance to proposed change (Keen, 1981). This tends to be characterised by low levels of cooperation, by prolonged negotiations and discussions relating to the change, by the raising of tendentious or spurious objections to elements of the proposals and by the refusal to accept responsible roles in the implementation of the system. Motivation in the group can drop and, with it, the efficiency of the work unit.

(c) Development of informal systems. The most common way for the user group to regain control over its work situation and reduce its uncertainty with regard to the new systems is to develop its own information system. These systems often parallel or even replace the formal system. In organisations which have developed networks of informal (and often unauthorised systems) the formal computer system becomes degraded and ineffective because the user group puts little effort into keeping it accurate or up to schedule.

DP specialists faced with the relationship difficulties described above begin to feel isolated within the organisation. They may respond to their isolation:

(a) by taking a rather authoritarian approach. Faced

by lack of confidence in themselves, and lacking confidence in the user, but having been given the power to change systems (indeed it is their raison d'être) they adopt an increasingly didactic and even authoritarian stance. An authoritarian approach may be effective in the short run, but ultimately tends to widen the gap between user and specialist.

(b) by designing systems on the basis of their own perception of the needs of the organisation, underpinned by their own value system. This results in a design which may fail to meet the real needs of the user.

(c) by having an exaggerated confidence in their design. The absence of informed and constructive feedback from the user may give the DP specialist an unwarranted confidence that the design is either acceptable to the user or workable in the long run.

The individual user may respond to uncertainty regarding his own future, i.e. what his career prospects will be, how he will cope with the new work situation, and the new relationships he may have to establish:

(a) by physical withdrawal: he may quit the job, or indulge in absenteeism. For the organisation, physical withdrawal on even a small scale can be very expensive. Many firms underestimate the cost of labour turnover (Hopwood, 1980) and the effects on the efficiency of the organisation.

(b) by mental withdrawal indicated by low motivation and efficiency, or apathy.

(c) by displaying signs of psychological stress reflected in high sickness statistics and low efficiency.

(d) by what is sometimes called projection. He may blame the system as the cause of all his difficulties.

(e) by aggression. He may actually try to sabotage or destroy the system by aggression.

Finally, the individual EDP specialist copes with the isolation he experiences vis-à-vis the rest of the organisation:

(a) by looking for a new job. The average duration of employment of an EDP specialist in an organisation is still low, very much lower than that of other groups of workers in the same industry. The cost of replacement in times of shortage of professional EDP staff is very high. The cost in terms of projects not completed in time may be higher still.

(b) by giving his loyalty to the profession rather than to his employer.

## The Overall Impact

The impact of all the adverse features described above has the result that the new system operates at low efficiency when introduced, needs considerable maintenance in order to make it workable and will have cost much more to introduce than was first estimated. Within the organisation this can lead to a low level of confidence in computer systems which will make it even more difficult to introduce future systems.

Of course, the model and the above explanation describe the worst kind of situation, but nevertheless some of the situations described above follow naturally from the perceived roles and needs of users and EDP specialists. The EDP specialist tends to gain esteem, and will be judged, by his peers, on the basis of his success in introducing technical innovations. To further his career in his chosen profession he tends to push the technology to its limit - he advances through innovation. In contrast the typical user (say a line manager) can best succeed in terms of achievements on which he is judged in situations of relative stability. Hence to further his own objectives he will often attempt to reduce uncertainty and avert risk - while innovation implies both risk and uncertainty.

It is interesting to note that the EDP manager, in his role as line manager of the EDP function, takes on the risk-averting and uncertainty-reducing role when faced with innovations in the organisation or techniques of the EDP function itself. He too attempts to preserve the status quo by using counter-implementation techniques (Keen, 1980). Some of the elements described are, therefore, present in all new system implementations. In general the less the different categories of users are involved in the design process, the more the situation described becomes the typical situation.

## The Shared Approach

Participation by users in the design process is a powerful technique to avoid the isolation of the DP specialist and the loss of certainty and control by the users, and to help strike a balance between the specialist's need to innovate, and the line manager's requirement for stability. The model in Figure 2.3 shows this situation, where users form part of the design team so that they share the control of the analysis and design process. As a result, conflicts relating to differing objectives are brought out into the open, and this provides an opportunity for negotiation and resolution of the differences. Users gain in confidence as they learn to cope with the problems of design themselves and have more confidence in the DP specialists because they are

**Figure 2.3: System Design with User Participation**

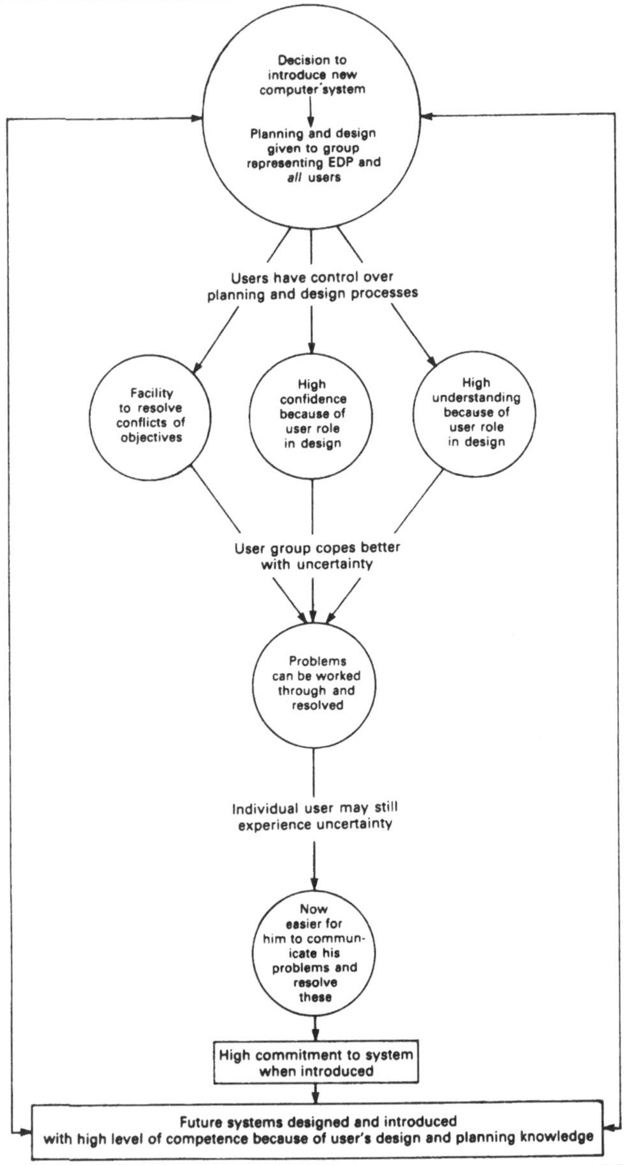

perceived as helpers rather than opponents. The DP specialists lose their isolation and become more identified with the organisation.

Because users do not lose control, and because they have a clearer vision of what the new system will do to them, the extent of uncertainty is limited. Uncertainty will still exist because an innovative system cannot have precisely predicted outcomes, but the group of users and DP specialists has an improved capability of communication and of resolving problems. Users are more likely to regard future changes as a worthwhile challenge, because they have themselves played a part in setting the objectives for the systems, and in evaluating the design. Hence, their response to uncertainty will be positive, rather than an attempt to retain the status quo by means of counter-implementation strategies.

Above all, users will tend to have a high commitment to make the system work. Users also learn from the experience of designing systems, and achieve a high level of competence which leads to improved design of future systems.

## The Participative Process

Since participation by users is so important (Land, 1982; Land and Hirschheim, 1983), how can it be achieved? In practice, participation is effected at many levels and takes many forms. There is no simple prescription for the way participation should be introduced or practised. Introducing systems change into a large unit of public administration, such as the Department of Inland Revenue, with 50,000 employees scattered throughout the British Isles, must be different from the introduction of, say, new office technology to a company employing 150 people. Introducing change to a medium-sized family-owned company, with a history of paternalistic concern for its workers, must be different from introducing the same type of change into a company of equal size, but having a strong trade union and a history of management/union conflict.

Nevertheless, it is possible to suggest a general organisational framework within which to consider the participative process. A distinction can be drawn between participation in decision making, where the participative process is concentrated on taking part in making decisions about a project (as when the participants are invited to assist in the choice between a number of alternative designs suggested by the designers), and participation in the analysis and design and implementation process.

## FORMS OF PARTICIPATION

### Participation in Decision Making

Perhaps the most common form of participation (Land, 1982) is that know as consultative. The participants are invited to give evidence to the decision-makers, either by answering questions (interviews or questionnaires), or by offering evidence directly, and by subjecting evidence provided by other interest groups to cross-examination. The evidence is taken into account when the decisions are made. Ideally, the grounds for the decision reached should be made available to the participants. In this situation participation is often confined to special interest groups identified as being affected by the project under discussion.

Much rarer is the democratic form of participative decision making in which all participants have an equal voice in the decision process. Decisions may be taken on the basis of ballots or votes of the participants, but the implementation of the decision is in the hands of some authority or agency.

The third kind of participation in decision making is called the responsible form. The participants are given full authority to make decisions as they see fit and to involve other interest groups or specialists as advisers to help them make decisions. Responsible participation is seen most freqμently, for example, in organisations which give departmental managers and their subordinates authority to acquire their own data processing facilities in the form of personal computers.

### Participation in Systems Analysis and Design

Participation in analysis and design can occur at three different organisational levels (Land and Hirschheim, 1983): at the top where it is concerned with strategic planning; at the middle where it covers systems definition for a number of divisions, functions or departments; and at the bottom where it relates to the detailed design of an organisational sub-system such as a single department or function.

The participative approach can be used at all three of these levels, although it may take a different form depending on whether it is concerned with higher or lower level systems. These different forms have been named consultative participation, representative participation and consensus participation (Mumford and Henshall, 1979). The consultative approach is seen as most appropriate for securing agreement on strategic planning objectives. Here the major planning decisions are taken by senior management, probably at Board level, whose position in the hierarchy enables them to take a broad view of the enterprise's future needs. However, they will only take these decisions after extensive consultation with interested groups lower down the organisational hierarchy and a consultative structure must exist or be created so that this sounding out of opinion can be thorough and accurate.

Representative participation is seen as appropriate at the system definition stage when powerful interest groups at the middle management level will wish to express an opinion on where system boundaries are to be drawn and on the broad form any future system should take. Representative design teams will include selected or elected representatives of all grades of staff and all trade union interests in the departments which a new system will affect.

Consensus participation permits all the staff in a department to play a part in the design of a new work system. They are specially involved when efficiency and job satisfaction needs are being diagnosed through feedback and discussion in smaller groups.

As the design team formulates alternative design strategies these are discussed at staff meetings and the choice of work organisation and task structure to be associated with the technical part of the system will be greatly influenced by the views of the staff. Experience has shown that an agreement on a new system solution does not always emerge easily - conflicts which result from different interests within an organisation and even within a single department may have to be resolved first (Mumford and Henshall, 1979). Consensus participation involves both users and DP specialists, but the responsibility for design and implementation is carried by the user group.

## Forward Planning

The process of forward planning, including systems design, implementation and evaluation, should be carried out by two types of teams (Mumford et al, 1978). The first team is responsible for steering the project: it is the direct link between the senior management of the organisation and the team responsible for the detailed design. This steering group sets the basic organisational objectives and constraints under which the new system is to be developed. It makes the 'go', 'no go' or 'postpone' decision. The steering group will usually include the managers of affected departments, official representatives of trade unions and other major interests affected by the new system.

The second team is responsible for the detailed systems design and consists of representatives of the department in which the new computer system is to be introduced. This team defines the scope of the local problem, scans the environment for new opportunities or changing constraints, and analyses deficiencies in the current system. As a result it is able to define development goals in consultation with other groups likely to be affected, provide decision makers with assessments of the likely impacts of different design strategies on these goals, and design and test, by means of prototypes, the selected system with its associated work organisation.

Such a team will include members from the traditional DP department, but their function will be to transfer the required skills to other members rather than carry out the design themselves. Their function is that of technical consultants to the design team. At the same time they may set up standards to ensure that all systems designed in this manner harmonise effectively.

## TOOLS AND TECHNIQUES

Systems design is not merely a technical process involving the choice of hardware and the development of appropriate software - it requires the set of new (or changed) computer-based procedures to be inserted into an existing organisational framework. This includes a network of people carrying out a variety of tasks, playing different roles and having individual relationships and job satisfaction needs. In most cases, the introduction of a computer system requires the redesign of the functions and tasks which people at all levels in the organisation are expected to perform. It requires of the members of the design team the ability to identify and specify both the organisational and the social needs, thus creating a system that facilitates the satisfying of these needs.

For the target system to be truly effective it must, on the one hand, be regarded as efficient in the sense of productivity and quality, coordination and control, and in its ability to permit the organisation to develop and adapt to changing requirements. It must deliver the anticipated (usually economic) benefits to its sponsors. On the other hand, the target system cannot deliver the benefits unless it provides an environment for work in which people can achieve personal development and satisfaction. The design of a new computer application therefore requires the ability to create a system which uses information technology to assist in the attainment of efficent operating and decision making procedures, together with human effectiveness and satisfaction throughout the organisation as a whole.

Enid Mumford of the Manchester Business School and her collaborators have developed a range of tools and techniques for use by the design team. Here we provide an outline of the most important of the tools and the concepts which underlie them (Mumford et al, 1978; Mumford and Henshall, 1979; Mumford and Weir, 1979; Land et al, 1979).

## Describing the Essential Human System

The human system is defined as the network of roles and relationships necessary to achieve technical and economic objectives and meet the job satisfaction needs of people filling roles and involved in relationships. The design team has to describe each role and relationship within the functional area of the organisation under review, in terms of its function and the kinds and levels of knowledge and skill required to handle it. A useful framework for analysing roles is to consider them in relation to the following five types of activities which all functional units in the organisation require.

(a) Operational activities. These are the activities associated with producing the product, service or output which is the essential purpose of the system. Some of these activities may require a high degree of skill, others may be semi-skilled or unskilled. Some may be unstructured, and require a great deal of initiative, others may be formalised and leave very little discretion to the individual carrying out the activity.

(b) Problem avoidance or problem correction activities. All systems have weaknesses and have a tendency to go wrong. As far as possible procedures have to be devised for avoiding problems in the area of weakness. The problems which do arise need to be identified and corrective action taken. In many operational systems a significant proportion of total effort is devoted to trouble shooting. Here again different levels of skill and knowledge will be required. The trouble shooting activity may be combined with the operational activity, or a special trouble shooting function, such as progress chasing, may be created. Problem avoidance and problem correction activities are often found in the informal, undesigned part of the information system.

(c) Coordinating activities. These are activities associated with coordinating different functional units. No unit exists in isolation; each is host to a sequence of activities which together make up the system. Many of these will cross system boundaries, and therefore involve ensuring the successful interaction of the system with adjoining systems. Here again, the activity may be carried out as a part of an operational activity, or shared, perhaps, with a supervisory or control activity.

(d) Control activities. Control activities are those associated with ensuring the key objectives of the system are achieved and that the total system fits together and works as an effective unit. These can be described as supervisory activities, although this does not necessarily mean they will be undertaken by managers or supervisors. Where the operational activities are highly structured and capable of being programmed, the control activity can be taken over by a machine as part of the organisation's 'reflex control' system. Where the activities are subject to unpredictable variation, control tends to be more discretionary, and the control activity may be taken at a higher managerial level.

(e) Development activities. All systems change with time. Even where changes in the way the system has to operate occur as the result of unforeseen changes in circumstances, the implementation of the required change has to be planned, and the consequent new procedures have to be designed. Changes may be made to take advantage of new opportunities, to comply with new laws, to increase the efficiency of the organisation, and for many other reasons. If the changes are to be carried out effectively, and with minimum disturbance of the working system, development activities need to be specified. They may be taken by specialists, but often it is possible for the activity to be carried out, at least in part, by the non-specialist employee.

The task of the design team is to determine which part of the system shall carry out the identified tasks and activities. Some designers have attempted to disturb existing activities as little as possible, or have simply attempted to identify those tasks which appeared capable of programming, and allocated them to the computer part of the system, the remaining tasks being allocated to individuals in such a way as to minimise further change. In fact, such design methods may lead to unbalanced systems, which, for example, in reducing the job satisfaction of some of the users of the new system may result in a system which functions poorly.

The requirement to build a system which meets the approval of its users means the design team has to assemble clusters of activities so that they provide a logical and challenging set of tasks for groups or individuals. This may mean a task which is capable of being carried out by a computer is allocated to an individual (or group), because adding that task to the individual's responsibility enhances the effectiveness of the individual. There is evidence to suggest that it is a good design principle to incorporate a number of activities of different types into each group's, or individual's, job responsibility.

However, the actual design cannot be based on general principles alone. Each situation is different, and whereas one group may work well with and approve of one particular allocation of roles and tasks, another group may prefer a totally different mix. Hence it is important to analyse the features which individuals or groups regard as giving them job satisfaction. Job needs and expectations must be made explicit as part of the process of systems analysis. This requires each individual associated with the system to specify the kinds of satisfaction he or she would ideally like to receive from the work environment. Unless a very small group is involved, this information is best collected by asking users to complete questionnaires, and using the data collected in this way as the basis for small group discussion on how job satisfaction needs and expectations can best be achieved.

Job satisfaction has been defined as the fit between what an individual or group is seeking from the work situation and what is received (Mumford, 1972). An improvement in job satisfaction should always be a system objective. Any analysis of a system, prior to its redesign, should include the following information on job satisfaction.

(a) Needs associated with personality. Knowledge needs: how, ideally, would each individual or group forming part of the system like the existing skills and knowledge to be used? What opportunities would they like for these to be developed further? Psychological needs: what are their needs for responsibility, status, esteem, security and advancement, and how do they define these needs?

(b) Needs associated with competence and efficiency and rewards. Support and control needs: the kind of support services that users at every level believe would enable them to carry out their work responsibilities more efficiently. These support services include the information and materials necessary to work at a high level of competence, as well as supervisory support and good working conditions. Pay and reward needs: the level and structure of wages and salaries, and the relationship between performance and payment, are an important element of job satisfaction. Task needs: the kind of task structure that different groups of users find motivating, interesting and challenging. Do users want jobs which include elements of all five of the roles described above, or do they want jobs which are simple and repetitive, but require little mental effort?

(c) Needs associated with values. Ethical needs: do users share in the values and objectives of the organisation they work in? How do users at every level want to be treated by management? Do the organisation's policies on communication, consultation and participation meet employee expectations? Satisfaction in this area turns out to be crucial if a system is to be operated effectively for a long period.

The job satisfaction analysis assists the design team in identifying those areas of the work system in which the new design should aim to enhance job satisfaction, and those areas in which job satisfaction is already high and must be preserved.

## Describing the Essential Organisational System

Before an organisation can be moved from its present system to a new or revised system, it is important to understand and describe in detail the essential requirements of the unit which is to be redesigned. An essential requirement is one the unit must satisfy if it is to perform effectively the function for which it exists. The first step in any analysis is therefore to ask the question: what functions and what purposes does the unit serve? It is surprising to what extent different people working in the same organisation will provide different answers.

In analysing the requirements it is helpful to provide the design team with an analytical framework in the form of a number of concepts. The first of these is the concept of 'unit operation'. A unit operation is an interconnected, often integrated, set of activities or tasks associated with a major system function, and separated from other activities by some kind of boundary - perhaps a change of input, a different type of output, a change in location or change in time.

For example, if the major system function is the purchase of steel stock, the unit operations might be: calculate the type and quantity of steel needed; select possible suppliers and write letters asking for quotations; receive quotations, select best supplier and place orders; progress chase deliveries; receive deliveries and check quantities and qualities; receive invoices, and authorise payment.

Once unit operations have been identified the next level of analysis is to establish the nature of the activities associated with each unit operation. The design team should concentrate on the essential activities and requirements rather than on existing technologies, procedures or organisational structure. Many of these will be changed in the redesign phase. The analysis of each unit operation is best carried out in terms of the five types of activity used in the analysis of roles described earlier: operational activities; problem avoidance and problem solving activities; coordinating activities; control activities; development activities.

The operational activity for the unit operation 'select possible supplier and write for quotation' consists of searching through a list of possible suppliers, finding out which supplier stocks the item under review, and writing a letter asking for a quotation. The problem avoidance activity is concerned with ensuring that all relevant suppliers are written to, and that the correct items are listed for quotation. The coordination activity ensures that the previous unit operation provides the correct information at the right time. The control activity sets out the standards for the work to be done and ensures that the operation is carried out to the standards. The development activity tries to find methods of carrying out the unit operation more efficiently, or copes with changes in the environment. Of course this list of activities is not comprehensive, the problem-solving activity may have to deal with a steel strike, and the development activity to 'think up' a design that can cope with such circumstances.

The same framework of unit operations and activities can be used to establish the information requirements of the major functions being analysed. The classification of information described earlier is used to identify the information needed to support each activity in the unit operation. The design team has to identify, for example, the descriptive information needed to select a supplier, or the statistical information needed to ensure the supplier has a good reliability record. At the same time the analysis should indicate which elements of information are formal or lend themselves to formalisation, and which elements are essentially informal.

The analysis of the problem avoidance and problem solving activities is aided by a technique called 'variance analysis'. Variance analysis is used to identify, for each unit operation, the potential problems that can occur and, most importantly, the effect of any such problem on the major systems function being examined. Thus, the consequence of failure to identify correctly all possible suppliers of steel bar may be that a better quotation is missed. The consequence of neglecting to carry out a quality control check on delivered steel bars may be the subsequent collapse of a block of flats. The design team uses variance analysis to identify those aspects of the system that require special attention in the design of the new system.

**Future Analysis**
(Land *et al*, 1979)

A successful system is one which continues to be effective over its expected lifetime. In practice, the problem of maintaining a system's effectiveness in the context of changing technology and changing requirements is regarded as one of the most difficult tasks of the design team. One way the design team can be helped is to provide it with a systematic way of exploring possible futures, and with a systematic method for testing the potential robustness of the system undergoing design. The analysis is carried out in two stages.

In stage one the design team attempts to identify the kind of changes which the major business function is subject to. Such change may take the form of: changes in available information technology; changes in object system technology;

changes in legislation and regulations; changes in the economic climate; changes in the competitive position; changes in management; changes in attitudes; and changes in organisational structure.

The design team has to select and co-opt experts in each of the possible change areas. The objective is to build up some possible scenarios for the future, and to do this the team may employ a number of forecasting techniques. The analysis cannot give an accurate picture of the future, but will provide the design team with a number of target scenarios and hence enable the team to make design choices. The team may decide to build a system which is capable of supporting several of the possible scenarios. Such a design may be more expensive than one which optimises on a single view of the future, but it will have a better chance of surviving with less expensive (and unplanned) maintenance. On the other hand, the design team may decide to build the system in such a way that components of it can be discarded if they no longer support the needs of the organisation. Or again, the team can decide to reduce the expected life-span of the system.

In stage two the design team concentrates on the developing design of the system. Each facet of the system has to be examined in detail to check what would be the effect of a change in a design parameter. For example, the team would have to check the effect on response time of a range of different activity levels, or the effect of the introduction of a new method of computing freight rates. The team has to conduct a structured walk-through of the design. As a result of the analysis the design team can list those elements which are most sensitive to change, and those elements of the proposed system where such changes would have the maximum effect on the organisation. A particular element in the system may be very difficult to change, in response to a revised need, but the impact of failure to accommodate the need may be trivial as far as the organisation is concerned if it is easy to provide a manual 'fix' for the problem. The analysis helps the team to determine its design strategies.

## Setting Objectives and Evaluating Strategies

Most information systems serve a variety of users who may have very different perceptions regarding the value to themselves or to the organisation of the facilities provided by the system, or of the way the system is designed. Each user group will tend to rate as most important the objectives which further its own interests and this potential conflict of goals must be recognised at the design stage and dealt with by the design team. The ideal design is one that meets each group's most important objectives, but this is not always possible, and conflict often arises. The greatest danger to the success of the system is that the conflict is not recognised until the system has been implemented. Early recognition of problems of conflict can lead to discussions between the interested parties, and it may be possible to reach agreement on priority objectives.

However, before the design team can choose which of a number of alternative designs to implement, it must evaluate the extent to which the different designs meet design targets. For example, a design team has proposed two ways of providing a customer service function: design one is based on a number of multi-task groups each capable of servicing all the needs of designated types of customers; the multi-task group is supported by a realtime tele-ordering system. Design two is based on specialist groups carrying out designated functions for all customers, in which, for example, one group is responsible for all data entry. The first design rates highly in terms of meeting systems goals such as increasing job satisfaction by enriching jobs (the multi-task group design) and providing customers with a single focus in the organisation. The second design rates well in terms of productivity targets through the special skills developed by the functional specialists, such as data entry clerks. The final choice of systems must depend on which systems goals are regarded as the most important.

John Hawgood of the University of Durham has developed a graphic aid to this process, which consists of a rectangular plot of the predicted performance of alternative designs, against the relative importance of the objectives to the different interest groups (Mumford et al, 1978). The plots for two different groups when alternative designs are being evaluated are shown in Figure 2.4. This suggests the position to be:

Options:
- x No change in current policy
- y Multi-task groups
- z Specialist functions groups

Objectives:
- a Reduce cost of system
- b Improve job satisfaction of sales clerks

The horizontal scale can be labelled 'unimportant', 'fairly important', 'very important' and 'vital'. The vertical scale indicates the extent to which the design objective is being met.

The top graph in Figure 2.4 displays the value the clerks put to the systems options. It shows that as far as the clerks are concerned the first objective (a) is given the value 'fairly important', but that they regard the second objective (b) as 'vital'. The accountants, on the other

**Figure 2.4: Evaluation Graph**

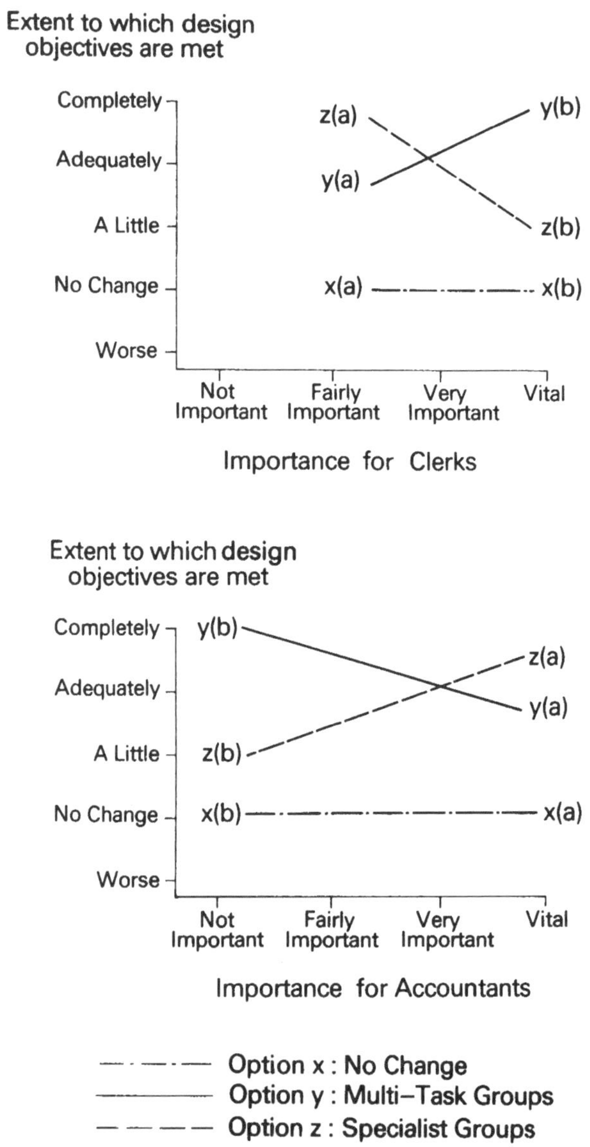

hand, regard the reduction of costs as the 'vital' objective and have not really considered the job satisfaction objective as a valid objective of systems design.

On the basis of the graph alone the design team might well chose the multi-task group design, because both the clerks and accountants would be better off. However, the decision makers might decide that the views of the accountants ranked higher than those of the clerks and attach more weight to the fact that option 'z' provides greater cost reductions than option 'y'. The ultimate purpose of the procedure is to guide the decision makers in their choice of design strategy. The design team may have particular criteria in mind when making such a choice. They may decide, for example, that the solution chosen must be regarded as an improvement over the current system by all participants even though another design would have yielded a higher return to some groups. The final choice of policy or system may also take into account factors other than those prescribed by the design team. Where there is an unresolved conflict of interest between different groups a political judgement may have to be made.

The decision process itself varies from organisation to organisation. The final decision may be left to the steering group, or may be the result of negotiation and bargaining between groups, or may be the subject of a Technology Agreement, or may be left to the individual with responsibility for the project. As a result of the processes described above, decision-making will be firmly based on an evaluation of the preferences of each group liable to be affected by the system.

## HUMAN FACTOR ENGINEERING OR ERGONOMICS

It has been evident for many years that the performance of a machine operator is significantly affected by the way the design of the machine, and the machine environment, relates to the operator, both in terms of the operator's physical and mental (psychological) attributes.

The study of the efficiency of a person in his working environment has become known as 'ergonomics', and the design of machine systems which have the capability of being used efficiently by human operators has become known as 'human factor engineering'.

A great deal of work has been done to establish some of the important variables which determine how successfully an individual can operate a machine, or a system of machines such as, for example, the control room of a nuclear power station.

The standard layout of the typewriter keyboard - the QWERTY layout - was devised in the early days of the typewriter to effect a compromise between the mechanical problem of clashing keys, and the need to spread the letters so as to make the best use of the typists strongest fingers, given the frequency of use of different letters of the alphabet. It is interesting to note that the QWERTY layout still dominates the design of keyboards for micro computers, though the original design problem based on a mechanical device is no longer relevant. The layout of a keyboard is a good example of the application of ergonomics to the design of a specific machine feature.

The well known Hawthorn experiments conducted by Elton Mayo (Roethlisberger and Dickson, 1939) in the 1930s were concerned with the influence of the level of illumination on the productivity of the work force of a machine shop. Mayo found that the greatest influence on productivity was not (at least within a certain range) the level of illumination, but the fact that the group of workers participating in the experiment saw themselves as the subjects of the experiment. The Hawthorn experiment showed that psychological factors were at least as important as technical factors in determining the efficiency of the workshop.

In recent years a number of research groups have developed a special interest in the ergonomics of computer systems (Shackel, 1984). In the UK these include the Human Sciences and Advanced Technology Unit (HUSAT) at Loughborough University of Technology and the Medical Research Council Units at Sheffield University and Cambridge University. The kind of questions to which ergonomists address themselves include:

(a) The layout of an operating console or work station. The buttons, keys, switches, displays and input and output mechanisms of the device must be designed to minimise operator effort. The keyboard of a terminal, for example, should ensure the most frequently used characters are distributed to be used by the strongest fingers of the operator in such a way that it does not provide too much stress for one or two fingers; it must provide a clear and unambiguous mode of operation for the operator. If a sequence of operation is required the order should be obvious from the layout and labelling of the switches and keys. The code of a command or editing language, for example, for a word processing system should provide clues to the operator, perhaps by means of a mnemonic code, of the function of the command; make it obvious to the operator when emergency action is required, and make emergency action easy by placing, for example, the cut-off button in an accessible place, but at the same time, not so accessible that it can be hit by accident during normal operations.

(b) Provision of safety and fail-safe measures to ensure against accidental misuse or misoperation, or damage to the health of the operator. For example, studies are being carried out on the effects of different display characteristics - flicker, colour, character size, number of characters on the screen, light intensity, speed of display change - on the operator from the point of view of the operator performance, operator health, and long-term operator behavioural symptoms, such as stress, fatigue, eye strain, and even mental health.

(c) Providing the operator with 'help' or 'show me' facilities which explain how to get out of a problem situation if the operator has misoperated the system or does not know how to progress (take the next step), perhaps because an unusual situation has arisen, or even because the operator has forgotten the correct operating procedure.

(d) Behavioural attributes of the operator vis-à-vis the device. It has been recognised, for example, that a machine has to interact with the user. For this reason electronic keyboards, which can be totally silent, have a click incorporated so that the operator gets some feedback when a key is depressed. Response time, and the variability of response time affect operator performance and operator perception and satisfaction.
The operator's behaviour in relation to the machine system is dependent on a range of physical, psychological, learning and cultural factors which are being investigated, but are still very imperfectly understood. At the same time the rapid changes taking place in the technology constantly create new problems for the designer to solve.

(e) Impact of the environmental factors on the user. These factors include: noise - both background noise and the noise made by the machine itself (too much noise can spoil concentration, too little can also be harmful); temperature, humidity, illumination, direction of light; the styling of the machine or work station. A machine with clean, uncluttered lines and a satisfactory styling is more happily used than one which is purely functional. Similarly, the type of surroundings affect the behaviour of the user. Well designed surroundings lead to better results, both in terms of quality of life and level of performance, than cluttered, dirty surroundings.

(f) The level of skills needed and how they can be acquired. The operating mode of the system must be fitted to the level of skill and experience of the users of the system. That means a system may have to have a variety of operating modes or procedures to fit in with the skills of users with a wide range of skills and experience. For example an information retrieval system might have a menu based guidance system to help an inexperienced user to 'navigate' through the system, and at the same time have a very concise command language for everyday, experienced users.

The very rapid diffusion of information technology through offices, factories and the home has led to an enormous increase in the number of non-specialist users interacting directly with computer devices. The problems of providing these users with systems they can use effectively has given a very significant boost to the study of ergonomics and human factor engineering (Shackel, 1984).

The emphasis attached to the topic is indicated by the recognition in the Alvey Report (1982) on Advanced Information Technology of the man/machine interface as one of the four 'enabling' technologies on which the future of information technology is to be based. Today ergonomic studies range from the measurements of the eye movements of a VDU operator in order to aid the design of better screens, to the study of the effect of variations of response time on the error rate of a terminal operator; to studies of the effect of different designs of office chairs on the rate at which word-processor operators become fatigued, to the study of man-machine dialogues on the willingness of 'naive' users to become regular clients of an information retrieval service.

## CONCLUSION

The object of good systems design must be to develop systems which enable an organisation to utilise its resources more effectively and at the same time improve the quality of work of those who work for the organisation. The previous sections of this paper have suggested some approaches to design which attempt to achieve such objectives. However, good systems design alone cannot achieve all the desired technical and social objectives.

A great deal has been written about the possible impact of information technology, and there seem to be two schools of thought on the social impact of the technology. The first school, whose views are articulated very clearly by writers like Cooley (1980), see the diffusion of information technology as a continuous process of rationalisation and as such a part of the process triggered by the industrial revolution. The earlier phase of the revolution reproduced and replaced the physical strength and manual skills of the human worker by machines, and more recently by robots. The first industrial revolution was characterised by the factory system which resulted in the increased control over the workforce by the employers. The system culminated in the almost complete abdication of formal control over his job by the worker on the assembly line under Taylor's principle of scientific management.

The only way the worker could maintain a position approaching equality was by organising into unions and taking an opposing stance to management.

Those who belong to the first school believe the same process is now overtaking white-collar, management and professional workers. The school is divided into optimists and pessimists. The optimists believe, like Cooley, that the technology is neutral, but that it is the capitalist system which uses the technology in a way which increases the control of the employer over the work process and the worker, in order to achieve higher levels of private profit (or ensure survival against new competition). Because the technology is neutral, they believe it is possible to organise the workers (through the unions) to choose alternative, humanistic ways of using the technology, thus achieving both social and technical goals.

Rosenbrock (1982) has shown that it is possible to design computer controlled, manufacturing processes which utilise the skills of workers, and which enhance rather than reduce the control the worker has over the job.

The pessimists (Braverman, 1971) believe that the process of industrialisation is deterministic and irreversible: social controls are bound to increase if the new technologies are to achieve their technical ends, and will result in a progressive degradation of work. It is believed that there is a technological imperative, whereby the proper utilisation of the technology demands increased control over the actions of the worker.

The second school takes a contingency approach. It notes the enormous variation in experience and outcomes with the introduction of information technology, and suggests that a wide range of factors underlie these experiences. This view is supported by a study of the impact of information technology on actual or perceived social control (Land et al, 1983). The study identified the following factors as contributing to the way technology is introduced and how it is perceived.

(a) The extent to which those who work in the organisation share its goals and values. Where values are shared there is a better chance of the new technology being accepted, and for the employees to get satisfaction from improved efficency. At the same time, shared values imply that management gets satisfaction from seeing the technology used in a way which enhances the job satisfaction of its employees. Evidence from case studies (Bird, 1980; Land et al, 1983) provide support for this conjecture.

The contrary case - where goals and values are not shared - has an opposite effect. Change is resisted, and counter-implementation strategies employed. Employees regard the introduction of computer systems as a threat, and at the same time use the introduction of such systems as an opportunity to demonstrate their independence, and, where possible, their power. They get satisfaction from winning battles against management. Management seeks to overcome resistance by taking a more authoritarian stance and by increasing control over the work situation. The extent of shared values is itself contingent on other factors. These include:

The industrial relations climate prevailing in the country, the industry, or the workshop. Historical, economic, the relative power of unions versus management, and personal factors can determine what the climate is like at any moment. Evidence from case studies (Land et al, 1983) demonstrates that industrial relations can range from excellent to catastrophic, even in different locations of one enterprise.

Management style. An authoritarian style mitigates against shared goals. On the other hand both paternalistic and democratic styles can encourage it.

Personal relations. Good personal relations within a department can encourage shared goals. Poor relations, even where the general industrial relation climate is good, can reduce the perception of shared goals.

Management distance. A remote management, either physically remote, but more importantly one which erects barriers between itself and its employees, such as separate dining rooms for managers and workers, is less likely to achieve shared goals than a management which attempts to reduce barriers, by, for example, sharing facilities with its employees. Management in the UK, perhaps because of the existing class structure, is reputed to erect more barriers than management in some other industrial countries. The success of Japan is often ascribed to consensus and conformity, and certainly Japanese management attempts to avoid the appearance of remoteness.

Management goals. Where management goals are narrowly defined in economic terms and where information technology is introduced primarily to reduce the work force, or reduce costs, shared goals, even if they existed beforehand, may cease to be shared.

Cultural and political factors. Different cultures have different behavioural norms and expectations. In some societies deference to authority is the norm, and an authoritarian style is expected and hence accepted.

In other societies it is expected that those who have authority seek a consensus with those in subordinate positions. In other societies those who have authority seek to ensure a shared ideology and shared values, by a process of conditioning starting at an early age, and any dissent from the prevailing ideology is discouraged by the harsh treatment of the dissenter.

(b) The approach chosen for the introduction of the technology. An approach which takes account of social as well as technical and financial objectives, and which encourages participation in design and implementation, is more likely to produce a system which is both widely accepted, and which achieves a high level of organisational performance. Some critics (Kraft, 1979) have suggested that such approaches are manipulative, and are designed to gain approval through a pretended sharing of decisions when the real decisions and power are still in the hands of the employers. The conventional approach, however, can create conflict and result in systems which do not perform at the required level and which fail to earn an adequate return on the resources invested in them.

(c) The philosophy or principles which underlie the way systems are expected to operate. The assumptions on which systems design is often based are derived from the principles of scientific management. The outcome is systems which seek to minimise the users' independent judgement, which tend to be prescriptive, and which use the technology to control and measure the performance of the operator or user.

Even systems designed for the use of management have tended to be prescriptive, and to replace the decision-making tasks of at least junior and middle management by computer-based decision procedures. For example, the manager of a retail store loses the responsibility for provisioning the shop, that task being taken over by the central computer using an inventory control algorithm.

In recent years an alternative strategy has been formulated. This is based on the realisation that many decision processes depend on data from a wide variety of sources, some from the designed information system, some from the informal system. In many situations it is impossible to predetermine the precise decision process. Conversely, it is possible to provide the decision maker with a variety of computer aids. Such 'decision support systems' can include a variety of facilities - data bases which can be interrogated by means of easy-to-use query languages, modelling and simulation facilities which enable the decision maker to ask 'what if' questions and use statistical techniques to extrapolate trends.

(d) The extent to which organisations are used to technological and organisational change. An organisation which is used to change is more likely to assimilate change stemming from the introduction of new information technology, without creating adverse reactions to its initiation, than an organisation where the pace of change is slow. Because people of all levels working in an organisation not used to change may be less good at coping with the uncertainties engendered by the change process, projects run into trouble, and it may be felt necessary to exert more pressure and to impose tighter controls to get the new system implemented.

(e) Economic factors play a key role in determining the kind of systems to be implemented, and in the method of implementation. They dominate the selection of goals for the new system. The condition of an enterprise's balance sheet, or movements in the market share of its products, may dominate the choice of application and the method of implementation. Efficiency and cost saving goals become paramount and overshadow any consideration of other factors. Short-term considerations may be allowed to dominate the design process, and inadequate attention may be paid to organisational and social factors, leading to the design of systems which are incapable of gaining the approval of those who have to work with them.

(f) Government regulations and legislation which can affect the design of systems and some of their social impact through laws relating to privacy, and which can have an impact on implementation methods through government sponsored measures such as the German co-determination agreements, and the Norwegian Data Acts. These measures try to ensure that new information systems receive the assent of employees before implementation. Laws which attempt to curb the general powers of trade unions can have the effect of reducing the power of employees to resist systems which they regard as adverse, and increase the opportunity for managements to increase their control over the work force.

(g) This affects the power of trade unions to make conditions relating to the introduction of information technology. Likewise the extent of a trade union's ability to play a role in determining the kind of system which is to be implemented depends on the following:-

The union's knowledge and understanding of the technology. In the UK unions are relatively uninformed, and the role in designing systems is therefore limited. Unions, in particular white collar unions, are attempting to gain more understanding of the technology. In some Scandinavian countries the unions are much better informed, and as a result have the capability of effectively criticising the plans of management, or of putting forward alternative designs. It is interesting to note that there is a willingness of university researchers in Scandinavia to cooperate with the unions in training and helping the unions.

The extent to which management is prepared to divulge details of its plans and aims to the unions. Some managements are willing to involve the unions in the change process, but many employers regard interference in the planning process by the unions as an infringement of their own right to manage.

The power of a union to insist that it play a part in the introduction of a new system. In some countries that power is supported through government legislation or sponsorship, as with the Swedish and West German co-determination agreements. In other cases the union's power depends on its overall bargaining strength vis à vis management, and that depends both on local conditions and the general position of unions in the economy.

Overall, in the UK and USA, the impact of unions on the introduction of information technology seems to be slight, even for white collar unions which have had the greatest success in prevailing on managements to come to Technology Agreements.

This list of contingency factors cannot be exhaustive, but it probably highlights the more important factors. Of course the factors are interdependent, and the actual outcome in any situation will be determined by a mixture of factors. What the approach suggests is that how effective a new system will be, or how its users will perceive it, is highly complex and difficult to predict. Nevertheless there are a number of ways in which it is possible to improve the change of design and implementation of information systems which are organisationally effective, and which at the same time enhance the quality of life of those who operate and use the systems.

## REFERENCES

Alvey, J. (Chairman) (1982) A Programme for Advanced Information Technology, The Report of the Alvey Committee, HMSO

Argyris, C. and Schon, D. (1974) Theory in Practice: Increasing Professional Effectiveness, Jossey-Bass

Bird, E. (1980) Information Technology in the Office: The Impact on Women's Jobs, London Equal Opportunity Commission

Bramer, M.A. (1981) 'A Survey and Critical Review of Expert Systems Research', in Parslow, R.D. (ed.) Information Technology for the Eighties, Heyden

Braverman, H. (1971) Labour and Monopoly Capital: The Degradation of Work in the Twentieth Century, Monthly Review Press, New York

Cooley, M.J.E. (1980) Architect or Bee, Langley Technical Services, Slough

Dickson, G. and Simmons, J. (1970) 'The Behavioral Side of MIS: Some Aspects of the "People Problem"', Business Horizons, August, 59-71

Earl, M. and Hopwood, A. (1979) 'From Management Information to Information Management', in Lucas, H., Land, F.F., Lincoln, T. and Supper, K. (eds.) The Information Systems Environment, North Holland

Feigenbaum, E.A. and McCorduck P. (1983) The Fifth Generation, Addison-Wesley

Hawgood, J. (1974) 'Quinquevalent Quantification of Computer Benefits', in Freilink, A. (ed.) Economics of Informatics, North Holland

Hedberg, B. and Mumford, E. (1975) 'The Design of Computer Systems: Man's Vision of Man as an Integral Part of the Design Process', in Mumford, E. and Sackman, H. (eds.) Human Choice and Computers, North Holland

Hirschheim, R. (1983) 'Computers and Privacy', Computer Bulletin, March

Hopwood, A. (1980) Towards Assessing the Economic Cost of New Forms of Work Organisation, Unpublished Monograph

Hoyer, R. (1979) 'User Participation: Why is Development so Slow? The Dynamics of the Development of End User Control', in Lucas, H., Land, F.F., Lincoln T., and Supper, K. (eds.), The Computer Systems Environment, North Holland

Kall, C.O. (1984) 'Conceptual Data Modelling as an Obstacle to Organisational Decentralisation', Proceedings of IFIP W.G. 6.3 INTERACT Conference, (2), London, September, 289-93

Keen, P.G.W. (1981) 'Information Systems and Organisational Change', Communications of the ACM, 24 (1), January

Kerola, P. and Taggart, W.M. (1982) 'Human Information Processing Styles in the Information Systems Development Process', in Hawgood, J. (ed) Evolutionary Information Systems, North Holland

Kilmann, R.H. and Mitroff, I.I. (1976) 'Quantitative versus Qualitative Analysis for Management Science: Different Forms for Different Psychological Types', TIMS Interfaces, February

Kraft, P. (1979) 'Challenging the Mumford Democrats at Derby Works', Computing, August 2nd

Land, F.F. (1976) 'Evaluation of Systems Goals in Determining a Design Strategy for Computer-Based Information Systems', Computer Journal, 19 (4), November

Land, F.F. (1982) 'Notes on Participation', Computer Journal, Vol. 25, No. 2, February

Land, F.F. (1984) 'The Information Systems Domain', in Wood-Harper, A.T. and Episkopou, D.M. (eds.) Issues and Methods in Information Systems, Report from IFIP Work Group 8.2 Meeting at University of Michigan, Ann Arbor, December 1982, published by School of Computing Studies and Accountancy, University of East Anglia, September

Land, F.F., Detjejaruwat, N. and Smith, C. (1983) 'Factors Affecting Social Control: The Reasons and Values', Systems, Objectives, Solutions, 3 (1) and 3 (6)

Land, F.F. and Hirschheim, R. (1983) 'Participative Systems Design: Rationale, Tools, and Techniques', Journal of Applied Systems Analysis, 10, 91-107

Land, F.F. and Kennedy-McGregor, M. (1981) 'Effective Use of Internal Information', in Pappenheim, A. (ed.) Business Information Systems, INFOTECH State of the Art Report, 9 (7)

Land, F.F., Mumford, E. and Hawgood, J. (1979) 'Training the Systems Analysts of the 1980's: Four New Design Tools to Assist the Design Process', in Lucas, H., Land, F.F., Lincoln, T. and Supper, K. (eds.) The Information Systems Environment, North Holland

Lawrence, M., Edmundson, R. and O'Connor, M. (1984) 'Problem Partitioning in the Design of a Forecasting Decision Support System', in Proceedings of Joint International Symposium on Information Systems, Sidney, April

Lindop, N. (Chairman) (1978) Report of the Committee on Data Protection, Cmnd. 7341, HMSO

Marchetti, C. (1981) 'Society as a Learning System: Discovery, Invention and Innovation Cycles Revisited', Invited Paper presented at the Conference "Market and Product Innovation Facing Social and Technological Change", Turin, April

Mintzberg, H. (1974) How Managers Manage, Harper & Row

Mumford, E. (1972) 'Job Satisfaction: A Method of Analysis', Personnel Review, No. 3

Mumford, E. (1981) Values, Technology and Work, Martinus Nijhoff

Mumford, E. and Henshall, D. (1979) A Participative Approach to Computer Systems Design: A Case Study of the Introduction of a New Computer System, Associated Business Press

Mumford, E., Land, F.F. and Hawgood, J. (1978) 'A Participative Approach to the Design of Computer Systems', Impact of Science on Society, 18 (3)

Mumford, E. and Weir, M. (1979) Computer Systems in Work Design - The ETHICS Method, Associated Business Press

Roethlisberger, P.J. and Dickson, W.J. (1939) Management and the Worker, Harvard University Press

Rosenbrock, H. (1982) 'Technology Policy and Options', in Bjorn-Andersen, N., Earl. M., Holst, O. and Mumford, E. (eds.) Information Society: For Richer for Poorer, North Holland

Shackel, B. (1984) 'Designing for People in the Age of Information', Proceedings of IFIP W.G. 6.3 INTERACT Conference, Vol. 1, London, September, 6-15

Stamper, R.K. (1979) 'Towards a Semantic Normal Form', in Bracci, G. and Nijesen, G.M. (eds.) Data Base Architecture, North Holland

Williams, R. and Moseley, R. (1982) 'The Trade Union Response to Information Technology: Technology Agreements', Bjorn-Andersen, N., Earl, M., Holst, O. and Mumford, E. (eds.) Information Society: For Richer for Poorer, North Holland

# 3. Planning, Control and Technological Change

by Roger Mansfield

## INTRODUCTION

This chapter starts with the proposition that information is vital to successful management. If this is the case, the recent dramatic developments in various aspects of information technology present enormous opportunities for augmenting managerial effectiveness, and hence for improving organisational efficiency and performance.

It is commonplace to point out that the successful practice of management in any organisation depends on the ability to obtain, process and utilise information. At the extreme, without information, attempts to initiate or control any activity can be little more than random behaviour, since ignorance or uncertainty erodes the ability of managers to manage. This is particularly true for senior managers involved in policy-making and top level organisational control, although not always fully reflected in practice in some organisations. It follows that there are likely to be considerable pressures in any organisation towards the creation and maintenance of an information system for management.

There is, of course, nothing particularly new or original in the sentiments expressed above. Indeed, managers have for a long time expended considerable time, effort and money in gathering and processing information. They have often set up elaborate information systems to routinise such operations. These managerial actions have been particularly noticeable in large organisations where the scale of operation has been sufficient to spread the associated costs over a large volume of output. At the same time the inevitable complexity associated with size has made the requirement for such systems that much more compelling in such organisations. Since the advent of electronic data processing, some parts of such systems have been computerised. Indeed very large sums of money are devoted to this quite routinely by very large organisations. This has given the facility for handling large quantities of information both rapidly and accurately.

What is new in the present day situation is that, with the latest technological developments, the data handling and transmission capability of management information systems has increased dramatically. At the same time the technology and associated software have become significantly more user-friendly thus giving the possibility of designing systems which allow almost instant access to large bodies of data to almost anyone in an organisation - at least this is so in theory.

These changes can be seen to be the very rapid cumulative outcome of a series of interconnected quantitative changes which have dramatically increased the speed, reliability and power of computing systems whilst their real cost has progressively decreased. At the same time communication facilities have been improved by at least an order of magnitude. Taken together these developments have led to a qualitative change in the potential information resources available to management.

The possible applications of the new technology are, at least in theory, relevant to virtually every organisational activity in almost every organisation. However, attempts to exploit such potential have been very uneven. Up to the present it would seem that the new developments in technology have been used most readily in production areas (Sorge et al, 1983) and offices (Long, 1984) to facilitate improvements in the efficiency of relatively routine operations to reduce labour costs, speed up outputs or provide for a higher quality of work. In addition the new technology has been used significantly in many record-keeping, data processing and information systems areas, particularly where financial or other quantitative data are involved (Earl, 1984).

However, the areas of organisational activity which may ultimately be most significantly changed by the new technology are those that relate to higher management decision-making, and encompass the basic planning and control processes on which other organisational activities ultimately depend (Mansfield, 1984) and which, in the last analysis, have the greatest implications for organisational effectiveness. It is to a discussion of the issues relating to this broad area of potential applications that most of the present chapter is devoted. However, before moving on to that, it may be useful to sketch briefly an outline of the nature of the new technology which may eventually make a complete rearrangement of methods of executing the top management task possible or even essential.

## THE NATURE OF THE NEW TECHNOLOGY

Technological development in recent years has been both dramatic and exceedingly rapid. Of particular consequence to the present discussion has been the apparently ever accelerating changes in both computer and communication technologies, largely, but certainly not exclusively, based on the silicon chip. The potential embodied in the developments in hardware are amazing and far outstrip both software developments and even more particularly the utilisation of the new technology by management. At the same time as the power and speed of information technology hardware has been greatly enhanced, the price of equipment in real terms, and often even in actual money, has decreased. In many cases the reduction in cost has been very considerable, thus putting many items of equipment well within the scope of even very small businesses. These trends would still seem to be continuing, and at the present time developments using gallium arsenide or, more radically, optical techniques may well make even silicon-based hardware obsolete in its capability.

Perhaps the most significant element in the new technology thus far has been the development of smaller, faster, cheaper and more powerful computers, such that the latest generation of microcomputers have a quite amazing capability. This, coupled with increasingly more sophisticated software, has allowed a wide range of employees to have immediate access to a tremendous range of information and information processing capability. The implications of this have been made all the more dramatic by the concurrent developments in communications technology which allow these microcomputers to be networked to provide whole systems of interlinked devices. The available technology now means it is no longer a dream or science fiction to envisage senior executives being able to get detailed current production or sales figures flashed on to a VDU on their desks at the press of a button in order to keep track of the minute by minute operations of a company. This is true even where some of the operating sites are located in far distant parts of the world.

The technology, at least in terms of hardware, has already been developed to such an extent that the whole nature of the practice of management could be changed. Indeed as long ago as 1960, Simon (1960) suggested that in a few years (from then) it would be possible to computerise virtually all non-manual organisational operations including all types of decision-making.

As far as can be ascertained, however, the reality of management in most functional areas and particularly in the general management area has so far not in fact altered to any particularly dramatic extent. This would seem to be the case for three main reasons. Firstly there is a lack of sufficiently sophisticated software to deal with many managerial problems, and there is a relatively high cost associated with the development of software in this area.

Second, there are a large number of organisational, social and psychological factors which militate against very rapid change. Finally, the nature of apparent possibilities suggests that the balance of economic factors is against the widespread adoption of the new technology in many managerial areas of responsibility at the present time. These issues will be considered further at a later point, but as a next step in the discussion, attention will be focused on the nature of the general management task and its information requirements in order that the relevance of the developments in technology outlined above can be examined.

## THE GENERAL MANAGEMENT TASK

In any organisation, of whatever size, the basic task of general management involves (1) the setting of objectives; (2) the development of strategies to accomplish those objectives; (3) the design of organizational structures and administrative systems to assist in the accomplishment of those strategies; (4) arranging for the staffing of those structures and the development of personnel; (5) the giving of direction and the exercise of leadership in pursuit of the accomplishment of strategic objectives; and (6) the monitoring and control of organisational performance. Thus, overall, the task of general management must be seen as a combination of planning, coordination and control.

In order to accomplish its task, general management must involve and coordinate the activities of a number of functional areas. Most obvious amongst these are those involved in the major operational tasks of the organisation, such as production and sales. Also, there are those support functions directly linked to the productive areas such as marketing, quality control and industrial engineering. In addition, there are the more general support functions such as personnel, accounting, and corporate planning. In large organisations it is generally the case that each of these functional tasks is carried out by departments of significant size. On the other hand, in the smallest companies the managing director or general manager typically performs many, or even all, of the non-productive functions himself. Irrespective of who carries out the variety of functional tasks involved, however, it is clear that some aspects of the tasks associated with the latter category of support functions form an integral part of the overall general management task, although not always of the jobs of general managers. This must be true because of their linkages to the fundamental areas of policy-making and control.

The outline sketched in thus far should be sufficient to make clear that any serious consideration of the variety of tasks involved in general management from objective setting through to performance monitoring immediately involves a significant requirement for a very high level of information input. Without information general management can hardly begin.

Given the scenario sketched out above, it is clearly important to examine the nature of the information used by general management, and, perhaps more importantly, the information system which supplies general management with the data upon which decisions are, can be or should be based. In pursuit of this objective, it is important first to note that, in general terms, organisational personnel gather information as a consequence of one or other of two logics. On the one hand it may be done as a side-product of carrying out other functional duties within the organisation. On the other hand information gathering may be an additional functional task very specifically designed and executed in order to increase the knowledge-base of the organisation's management. In either case the data may be used in order to aid both strategic and tactical decision-making as well as to aid the control of organisational activities and performance. To this end, it must be noted that in both cases the collection, transmission and processing of such data can and should be planned and regulated to improve the reliability and relevance of the end-product information for senior management.

In order to further consider top management's information requirements, it is also useful to distinguish between information on aspects of the organisational environment and information concerning the functioning of the organisation and the behaviour of its employees, that is to differentiate between information regarding external factors on the one hand, and information relating to internal factors on the other. Such a distinction is likely to be important in terms of the information itself, the problems of collecting it, and the strategic use to which it may be put.

Considering the two dichotomised dimensions just identified provides us with a four-fold categorisation of information sources which provide information relevant to the top management task. This is based partly on the processes of information gathering and partly on the distinction between internal and external sources.

The four categories are shown in Table 3.1. Firstly, there is information gathered from, or regarding, external factors, which is collected as a consequence of people carrying out their normal tasks. Examples would be sales figures and reports from salesmen on customers. Secondly, there is information regarding external factors collected as a consequence of deliberate information gathering efforts, such as market research. Thirdly, there is information with regard to internal matters gathered as a by-product of the normal execution of the company's business, such as

**Table 3.1: Categorisation of Management Information Sources**

| | External | Internal |
|---|---|---|
| Gathered as a side-product | e.g Sales figures | e.g. Personnel records |
| Deliberately gathered | e.g. Market research data | e.g. Productivity rates |

personnel records. Fourthly, there is information on internal functioning gathered as a consequence of deliberate information gathering, such as productivity rates. All these sorts of information have relevance to particular functional areas and would be used in most organisations by a variety of managers in many functional areas at different levels in the hierarchy. However, all of them, appropriately processed, would be relevant to the overall top management task of policy making and control.

At this point it must be noted that in terms of the way the information is treated, and in some cases the nature of the information required, it is useful both analytically and practically to distinguish between that element of the top management task relating to policy making on the one hand and that element of the task relating to organisational control on the other. This may have utility not only because the information requirements of the two are somewhat different, but also because the implications of the new developments in information technology may vary considerably in the two cases.

## INFORMATION FOR POLICY MAKING

It is almost true by definition that policy making is about the future. More than that, it is typically very often about the medium and long-term future. This means that information has to be gathered which allows prediction of one sort or another about future events. In many cases such predictions must stretch many years ahead. Clearly such requirements will necessitate some form of forecasting process of greater or lesser complexity, and also suggest that the data will need to be processed to a considerably greater extent than would be needed in the case of decision making about the present or the immediate future.

Clearly where the forecasts of the medium and long-term future are to be created by the manipulation of data, the question of probabilities or uncertainty becomes a very significant factor, even where the data themselves are deemed to provide reliable and accurate indications of current situations. Using such information to predict the future must inevitably create a probability of less than one that the estimates or forecasts are accurate. In many cases such probabilities may be dramatically less than one. Clearly where this is the case, top managers may be inclined to treat such forecasts with cynicism or indeed to disregard them completely. Even where precise estimates of the probabilities involved and also of the range of possible variation can in reality be defined with accuracy, it is likely that many managers will view the ensuing forecasts with a certain lack of faith.

One of the clear implications associated with the ability to manipulate data in highly sophisticated ways using modern computer technology is that the final output may be well removed from the initial inputs to the process in both form and kind. Also the processes involved may seem incomprehensible to all but statisticians and computer programmers. Hence if top managers have insufficient faith in this manipulation process, they will tend to a considerable extent to disregard the outcomes and thus rely on personal judgement for making policy-making decisions. In the case of many senior managers this would seem to be true even where the cost to the organisation of supplying the information they ignore is considerable. In such instances it is often also true that the veracity of the computer output may be greater, when viewed objectively, than that stemming from the only partly articulated judgemental logic of a senior executive.

It must of course be noted that the sort of information required for policy-making decisions would not normally be required on a continuous basis, as corporate plans are rarely modified on a day to day basis, but rather annually or on some other relatively long-term time scale. This last point taken in conjunction with the need to develop medium and long-term forecasts suggests particular requirements of the new technology which will be considered further below.

## INFORMATION FOR CONTROL

The information requirements for control in organisations are generally somewhat different in a number of respects from those for policy making. Firstly, the information required is typically about the immediate past or the present or occasionally about the immediate future. The essence of such information is that it should be in a form which allows for the monitoring of relevant organisational activities, inputs and outputs, such that remedial action could be taken rapidly and efficiently where required. In cybernetic terms it is the basis upon which negative feedback can be given in order to keep the organisation on course for the achievement of strategic objectives. It follows from this that the information required in most cases needs to be more detailed than that required for policy making. This is typically true as nothing less than detailed and immediate information will facilitate the sort of immediate corrections required to prevent the organisation getting well off course. It follows therefore that information collection, processing and interpretation for control purposes, if not actually continuous, must become routine in any organisation. It should be capable of providing feedback on a timescale geared to that of the natural operating cycles within the organisation.

There can be no doubt that in this area the opportunities created by modern technology have dramatically improved the possibilities of control systems operating effectively, efficiently and rapidly in organisations. In the vast majority of concerns, there can be no doubt that output measures, whether for manufacturing or for service organisations, can be placed into some computational network, and thus be capable of rapid interrogation by senior management. As Heery (1985) has argued, 'Computers have been considered to hold this potential essentially because of the opportunities they present for greater and more rapid information capture, storage, analysis and distributing so as to increase the visibility of operations at the base of the enterprise to those at its peak.' It is perhaps in this area of control that the prediction made a long time ago by Herbert Simon (1960) that electronic data processing would remove the role of middle management may, at last, come partly true. Certainly with regard to some functional activities this has been suggested to be happening (Purcell, 1979).

## GATHERING AND PROCESSING INFORMATION

It is worth digressing at this stage in the argument, to consider very briefly the ways in which the new technology has effected the methods by which data can be gathered, processed and output. It is perhaps easiest to start by considering the processing area. Here, it is clear that where the information is, or can be, converted into a numerical form, then modern computational equipment and software allows it to be rapidly manipulated and transformed into almost any form of end product required. For this to be useful for management an appropriate model or algorithm must be available to guide the computational steps carried out. This proviso is most likely to cause problems in the policy-making area where sufficiently complex computer models are difficult to develop. However, that problem will be considered further below.

Where the information cannot on the basis of present knowledge be transformed in any reasonable way into a numerical form, then the processing is more difficult and is likely to involve substantially less data manipulation or reduction. Nonetheless, modern software developments are rapidly improving one's ability to process non-quantitative material. However, with both quantitative and qualitative types of information, it is increasingly the case that many of the key problems relate on the one hand to the collection and input of the raw data in the first instance in a reliable, rapid and economic way and on the other hand to the interpretation and utilisation of the processed data at the other end. In many cases, the intermediate processing would appear to be relatively non-problematic, at least by comparison.

In examining these problems let us first turn to the question of information gathering. Remembering the four-fold classification suggested earlier (Table 3.1) it is perhaps useful to see the extent to which modern technology has made the possibilities of these processes greater and the problems that are still involved. The first category related to information from or regarding external factors collected by personnel employed by the organisation carrying out their normal tasks. Much of such information will of its nature be of a quantitative kind such as sales reported, complaints received, and so on. A certain amount, however, will involve subjective assessments made by personnel such as salesmen about such factors as potential trends in the market place. The former type of information can normally be input without difficulty via keyboards and processed easily by any computational system. However, the latter type of data is obviously subject to much greater difficulties. There is clearly a danger in accepting subjective, possibly intuitive, reports and entering them into the information processing system. On the other hand to ignore such ideas may be equally dangerous. In the last analysis, what is required is a way of placing probabilities on the opinions of a large number of organisational personnel even if these are themselves subjective estimates.

The second category related to information regarding external factors collected by deliberate action over and above the immediate requirements of the organisation's functioning. In the main such information may be capable of quantification and thus relatively routine processing. However, particularly where senior personnel are involved in making judgemental assessments of the way external factors are changing, the information may again be both qualitative and subjective and again create problems in terms of utilisation within any data processing system.

The third and fourth categories of information, in as much as they relate to the present or past, should generally be more likely to involve data collection on a relatively routine quantitative basis. Thus, for example, production figures and absenteeism statistics can normally be obtained in a routine quantitative form. However, where the information is used to indicate future trends, then again there may be a significant subjective element which may be difficult to quantify and to process in a computer-based system. In the main, the greater the predictive element the greater will be the subjective component of the information and hence the greater the difficulty in dealing with the information automatically by electronic data processing in any way which can give reliable answers.

Clearly one of the key issues in collecting and inputting information for any purpose must be the ways and means by which this can be done. In many areas the data is still effectively collected by older techniques and then scores representing that data punched through keyboards into a variety of communication and computational systems. However, two recent technological developments have changed and enhanced the possibilities for an individual organisation to collect information. Firstly, there are now a variety of automatic transducers which can assess on-going situations and automatically feed electronic signals into a computer system. Perhaps the simplest versions of these are likely to occur in the production area, where, for example, each component produced could be inspected and counted automatically, using mechanical or visual detectors, and the information fed back into a central system.

A much more significant development may eventually come from the possibility of networking computational systems, not only within organisations, but between organisations. Thus customers' computers could be connected directly to the sales department and thus information from such sources fed into the central computing network of an organization. This would in theory lead to considerable cost savings for both customers and sellers. However, there could be dangers with such a system for both, as they would possibly be unable to protect their own computer-based information from being read and indeed from being modified by outsiders. It would seem likely, at least for the moment, that this security problem will prevent many organisations from networking their computers with those of other organisations despite the potential for considerable savings in time, manpower and money.

## THE NEW TECHNOLOGY: THE ULTIMATE CHALLENGE

Without any doubt the application of the new technology developed in the areas of communication and computation and all related areas could, at least in theory, be used to revolutionalise the basic tasks of strategic management, planning and control in a large number, if not all, organisational settings. The hardware capability is unquestionably already developed, the software capability is in process of development. The problems of implementation are probably at least ninety per cent in the area of management, particularly relating to social and psychological acceptance. It is plausible to suggest that only ten per cent of the problems are in the areas of hardware and software development.

As has already been pointed out, the task of top management requires the greatest information inputs of any managerial function. Partly because of this, and partly in spite of it, the use of the new technology has been, and is likely to continue to be, limited in this area. Where, as may be sometimes the case with functional decision making in production or accounting, the problem may be defined with precision and the information requirements clearly stipulated, then the new technology lends itself in a relatively easy and straightforward way to the assistance of management and managerial decision making. In that much broader area in which top management is involved, the problem is less definable. Also the information requirements, although enormous, are less easily capable of precise definition. This being the case, there can be no doubt that there must be an element of judgement that must enter in. This will continue to be the case in the forseeable future. Apart from the limitations that have been mentioned already regarding the development of software, and the difficulties of dealing with qualitative and quasi-quantitative information, the area where the new technology has most limited immediate and direct application is where a mixture of hard information heuristics and judgement is required. The mixing of different types and qualities of data and processing models, in and of itself, causes considerable problems.

Clearly the key ingredient, or perhaps the joker in the pack, is the concept of judgement. All too often this ill-defined, and perhaps undefinable, notion is used as an excuse for making decisions on the basis of intuition or guesswork rather than by an exhaustive examination of what data is available and the most modern decision-making models. The complexity of the problems and the need for enormous quantities of information may, and often does, have the counter-productive consequence of leading senior managers to ignore much of the information that is available on the grounds that it is incomplete. It would seem intuitively obvious, although probably unprovable with the present state of knowledge, that some information must always be better than none; and a great deal of information, even if incomplete, must always be better than some. Almost instinctively, however, many senior managers may revolt against this notion. They appear to believe that when uncertainty cannot be removed, either by hard information or generally acceptable decision-making rules, then judgement must be allowed free rein, even where this means disregarding what information or part of what information is actually available.

If such prejudices are to be overcome, considerable attention has to be given to the overall way in which modern, technologically-based, management information systems can be designed and utilised for senior management decision making. The processes that must be involved are, first, the collection of information, including in some cases its creation by such activities as research. Second, there is the coding of such information for utilisation by a computer system. Third, there is the transmission of such information from the point of input to the point of processing and then on to the point of utilisation. Fourth, there is the processing and manipulation of the information. Fifth and finally, there is the retrieval and utilisation of the information.

We have already briefly considered the question of data collection, but it is worth reiterating the point that it is clearly essential to develop an overall strategy on the basis of which to decide on the nature and extent of the data collection process. As with many of the other issues that must be considered, it should be noted that data may be collected for a variety of different purposes. In the context of senior management decision making it is essential that the needs of that process are identified and, where necessary, additional data collected over and above that which may be required for operational or functional requirements.

There can be little doubt that any data collection process may be subject to error. This may occur either as a consequence of pure mistakes, or as a consequence of bias, whether accidental or deliberate, being entered into the information. It is essential, particularly where the information is to be utilised for senior management decision making, that care be taken in the design of data collection systems to ensure that the inevitable risks of inaccuracies are minimised. Also it is desirable to ascertain the maximum extent of error possible with regard to each type of data. Whether the inaccuracies are liable to be random or systematic should also be assessed.

The second stage in the process involves the coding of information to allow it to be entered into a computer system and used by that system. In some cases the coding is an entirely straightforward, largely manual task, and merely converts information into machine-readable language. However, in many cases, particularly where non-quantitative information is being utilised, the coding inevitably extracts only part of the information that has been collected and thus there is a possibility of data loss occurring at this stage. Thus, for example, a complex statement by a customer concerning the quality of goods may at the extreme be converted into a simple 'yes/no' statement on the acceptability of the goods received. At this stage, therefore, great care must be used in the design of coding systems such that information which will later be valuable for decision-making should not be excluded. It is also important that no additional inaccuracies or biases are unnecessarily built into the data available at this stage.

The third stage of data transmission is, with modern technology, increasingly less of a problem. With the multitude of aids now available it is possible to transmit very large quantities of data at very high speed from one part of the world to another, without adding inaccuracies. Clearly care must be taken in the design of such systems, but in this area the technology has advanced to such an extent that the problems are typically likely to be limited. It must, however, be the case that, where speed and reliability of transmission are important, there should be alternative back-up systems available, in case the prime transmission system should break down. Such requirements are most likely to be needed for operational decision making or for top management control as opposed to top management policy making, where in most cases the time scale can afford to be rather more relaxed.

As has already been noted, in the fourth stage of processing and manipulating data very few problems will be likely to arise because of the lack of computing power or hardware deficiencies. Even relatively small computers can, in this day and age, process large amounts of information in complex ways at tremendously high speeds. The difficulties that may and do arise are typically ones associated with the problems of programming the data processing, such that it is executed in a way which will be useful and beneficial for senior management in carrying out their twin tasks of policy making and control. Unless this data manipulation is guided by a viable model of the organisation's activities, it is liable sooner or later to lead to serious problems in the decision-making processes. With this in mind, it is useful to analyse the issues involved with considerable care. Following this approach suggests that, in the general area of data processing and manipulation for senior management decision making, four particular problem areas can be identified. It is clearly vital that each is treated appropriately if serious misinformation is not to be passed on to senior managers.

The first of these problems or questions relates to the question of data reduction. Inevitably the data that will be collected by an organisation will be substantially greater than that which any senior manager would ever wish to look at. This will be particularly true in large organisations. Clearly senior managers will need to have this data presented to them in summary form. In other words they will not wish to know, for example, which operative produced how many items, in one shift, in one plant on a particular day. They are much more likely to be interested in average rates of production, average rates of productivity, average production costs, and so on.

However, the question of averaging in order to achieve the summary data may in many cases, if not treated with care, lead to dramatically misleading answers. A simple-minded example will serve to illustrate this point. If one considers a company which owns two plants producing the same products at the same time, then to give an average production figure for the two would be useful information where the two plants were operating at approximately the same level of efficiency, productivity, and manning. If, however, one was dramatically more efficient than the other, then an average figure could well lead to misleading decisions at senior level. This, of course, is a very simple example and there are many that could be mentioned where the complexity is very much greater and the potential for misleading senior managers is much more hidden by the data manipulation processes involved. The same problem potentially arises with any other method of data reduction as well as that of averaging.

The second issue is in reality very similar to the data reduction problem and it relates to the general problem of aggregation. How can different sorts of information be aggregated in order to provide meaningful summary data for decision making? The problems of aggregation are well-known in social science and without doubt can lead to serious mistakes being made. Again, a simple example will serve to illustrate the point. It is generally straightforward to count the number of finished cars coming off the end of an assembly line. However, it will not necessarily be easy to interpret the total if within it are numbers of cars of a variety of different models. The utility of the total as a piece of management information will diminish further if the mix of models is constantly changing.

Both the data reduction and aggregation issues relate very much to the third issue of the choice of units of analysis. One has to decide about what analytical units information is required for senior management decision making. Is it appropriate to know production figures factory by factory, or is it needed on a much more detailed basis or a much broader basis? The decision depends, of course, both on the nature of the problems that are faced by the company and also the extent of variability within categories that might be put together to provide a single unit of analysis. These three issues, although difficult to handle, are, in the main, capable of analysis by statistical techniques. With modern computer systems this can be done automatically at high speed at relatively low cost.

The fourth issue may in the end be much more difficult and perhaps much more important for senior management to consider. This relates to the extent to which extrapolation can be utilised in order to make predictions outside the data base in order to guide senior management in decision making. Extrapolation and kindred processes may have to be used for a variety of different reasons, but the most common and probably the most consequential for policy decision making is extrapolation into the future. Without doubt many of the factors which are relevant to senior management decision making trend in tolerably smooth ways. Under such circumstances extrapolation for short periods into the future is likely to prove a fairly reliable basis for forecasting. However, there are many indicators and factors which fluctuate in a way which does not allow for extrapolation without a very sophisticated model. In addition it will be true that in virtually all cases the temptation to rely on extrapolation is likely to create more problems as the length of time over which the extrapolation takes place increases.

It is clear, therefore, that in the processing and manipulation stage the possibilities for inaccurate and misleading information to be created and passed on towards senior management are very considerable. Iterative approaches to these various problems may well reduce the difficulties and provide a greater reliability as well as better estimates of the inaccuracies that may still be involved. However, from the point of view of the senior manager, it is very often the problem that he is not fully conversant with the way in which this processing occurs or the models on which it is based. As a consequence of this he may have difficulty checking the output information and may in any case distrust it.

The final stage in the process involves the retrieval and utilisation of the information. Here again problems may well exist. In the very recent 'old days' it was conventional that retrieval involved the printing-out of vast quantities of information. This very often left senior managers' desks invisible below a heap of computer printout, often leading to significant problems of overload. The senior executive, particularly the less sophisticated and trained senior executive, was typically unable to sift rapidly through the vast amount of data apparently provided him in printouts. As a consequence he all too often would either ignore it completely or sift it in a somewhat biased or even random way.

However, it is now increasingly possible with modern technology to provide senior executives, not with data as such, but with a facility to interrogate information stores held within the computer system. This, on the face of it, would seem a much more satisfactory approach, but it can only work satisfactorily where the senior managers involved are exceedingly knowledgeable about the overall store of information held within the system, also understanding its relevance, accuracy and the ways in which it can be retrieved. In the last analysis, given what has already been said, it is clear that the potential for the utilisation of modern information technology for aiding, and possibly even making, senior management policy decisions, is enormous. It is equally clear that the potential pitfalls and problems are large.

In the main senior managers will be left with three potential problems concerning the information they can retrieve. First, there is the question of inaccuracy which can, at the extreme, invalidate the whole basis on which particular decisions are made. The issue of inaccuracy, becomes dramatically more of a problem when the managers are not aware of the likely inaccuracies, or the extent to which information can be inaccurate. Second, there is the danger of overloading, where managers are provided with too much information for them to sift and consider in the time available. Third, there is the apparently opposite difficulty of lack of information, where some of the things the managers would like to know cannot be gleaned from the system. Perhaps paradoxically both these second and third problems can occur at the same time where managers are supplied with too much information which nonetheless lacks some critical elements within it.

There is nothing new about any of these problems and they do not specifically relate in any way either to modern management information systems or to the new technology. However, given the suspicion of change which is often present in senior managers, just as in other people, they may feel less able to cope with the form of some of the problems with which they are now confronted than with those they have come to learn to deal with in their earlier careers.

## THE LIMITS TO RATIONALITY

The last point made emphasises the fact that managerial decision-making can only be rational to a limited extent. It is perhaps best characterised as being a product of bounded rationality (Simon, 1960). That is, attempts to make decisions on a wholly rational basis are limited by the inevitable incompleteness of the information available, and a variety of social, political and psychological pressures. The reasons why senior management will rarely, if ever, have complete information for decision-making have been rehearsed many times (e.g. Mansfield, 1986). This being the case they will not be examined here. However amongst the more important of them are the limits to scientific knowledge at any point in time, the cost of gathering information and the problems of predicting the future.

These limitations on the rationality of decision-making not only introduce a significant political element into the process, but also mean that management is as much an art as a science. The implications of this mean that there may be disjunction between the nature of the management information system and the process of top management. This would seem likely as information systems are designed to be essentially logical and rational, whereas as we have already noted management decision-making will be characterised by bounded rationality.

This disjunction is likely to lead to organisationally dysfunctional consequences unless faced in an explicit way. Weick (1969) argued that equivocality stemming from such sources can only be encompassed by moving to a higher level of abstraction, which in this case would involve the development of more complex models of analysis. In the absence of such highly sophisticated models, management will have to continue to exercise its art in using the products of systematic, ostensibly rational, information systems in order to make decisions within an incompletely known and understood situation.

In addition to the difficulties already mentioned there may be informational inadequacies stemming from the lack of cooperation of the actors in the situation. It has been widely demonstrated that information is a scarce resource, the possession of which gives power (Pettigrew, 1973). The consequences of this in a highly integrated computerised management information system may cause various participants to manipulate inputs or the system itself in order to obtain outcomes valued by them.

It should also be noted that the creation and operation of a computerised management information system may itself alter the balance of power within an organisation with implications for both strategic decision-making and control. Such shifts may be towards centralisation as was suggested to be the typical outcome of the older main-frame computer systems (Mumford and Banks, 1967); or towards decentralisation as may be the outcome of networked micro-computer systems (Edwards, 1982). Equally shifts may take place laterally between functional areas as different areas of information are routinely fed into the system (Heery, 1985). The complication stemming from the fact that information can be a source of power within organisations makes more difficult the full utilisation of the new technology by senior management. This is particularly likely until senior managers become sufficiently knowledgeable about the working of the modern technology-based management information systems to feel in control of them rather than controlled by them.

Nonetheless, there can be no doubt that the utilisation of modern technology for senior management decision-making will come. It is equally and most certainly without doubt that it will come very slowly. Indeed, it may take a whole generation of senior managers before it becomes effective in any given organisation. Nonetheless, all the logic of the trends we are currently experiencing with regard to changes in technology, and changes in the cost associated with technology, suggest that the economic balance of advantages and disadvantages will move steadily towards an acceptance of computerised information provision for policy-making of a high order, and probably, in the end, to the automatic making of many policy decisions.

## REFERENCES

Earl, M. (1984) 'Emerging Trends in Managing New Information Technologies', in Piercy, N. (ed.) The Management Implications of New Information Technology, Croom Helm/ Nichols, Beckenham

Edwards, C. (1982) Developing Microcomputer-Based Business Systems, Prentice-Hall, Englewood Cliffs, N.J.

Heery, E. (1985) 'Computers and the Industrial Relations Manager', Personnel Review, 14, 16-21

Long, R. J. (1984) 'The Application of Microelectronics to the Office', in Piercy, N. (ed.) The Management Implications of New Information Technology, Croom Helm, Beckenham

Mansfield, R. (1984) 'Changes in Information Technology, Organizational Design and Managerial Control', in Piercy, N. (ed.) The Management Implications of New Information Technology, Croom Helm/Nichols, Beckenham

Mansfield, R. (1986) Company Strategy and Organizational Design, Croom Helm, Beckenham

Mumford, E. and Banks, O. (1967) The Computer and the Clerk, Routledge and Kegan Paul, London

Pettigrew, A.M. (1973) The Politics of Organizational Decision Making, Tavistock, London

Purcell, J. (1979) 'Applying Control Systems to Industrial Relations', Journal of the Operational Research Society, 30, 1043

Simon, H. (1960) The New Science of Management Decision, Harper and Row, New York

Sorge, A., Hartman, G., Warner, M. and Nicholas, I. (1983) Microelectronics and Manpower in Manufacturing, Croom Helm, Beckenham

Weick, K. E. (1969) The Social Psychology of Organising, Addison-Wesley, Reading, Mass.

# 4. Organisational Aspects of Management Information Systems Change

by Annette Davies

## INTRODUCTION

Information has become an essential commodity in the modern organisation. The growing complexity of organisational activities and environments has greatly increased the amount and type of information that is required for optimal functioning. Systems of information acquisition, processing, retention and transmission have therefore been developed to cope with these complexities. The main uses of these systems are (a) data-processing, (b) supporting managerial decision-making, (c) acting as feedback and control systems (Brabb, 1976). These activities have been an obvious target for computerisation and, as Federico et al (1980) point out, computerised management information systems (CMIS) 'can provide managers with immediate access to the knowledge, information and data they need to make decisions, direct people and regulate operations, in order to better attain organisational goals'. The advent of microtechnology has revolutionised computing power in these areas.

Firstly, the main point is that microtechnology can be mass-produced and sold very cheaply for, while it has long been possible to apply computers to perform some of the functions of microtechnology, expense and bulk have always been deterrents. As well as the cost being drastically reduced, the performance of the present technology is also significantly superior. It affords much faster and more flexible information manipulation and, in terms of reliability, it far exceeds any engineering device to date. Microtechnology has a wide range of applications and is capable of performing any task which involves the reception, manipulation and transmission of information. There are predictions that such applications will lead to extensive automation of production processes as low cost microelectronics allow direct replacement of mechanical control systems. The designer's dream of using computers to monitor production as a whole is slowly becoming a reality. There is also considerable scope for the computerisation of offices, as much office work is amenable to improvement using information technology (Department of Employment, 1979).

However, perhaps the most dramatic developments encouraged by this 'new technology' are the convergence and integration of organisational functions (Barron and Curnow, 1979; Federico et al, 1980). Discrete stages of production and administrative processes such as order processing, product design, production scheduling, and stock control may be automatically linked and consolidated into one machine or closely linked group of machines.

Thus, it would seem that the elements of information systems are being transformed in terms of complexity, capacity, speed and flexibility. The successful implementation of information technology should apparently therefore improve organisational effectiveness, the logic being that better information use will lead to better decision-making in planning and control.

In addition, the effective use of technological advances constitutes a crucial competitive dimension. Companies which fail to adopt to changing technology may find themselves outpaced and outclassed by their more innovative competitors. However, such change is no easy task and many studies have shown that improvements and benefits may not always occur (Walton and Vittori, 1983). The central argument in this chapter is that there are dangers and difficulties in the process of incorporating technological advances and that the organisational context of the change may serve to undermine technical achievement.

## BEHAVIOURAL REACTIONS TO SYSTEMS CHANGE

The successful implementation of information technology is to some extent dependent on the behavioural reaction to the change. Incompatibility between people's needs, preferences and skills, on the one hand, and system requirements, on the other, will cause a variety of problems. For example, a decrease of skill requirements may lead to reduced motivation and a loss of status and self-esteem. Increased specialisation, which results in repetitive and isolated work, may produce alienation and unproductive conflict. Employees may react negatively to any increase in surveillance and control made possible by the new technological systems. Problems may emerge concerning what information should be included in the data-base, and who should have access to this information. In short, people may feel threatened by the new systems and fear the changes that could occur as a result of their implementation.

Most discussions of such behavioural problems, which are associated with information systems change, suggest that innovation often meets strong resistance from the people who are subject to it. Indeed, it has often been argued that the real problem of this type of change is not technical in origin, but arises out of the human changes which accompany technical innovations (Lawrence, 1969; Mumford, 1981).

Severe costs may be imposed upon workers, and these may be unevenly distributed amongst certain sections of the population. Although from an historical perspective technological change and modernisation may be equated with a better and healthier life for all, at a local level 'resistance to change' still occurs among employees who feel themselves to be the 'casualties of an industrial revolution, the benefits of which are not immediately evident' (Jenkins and Sherman, 1979).

The introduction of computerised technology has produced many recent examples of resistance and it would seem that, within organisations, managerial resistance in this area has been a much more significant factor than any 'worker' resistance.

For example, Shaiken (1980) showed how considerable resistance to computer technology had come from certain operating managers who saw their traditional authority in the workplace shattered by a compression of the work process and by the attempt of higher management to exert increased control over every aspect of production. Acts of resistance and sabotage can only serve to reduce the effectiveness of new information systems. The successful management of change must therefore aim at avoiding such resistance and at maximising acceptance.

## BEYOND TECHNOLOGICAL DETERMINISM

Numerous studies have shown that technology is an important determinant of organisational functioning and structure. However, the actual nature of technological impact may be highly variable, with the possibility of either positive or negative outcomes for the employees concerned. Information technology is no different. The impact of implementing new information systems is not an inevitable consequence of the particular technical system used. The process of design and implementation is influenced by a number of factors from within the target organisation. All systems work has to be carried out against this organisational background, and various aspects of the organisation, for example, its goals, structure and environment, will affect the designer's work and the outcome of the change. A simple model provided by Leavitt (1964) explains this dynamic very effectively. He suggests that an organisation is comprised of four interacting variables as shown in Figure 4.1. Any change in technology will influence, and be influenced by, the various task, structure and people elements within the organisation. The model illustrates quite clearly how changes in technological systems cannot be divorced from other organisational factors.

The importance of this interaction between the social and technical aspects of an organisation is also emphasised in Socio-Technical theory (Trist, 1981). According to this theory the best match needs to be sought between the requirements of social and technical sub-systems. It is suggested that tasks be distributed between man and machine components according to their respective capacities and costs. The design and implementation process should therefore deal with the total work system rather than a single element or a few elements of the technical sub-system alone.

**Figure 4.1: Interaction of Organisational Variables**

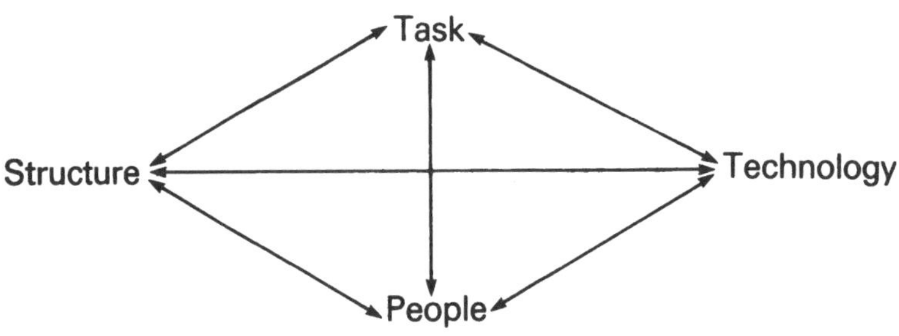


Source: Leavitt (1964)

## THE DESIGN AND IMPLEMENTATION PROCESS

Systems design shows all the characteristics of a problem-solving process. Its beginnings lie in the recognition of a problem or an opportunity and the belief that overall performance will be improved by the introduction of a new system. The process implies a set of objectives and requirements for the new system, although not everyone in the organisation may agree with these objectives. In fact, different interest groups in the organisation such as top management, system specialists, trade unions and users may all have their different objectives. The objectives adopted will depend on who participates in the process, and on what assumptions, in terms of human needs and organisational goals, lie behind the design solutions. A number of structural boundaries and constraints will also inevitably influence system requirements and the implementation process.

## Potential Participants in the Process

There are a number of interested groups when new computer systems are being introduced, and these groups may exert a great deal of influence on the design and implementation process. Many theorists have illustrated the discretion decision-makers have both in the design of technologies and in the organisation of jobs around the technical system. (Davis and Cherns, 1973; Child, 1972; Cooper, 1972). One of the influential groups will be the technical system designers who may be already employed by the organisation, or otherwise commissioned from outside to carry out a particular project. The job of these techical designers will be to define, design, formalise and specify the new system. While their work has an obvious influence on the system which emerges, it cannot be accomplished in isolation from other important groups in an organisation. As London (1973) pointed out:

> The technical aspects of an information system, e.g. document flows, data file characteristics, logical program branches are only the tip of the iceberg. The bulk of the iceberg in systems terms is the people, their jobs and their attitudes.

Therefore, other groups comprising the social environment of the organisation will need to be considered, as changes will be successfully implemented only through their decisions and actions. Important amongst these are the managerial and non-managerial users of the system. These groups will be the direct recipients of the effects of the system and as such will have an obvious interest in the process of design and implementation. They may have the power to severely restrict the speed and scope of the change and a number of studies have provided evidence showing that the impact of sophisticated technologies is often mediated by managerial actions or attitudes. Wedderburn and Crompton (1972), studying continuous process technology in three plants, found that individual management had a strong effect on the skill demands of new jobs. Similarly Hazelhurst, Bradbury and Corlett (1969), studying relationships between numerically controlled machines and job characteristics, concluded that policy decisions on the part of management affect the skill demanded of the operators as much, if not more, than the technology itself. For efficient and effective change, London (1973) emphasises the importance of the quality of managerial and non-managerial employees and the necessity of a good staff relations climate. The motivation and morale of users are other important considerations. The most sophisticated technical systems will become inefficient if user groups are dissatisfied and discontented with their operation.

Trade unions representing potential users will be another interested group. Since the late 1950s the British trade union movement has attempted to establish technological change as a major issue for collective bargaining. The approach advised by the Trade Union Congress in 1979, for combining the development of collective bargaining machinery with a response to technological change, was the pursuit of 'new technology agreements'. The purpose of such agreements is to provide minimum guarantees through negotiation. These typically refer to such procedural issues as: a joint agreement between management and union before the introduction of new systems; the full disclosure of information to the unions; and the use of trial periods to test new machines before full implementation. Important substantive issues refer to job security and no redundancies; increases in pay; reduction in working hours; retraining and improved health and safety standards. The trade union movement believes that it is their responsibility to ensure that the benefits of change are distributed equitably, and that the failure to satisfy these minimum demands may lead to resistance, acts of sabotage or strike action.

Other interested groups in the introduction of a new system will be the indirect users located within the organisation. Their relationship with the target department in terms of the flow and exchange of information is likely to change, with possible repercussions on the nature of their work. There are also indirect recipients outside the organisation, such as clients or customers, who will be affected by changes in organisational procedures and efficiency. All of these various groups could have an interest in the introduction of a new information system. Their reaction and behaviour will be influenced by their respective goals and values.

## Goals and Values of Participants

All aspects of systems change will be influenced by the values and goals of the different groups associated with the change. The groups described in the previous section may all have different 'models of man'. This refers to the way an individual or group assesses the needs, aspirations and competences of other individuals or groups and the adoption of a particular model has important implications for the allocation of tasks between people and machines. Two alternative models of man were identified by McGregor (1960).

He referred to these as Theory X and Theory Y. According to Theory X view, the average person has an inherent dislike of work and will avoid it if at all possible. Because of these characteristics, it is assumed that people must be coerced, controlled, directed or threatened with punishment if they are to be encouraged to work towards the achievement of organisational objectives. In contrast, the Theory Y view states that people will exercise self-direction and self-control in working towards objectives to which they are committed. They are thought to be capable of exercising a high degree of imagination, ingenuity and creativity in the solution of organisational problems. Under ideal conditions, they learn not only to accept responsibility but will even seek it out.

These viewpoints have clear implications when applied to the management of change. Many authors have therefore attempted to analyse the models of man which seem implicit in the design of new information systems. Most of the attention to date has been focused on systems designers. This group, like all other groups, will view their own behaviour and that of others in terms of certain assumptions about human beings, and about the way in which people interact with one another. Davis and Taylor (1972) maintained that the shape of technology is not predetermined by its own developmental 'laws', but that it substantially reflects the psychosocial assumptions of the systems designers.

Once certain requirements are built into the system, behaviour may follow the only path available, amply fulfilling the prophecy implied in the design. Thus, in part, the observed effects of technology on workers and organisations reflect the assumptions about men and social systems held by the designers of the technological system. Such psychosocial assumptions may not always be explicit and, as Davis and Taylor (1972) point out, it is not known to what extent engineers are aware of the assumptions they make in the design or choice of a technical system.

Nevertheless, many commentators accuse systems designers of widespread acceptance of the 'technological imperative', and believe that 'their assumptions about man which underlie their designs are often horrific' (Davis, 1971). Their allegiance to technology is thought to be a 'major influence on how they see the world and their own design responsibilities' (Boguslaw, 1965; Mumford, 1981). Davis (1971) described them as having 'no clear objectives concerning roles for men as men, although objectives are clearly defined for men as machines'. It has been argued that the vision of the future desired by many computer technologists was, and perhaps still is, one that embodied an increasingly sophisticated use of machines and the excitement of designing 'frontier of knowledge' systems. Mumford (1981) however, has indicated an inconsistency in this argument. Although she found that systems designers held a 'Theory X' view of man when designing new systems, she showed that they did neverthless recognise the importance of job satisfaction, the need for tasks to be meaningful and interesting. Mumford, therefore, concludes that systems designers may be working simultaneously with two inconsistent models of man - a practical model which resembles a 'Theory X' approach and a more theoretical model based on 'Theory Y' assumptions. She argues that this may indicate that systems designers would like to take a more humanistic view of systems design, but are prevented from doing so by the values of top management.

In the same study, Mumford also investigated the perceptions of the clerical users of the system. They, unlike top management and the systems designers, adopted a 'Theory Y' approach to the systems change. They showed an eagerness for challenging work and a desire to assume control of output and quality standards. If such considerations are to be given higher priority in the change process, the value systems of managers and designers will need to be changed. Mumford suggests that this may be achieved through a new approach to the training of systems engineers and the increased involvement of users and trade unionists in the process. She believes that engineers should consciously provide individual workers with opportunities for skill development, problem-solving, control, personal development and social relationships. Machines should certainly not prevent such activities taking place. Mumford is optimistic that this will be achieved and argues that the process is being made easier for two main reasons. Firstly, new developments in computer systems are allowing for more innovative designs and fewer technical constraints. Secondly, the power situation in organisations is altering as a result of a wider spread of knowledge through the increased use of computers.

## Structural Variables

The new information system will be influenced by the organisation's structure and technology, which will in turn be influenced by external environmental factors. Different organisations face different types of environment, and an important variable in need of consideration is the degree of uncertainty in that environment. This level of uncertainty will depend on such factors as: the rate of change experienced in the market; the rate at which the market is expanding; different types of competitive pressures and the degree of dependence on other institutions. The uncertainty generated will influence both the level at which decisions should be made, and the degree of integration or differentiation in the organisation. Organisations that do not meet these conditions are likely to be ineffective because the appropriate individuals will not have the information and authority they need for decision-making. To contribute to good decision-making, the information system must provide the right information to the individuals who need it. If the system fails to do this, it is often because the system has not been designed with the characteristics of the organisation and its environment in mind.

Thus, decisions relating to the design and implementation of new information systems cannot be divorced from important organisational variables. In fact, many theorists argue that the opportunities presented by information technology may only be grasped by dealing with this 'total organisation'. Recent research in innovative companies has also found evidence of this. Kanter (1985), in a study of innovative American corporations, concluded that innovation derives from the whole structure, culture and approach to problems which characterise an organisation. Innovative companies were found to emphasise integration rather than segmentalism, i.e. the integration of people, tasks, and structures to solve organisational problems. Similar research by Peters and Waterman (1982) showed that innovative companies are those which are especially adroit at responding to change of any sort in their environments. These companies were found to have a strong commitment to people, demanding involvement and initiative from all categories and levels of workers. In other words, these companies had ensured that there was a close and compatible relationship between the technical and social sub-system of their organisation.

## THE LINK BETWEEN SYSTEM DESIGN AND WORK DESIGN

During the past 20 years a great deal of literature has been generated around the topic of individual and organisational responses to increased automation and other forms of technological change. There is some evidence that the social system is built on a framework provided by the technical system and is heavily influenced by this framework. However, as we have already shown, this social system also has an independent life which in turn influences the operation of the technical system.

This interaction between the sub-systems was first illustrated in a series of research projects undertaken by the Tavistock Institute for the British coal mining industry in the 1950s. The research was instigated because of the negative effects which had resulted from the introduction of automated coal mining equipment at that time. There had been a failure to yield the anticipated increase in productivity and, since the change, men had left the mines in large numbers for more attractive opportunities in the factory world. Among those who remained, absenteeism averaged 20%

and labour disputes were frequent despite improved conditions of employment (Trist, 1981). The research indicated that technological change had destroyed the traditional structure of small self-regulating teams responsible for the whole coal-mining enterprise.

However, in a few of the mines a conscious change of 'work organisation' had occurred in response to the new technology and the negative effects outlined above had been avoided. In these cases, the miners, in order to adapt with best advantage to the technical conditions of the new seam, had evolved the form of autonomous work group which had been common before mechanisation. Resulting from this rejection of oppressive and bureaucratic work procedures, it was argued that organisations could 'choose' to disobey the technological imperative with positive economic, as well as human, results. There emerged a new paradigm of work (Emery, 1978), in which the best match would be sought between the requirements of the social and technical systems. This was in contrast to the old paradigm, which had led to an increase in bureaucratisation with each increase in scale and level of automation. Throughout the analysis it was emphasised that, when changes are being made in technology, one has to choose carefully from amongst a set of alternatives in the social system. The choice made, while enabling a new technology to be effectively exploited, simultaneously threaten, the existing social system. If this occurs, not only will productivity fall, but, as in the instance reported by Trist, voluntary absenteeism, the accident rate, and labour turnover may increase.

Most current work design strategies are closely linked to this socio-technical approach to organisations. Their success is dependent on finding a compromise between the demands of the organisation and the needs and desires of its members, so that the needs of both are jointly maximised. Those who advocate the benefits of new technology in improving the quality of working life lay great emphasis on this conscious process of work design in bringing about such improvements. It is argued that more sophisticated technology is able to provide a whole new work definition as the worker's role shifts from the tool and its guidance to the system and its maintenance, regulation and control (Davis and Taylor, 1972). In designing information systems, a crucial factor for consideration is the nature of the relationship between the human and computer components. As Federico et al (1980) point out: 'What needs to be established is the point at which the computer should replace man; the point at which it should assist him, and even the point at which it should not be used.'

An effective relationship between systems design and work design demands some knowledge of the psychological requirements individuals have of their work. These have been termed 'intrinsic characteristics' and a number have been identified. For example, Emery (1978) described six such needs as follows: (a) the need for the content of a job to be reasonably demanding in terms other than sheer endurance; (b) the need for people to be able to learn on the job and to go on learning; (c) the need for an area of decision-making that the individual can call his/her own; (d) the need for a certain degree of social support and for recognition in the workplace of the value of what the worker does; (e) the need to be able to relate what the worker does and produces to his/her social life, for it to have meaning and to afford dignity; and (f) the need for the worker to feel that the job leads to some sort of desirable future.

Sophisticated social analysis will need to be conducted alongside the technical analysis to determine the individual requirements in a particular organisation. It has been argued by a number of theorists, notably Mumford (1977), that computer technology is flexible enough to be adjusted to meet different human needs. The most popular work design strategies which satisfy the above set of needs are job enrichment and autonomous working groups. The aim of such strategies is to reverse existing divisions of labour without any reduction in productivity. With job enrichment, the worker's role is enlarged vertically as the worker is given responsibility for 'higher' level tasks previously done by supervisors. Autonomous work groups are similarly based on the general model of responsible, autonomous behaviour as a key element in productive organisations. However, here the emphasis is on group, rather than individual behaviour, with each group becoming multi-skilled and taking increased responsibility for a substantial area of production.

Autonomous group working was the approach adopted in the coal mining studies of the Tavistock school. The work group in that instance was responsible for all the activities associated with mining coal from a particular section of the coal face. These activities had normally been carried out by three different groups of miners, each group carrying out different tasks on different shifts. The autonomous group concept required each group to assume responsibility for the management of their own piece of the coal face. This involved the allocation of tasks and shifts on the basis of mutual agreement together with a joint problem-solving approach by the team when difficulties were encountered. Communication with management principally concerned agreeing how much coal the work group would produce, and how much they would be paid for doing the job. It is not difficult to see how this autonomous group concept may be helped through the computer's ability to provide work groups with accurate, up-to-date information, which they can use to effectively monitor their own performance and to set their own targets.

Information technology could therefore offer a challenge

for the redesign of work and improvements in the quality of working life. While such changes can be advantageous to employers, in terms of increased morale, they may even be a necessary prerequisite for the efficient running of a new system. If the information system is developed in conflict with the attitudes and needs of users, inaccuracies and errors may occur through boredom, anxiety or resistance. Therefore, consideration of the human factor during systems change will be ignored at the organisation's peril. Walton and Vittori (1983) suggest that, if this is acknowledged by organisations, new technology could present management with a positive organisational change opportunity. Again, as research in innovative companies has shown, systems design and implementation activities may then be used to move towards preconceived ideals or preferences. However, one necessary precondition for adopting this 'opportunity orientation' would seem to be a high level of participation between designers and users. Such participation is not without its problems and it is to this aspect of the design and implementation process that we now turn.

## PARTICIPATIVE SYSTEMS DESIGN (PSD)

Mumford (1979) defines PSD as 'the handing of responsibility for the design of a new work system to the employees who eventually will operate it'. She puts forward four principal arguments for the use of such an approach when new computer systems are being introduced. Firstly, there are arguments based on a set of humanistic values which state that people have a moral right to control their own destinies, and which maintain that this applies as much in the work situation as elsewhere. The value of increased participation is viewed as a means of optimising individual freedom and self determination within a collective context. Secondly, there are expediency arguments, which state that activities are ultimately controlled by those who perform them, and that people who do not have any involvement in decisions may decide to repeal them as soon as others leave the scene. The third argument relates to the location of knowledge, and states that the experts on operational factors such as task design are the people who actually do the jobs. Fourthly, it is suggested that involvement will act as a motivator and will lead to increases in productivity and efficiency.

However, the fundamental impetus for a participative approach to systems design is the realisation that the more conventional design process has not always worked. This conventional approach is characterised by minimising the amount of change and by focusing solely on the technology. The process is controlled exclusively by the systems analyst, and the user's only role will be to respond to the analyst's questions and to use the new system. Most authors who advocate a more active role for the user view the system development process as a change effort which has an impact on the human, as well as the technical, system of the organisation. They are concerned with changes on both these dimensions and, rather than trying to minimise such changes, they attempt to deal with them fully.

A great number of mechanisms for involving users in the design process have been proposed, each mechanism allowing a different degree of participation. At one extreme, there is a simple feedback mechanism by which the user is passed information as the design process progresses. At a minimum this means that users have an opportunity to review and comment on the design before it becomes final. One step beyond simple feedback is the notion of user liaison and steering committees. In the case of liaison, the bulk of the design work is done by the analyst, but a user is generally responsible for monitoring the development process and providing the user group's input to it. Mumford (1979) describes this approach as 'consultative design'. While most of the design decisions are still taken by the traditional systems design group, the objectives they set, and the eventual form the system takes, are greatly influenced by the needs of the user department.

The next logical step is to have a design group composed of users and analysts, preferably with a user at its head. Mumford labels this a 'representative design group' and has studied its effects in an international bank setting (Mumford, 1979). The study involved a group of clerks who were given the responsibility of designing a new, more motivating and satisfying work structure for a foreign exchange department. The catalyst for the change was a new on-line computer system. The clerks represented all grades and functions in their department and the task of this 'representative group' was to design a computer based system of work which improved both job satisfaction and efficiency. The technical part of the system was kept flexible enough to accept the form of work organisation decided by the user design group. The result was a number of autonomous groups with each group assuming responsibility for all the activities associated with buying and selling a particular currency. One particular problem of this form of participation is that of ensuring that all factions, including minorities, are represented, especially if representation is by election.

The fourth and final technique goes even further in involving the user. This is what Mumford (1979) terms 'consensus design' and it is a process by which all users are actively involved in the systems design process. A consensus design strategy embraces both representative and consultative design procedures and, as Mumford points out, the support of top management and of trade unions is vital for this approach to work. Employees are usually suspicious of management's motives for introducing new systems, and therefore they may become even more suspicious when they are asked to participate. There may also be problems relating to the role of the professional systems designers. As the process becomes more participative, the role of the designer is bound to change. Eventually he or she may become more of a consultant to the design group. The system designer may regard this change as a threat to his or her status and authority. Other important problems with increased participation relate to issues of time, money and expertise. Participation can be expensive and may increase the time taken to complete a project and, indeed, users or trade union representatives may not have adequate knowledge for contributing meaningfully to the process. In a recent study among trade unionists, it was concluded that one of the main reasons for their limited involvement in technological change was this lack of expertise in the area (Davies, 1985). This research also found that trade union strategies had not been clearly formulated and planned, and information was only received when management plans were fully developed and could not be changed. There was little evidence that trade unionists put forward any alternative plans and suggestions on how to handle the problems that the new technology created. In contrast, management was found to have highly trained specialists either employed or working as consultants. The unprepared trade unionist therefore had little hope of success.

PSD can thus reveal problems within an organisation which have not been previously realised or dealt with. The goals and objectives of systems designers, managers, users and trade union officials are also likely to differ. Such conflicts may not be easily resolved, making participation difficult. Thus, producing a significant policy for increasing participation and improving the quality of working life when changing technology is a complicated social and political undertaking. As Tipton (1982) concludes, changes in job content, other than of the most trivial kind, necessarily require the restructuring of traditional hierarchies of occupational prestige and control. It may even be argued that under capitalist market conditions, management-initiated schemes for adopting information technology must be viewed in the context of shareholder profitability. These schemes will be subjected to conventional business accounting techniques which concentrate on the individual firm and the relatively short-run period. In future, such political problems may become even more important as the group participating in the process widens, for example, as the general public become more involved.

## CONCLUSION

The design and implementation of sophisticated information systems is not simply a technological problem, but an organisational and political issue. We have seen in this chapter how the 'total organisation' needs to be confronted and consulted. This is the approach advocated by the socio-technical school in its attempt to find a positive relationship between the technical, human and administrative parts of the system. It has been argued that technical systems need not be designed according to a set of strict criteria related only to profit maximisation and control. Even when systems have been designed, there is still scope to introduce new methods of production and to change work organisation. However, innovative achievements in work design have never been easy and will involve a greater degree of confidence and expertise than is evident amongst trade unionists and user groups today. Mumford has also argued that there is a need for greater interest in this area from trade unions. There are indeed very few strikes over the routine nature of work, and few trade unions are making work interest and challenge their bargaining issues. Some lessons may be learned from current progress in Norway, where the Council of Nordic Trades Unions is calling for a programme of research into how computer technology could be used for improving the work environment, democratising working life and even developing democracy in society. The implications of information technology are certainly far-reaching and it is this writer's belief that the problem cannot be solved by top management or systems specialists alone. Effective systems design requires not only technical expertise but a broad understanding of organisations, their people, structures and environments. In this chapter it has been argued that a participative design process may go some way to achieving this understanding, and in creating new systems which are both productive for the organisation, and satisfying for users.

## REFERENCES

Barron, I. and Curnow, R. (1979) The Future with Microelectronics, Open University Press, Milton Keynes.

Boguslaw, R. (1965) The New Utopians, Prentice-Hall, Englewood Cliffs, N J

Brabb, G.J. (1976) Computers and Information Systems in Business, Houghton Mifflin Co., Boston

Child, J. (1972) 'Organisational Structure, Environment and Performance: The Role of Strategic Choice', Sociology, 6, pp. 131-157

Cooper, R. (1972) 'Man, task and technology', Human Relations, 25, pp. 131-157

Davies, A. (1985) Industrial Relations and New Technology, Croom Helm, Beckenham

Davis, L.E. (1971) 'Job Satisfaction Research: The Post-Industrial View', Industrial Relations, 10, pp. 176-193

Davis, L.E. and Cherns, A.B. (1973) The Quality of Work Life, Vols. I and II, Free Press, New York

Davis, L.E. and Taylor, J.C. (1972) Designs of Jobs, Penguin, Harmndsworth

Department of Employment (1979) The Manpower Implications of Micro-Electronic Technology, HMSO, London

Emery, F.E. (1972) Report on the Hunsfoss Report, Tavistock, London

Emery, F.E. (1978) The Emergence of a New Paradigm of Work, Centre of Continuing Education, Canberra, A.W.U.

Federico, P., Brun, K.E. and McCalla, D.B. (1980) Management Information Systems and Organisational Behaviour, Praeger, New York

Hazelhurst, R.J., Bradbury, R.J. and Corlett, E.N. (1969) 'A Comparison of the Skills of Machinists in Numerically Controlled and Conventional Machines', Occupational Psychology, 43, pp. 169-182

Jenkins, C. and Sherman, B. (1979) The Collapse of Work, Methuen, London

Kanter, R.M. (1985) The Change Masters - Corporate Entrepreneurs at Work, Allen and Unwin, London

Lawrence, P.R. (1969) 'How to Deal with Resistance to Change', Harvard Business Review, Jan/Feb, pp. 4-15

Leavitt, H. (1964) Applied Organisational Change in Industry - Structural, Technical and Human Approaches, Wiley, New York

London, K.R. (1973) The People Side of Systems, McGraw-Hill, London

McGregor, D. (1960) The Human Side of the Enterprise, McGraw-Hill, New York

Mumford, E. (1977) 'The Design of Work: New Approaches and New Needs', in J. Rijinsdorp (ed.) Case Studies in Automation Related to the Humanisation of Work, Proceedings of the IFAC Workshop, Pergammon Press, Netherlands, pp. 9-17

Mumford, E. (1979) 'Consensus Systems Design: An Evaluation of this Approach', in Szyperski, W. and Grochla, E. (eds.) Design and Implementation of Computer-based Information Systems, Sijthoff & Noordho 17, Netherlands

Mumford, E. (1981) Values, Technology and Work, Martinus Nijhoff, Hague

Peters, T.J. and Waterman, R.H. (1982) In Search of Excellence, Harper and Row, New York

Shaiken, H. (1980) Computer Technology and the Relations of Power in the Workplace, International Institute of Comparative Social Research, Berlin

Tipton, B. (1982) 'The Quality of Training and the Design of Work', Industrial Relations Journal, 13 (1), pp. 27-41

Trade Union Congress (TUC) (1979) Employment and Technology, Report by the TUC General Council

Trist, E. (1981) The Evolution of Socio-Technical Systems, Occasional Paper No. 2, June, University of Labour, Ontario

Walton, R.E. and Vittori, W. (1983) 'New Information Technology, Organisational Problem or Opportunity', Office: Technology and People, 1, pp. 249-273

Wedderburn, D., and Crompton, R. (1972) Workers' Attitudes and Technology, Cambridge, University Press

# II APPLICATIONS IN THEORY

# 5. The Adoption of Micro computer-Based Budgetary Systems in Small Companies: Organisational and Behavioural Considerations

by Roger Groves

## INTRODUCTION

The pace of the change in computer technology, both in hardware and software, is accelerating so rapidly that small business owners are in a position similar to that faced by their largest counterparts barely a few years ago.

On the software front, surveys by Grinyer and Wooller (1975) and Higgins and Finn (1977) provided plenty of evidence of the use of computer models in corporate or financial planning by financial departments of large UK companies, and a later study by Higgins and Opdebeeck (1984) showed how the microcomputer was becoming a tool of senior management in large UK companies.

Evidence of the small number of computers in use in small companies comes from a survey carried out by Micro Business which is shown in Table 5.1. Looked at in one way Table 5.1 indicates the thinness of computer coverage in small companies, but put the other way it indicates the vast potential market that still remains.

In-depth surveys of small companies are not usually easy to carry out on a large scale, so evidence supporting the opening remarks is far from complete and has to be based on smaller studies, some of which are on a regional basis (Hampton, 1985; Ho, 1985), as well as ad hoc personal experiences which get reported in the trade journals.

In larger companies there is empirical evidence regarding the changes that have occurred in attitudes to, and applications of, computer-based corporate modelling and other techniques (see, for example, Grinyer and Wooller, 1975, 1980; Bhaskar, 1978). Those financial techniques which were incorporated into the large corporate models, such as discounting models, financial ratio analysis, risk analysis and cash flow forecasting were useful aids to senior management in ad hoc company forecasting situations, and were available as such. Subsequently, software for these techniques was written so that they could be used on

**Table 5.1: Ownership of Business Computers**

| Number of Employees | Number of Companies | Percentage of companies with computers installed | Percentage of companies with computers that have more than one micro |
|---|---|---|---|
| 1 - 4 | 494,543 | 4 | 11 |
| 5 - 10 | 246,229 | 11 | 8 |
| 11 - 24 | 155,807 | 16 | 14 |
| 25 - 49 | 69,870 | 22 | 25 |
| 50 + | 69,220 | 47 | 69 |

Source: Micro Intelligence Survey on the Micro Business 1984 - 88

microcomputers, with the result that they are now being used on micros in large companies, and since they are marketed generally they are available for small companies.

Improvements in hardware, such as increases in memory capacity, have enabled microcomputers to handle large, spread-sheet programs and fair-sized company forecasting/ modelling packages and the like. Thus, what was once only in the domain of the large company because of the need for large computers is now becoming more and more available for the small company. The more sophisticated the software and the more advanced the hardware becomes, the more effect the introduction of a micro-computer and its library of programs will have on a small company.

As one might imagine, the management accounting applications used by the micro-users in the large firms centre predominantly on budgeting, via the spread-sheet, financial ratio analysis, future cost analysis, standard costing and stock control. These are all ad hoc programs, but there are moves in the big companies towards data base operating systems which may encompass an appropriate data base management system. These systems require considerable computer space which at the moment is beyond the scope of the average micro that a small business would want to buy. They also require a high level of sophistication in systems design and operation, the cost of which may be beyond the amount a small company may be prepared to pay or the capacity of its existing organisation. So although, in principle, the concept of a relational data base management system would be very appealing to a small company, the organisational and systems implications are considerable.

Similarly, with the advent of expert systems, though they may start with specialised uses available on only large machines, it is not beyond the wit of man to see them being used in a much more general mode on much smaller machines. It has to be said that at this stage there are some authors who are somewhat sceptical of the usefulness of expert systems in an accounting scenario (see Gambling, 1985; Gambling et al, 1985).

The introduction of microcomputers and computer-based accounting systems will have profound effects on the organisational and managerial structures of the small firm. Whether a small company is only going to acquire a microcomputer, or in the future decides to use a data base management system, or an expert system, does not matter the specific areas to be discussed here will still be pertinent.

The expression 'small firm' is taken here to mean firms with less than 50 employees and/or a turnover of less than £5 million. Conventionally writers have measured firm size either by value of sales, profits, or number of employees, but, because of the trend towards service industries with low manning and high value turnover, one has to use a mixed standard for the definition to be meaningful.

Small firms are idiosyncratic, each with their own internal organisational structure patterned by a number of factors such as the business the firm is in, the type of leadership given, the age of the firm, its historical antecedents, the length of service of the staff and their personal characteristics, and so on. The position of the auditor/accountant may also be critical since it is quite possible that a firm may initially record only the basic transactions of cash received or paid, bills received and unpaid and invoices tendered and unpaid. From this information the accountant/auditor then prepares a set of accounts which may have little relevance to management needs but at least minimises the tax liability. This lack of specialisation in the accounting area may also be true in the other functional areas of the small firm. Financial management under these circumstances is more likely a case of crisis management than controlled management.

It is not difficult then to see how the advent of financial recording and reporting packages, spread-sheet packages and modelling packages can be of help to the general management of a small firm. What can we then learn from the literature on the effects of the introduction of computer based systems into large organisations?

## COMPUTER BASED SYSTEMS

It is possible to go back to the 1950s and 1960s to find discussive articles predicting the impact of the introduction of computer systems in management information systems on the organisational and managerial aspects of a corporate entity (Leavitt and Whisler, 1958; Simon, 1965). There were subsequent empirical studies, in the main referring to large organisations, and sometimes reviewing only single cases. More recently, there have been some comparative surveys and analyses (for example, see Blau et al, 1976; Bruns and Waterhouse, 1975).

It is sometimes difficult to generalise from these works, since the results are usually situation specific and may even conflict with other findings. Because a computerised system was based often upon a single large central computer it is not surprising authors write about high degrees of centralisation and structuring in an organisation. But subsequently when remote terminals become more widely available, followed by stand-alone micros which may be networked, a different and decentralised organisation becomes possible. This onward march of technological development can often explain the conflicts found in the literature - for instance, compare Whisler (1970) with Bruns and Waterhouse (1975).

It is important to look at the company's rationale for acquiring a computer because the reasoning behind the acquisition will usually influence who uses the equipment and for what purposes. For example Ho (1985) found small accountancy practices in Wales were acquiring, or about to acquire, microcomputers to increase their audit productivity, to become cost-competitive and to counteract threats posed by similar sized firms already using this equipment. Thus, the main role of the equipment would be in the field of preparing client accounts, with a subsidiary role in the financial and managerial accounting needs of the firm. Therefore the main users of the equipment were to be audit managers and partners and not the partnership administrators, though they would be making some use of the equipment.

In this instance what the company was acquiring was a number of mobile work-stations which would impinge upon the work of certain individuals, but not produce any general reshuffling of the organisation. The amount of organisational change in the accounting and administrative areas depends upon the type of system that is being replaced. For example, in another small survey of small businesses in South Wales by Hampton (1985) one firm already had an accounting machine based financial reporting system, and conversion of this system into a micro-based system had little effect on the organisation on its members. However, the survey did not reveal whether the company intended to up-grade its reporting system and provide frequent information for management such as monthly accounts. The acquisition of a spread-sheet package to suit the company would not be difficult, but the introduction of a full budgetary process into which the spreadsheet would be incorporated could have far-reaching implications for the company.

Results of a study by Andersen and Pedersen (1980) (AP) support this contention that the introduction of a computer based system will change managerial roles and the organisational structure. The objectives of the AP study were to discover how tasks were influenced by the introduction of computer based management communication, and how influence patterns were changed when such an introduction was made.

Earlier studies, such as Blau et al (1976), were really only concerned with the locus of decision-making at any one specific hierarchical level, and so only focused on one facet of the complex combinations of interpersonal relationships that can be influenced by the introduction of a computerised information system. The AP study instead concentrated on changes in particular tasks within a managerial role, specifically production planning, scheduling and control. Most members of an organisation are subjected to the power of others as well as themselves exerting power over colleagues. The results of the study indicated that those involved in planning had their influence increased. This was a stated perception of both colleagues and planners themselves.

Planning by management in small companies in the past has not been seen as a primary task, so perhaps it is worth giving a slightly more detailed examination of this study to show its relevance to small companies. One of the bases of an individual's power is the status of that individual as an 'expert' in a field. The introduction of the computer-based system meant that information once provided by 'experts' is now being produced by the system to more people who are possibly more up-to-date than the 'experts' could be. So in AP's study the 'experts' in knowledge of production seem to suffer a decline in relative importance to the production planning department.

The form in which influence occurs can be changed as well, either through the influence channel or the means of influence. Channels of influence are factors such as the communication links used to convey influence. After the system was computerised it was found that there were fewer personal contacts, but more written reports and rules, and more formal meetings. The means of influence changed a little as well, with the planners gaining more control over activities and the managers giving fewer orders and less advice, but having more appeal to influential people. These results of increasing bureaucracy and reduction in flexibility are what many might have forecast but they do provide some pointers for consideration where small businesses are concerned. Finally, it was reported that the discretion of managers concerned with control in a corporate function was fettered as a result of greater forward planning, which also produced a reduction in slack resources and buffer stock held and caused a higher degree of formalisation.

The formal role of planner, or planning department, is unlikely to exist in most small companies, but should a budgetary system by introduced on the back of a spread-sheet package then the amount of planning undertaken will increase and will affect the roles of all individuals involved with the budget. The last statement assumes that the introduction of a system of budgetary control will be taken seriously by the company. Depending on the size of the company and its perceived needs it is quite conceivable that the organisation could be increased tu include a 'planner', or other persons who are taken on to accommodate the needs of the new systems, thus relieving existing staff of the planning tasks. This could have a significant impact on the organisation structure and the present interpersonal relationships. Likewise, small businesses tend not to be so bureaucratic, having fewer channels of influence, giving the staff greater flexibility and discretion, than their larger firm counterparts.

In a smaller company all these problems could appear simultaneously and be more immediate, since one is dealing with fewer people who are working much more closely together. It is also possible that due to the smaller numbers working in the small business, few, if any, of the employees may have a knowledge of the hardware, the software, or how to develop the system. Microcomputer salesmen are sometimes accused of understating the problems in the development of systems, or overstating their capabilities. Nevertheless, it should be borne in mind that the microcomputing industry is still in its infancy even if it is developing very quickly. This state of affairs means growing pains will be felt for a while yet, and be reflected in any one of a number of consequences (Edwards, 1983).

The cost of both the changeover and the subsequent operation could be inadequately estimated, and, due to lack of size and experience, impartial advice cannot be obtained. This point is also relevant to the analysis of the system to be installed, with the hardware required being the major focus of attention rather than the software and system. Inadequate analysis may be due just as much to the cost-cutting desires of the managing director, as to the inefficiency of the selling organisation. Potential problem areas such as security and maintenance of the system may have been neglected, or perhaps transaction volumes to be processed may have been underestimated, or over-optimistic forecasts made of what the hardware can achieve, which can leave the company in a situation, where, through not being able to process its sales invoices it cannot generate the cash necessary to stay alive - all scenarios to be avoided. The introduction of a new computer system will always affect the employees but such inadequate consideration can result in problems that can be long lasting and detrimental to the organisational health of the small company.

## Organisational Changes

The question of the effectiveness of the adaptation of the organisation, and the coping of the individuals in it, to the innovation of a computer-based accounting information system is an interesting one. The form and time period of the adaptation will be dependent upon the specific organisation, its leadership, the external and internal environment and the individuals within the organisation.

Ferris (1982) proposed a model of organisational response to the perception of environmental uncertainty which he tested in a study involving professional accounting firms. If one assumes that the introduction of a computer-based accounting information system is an uncertainty-producing event, then one could consider applying his model to that. Ferris' model suggests that outcomes of the perceptions of the dominant coalition are crucial to the type and quantity of coping behaviour that takes place on the introduction of the major event.

The implication for small firms is that the perceptions of its director(s) are important in ensuring that the organisational coping effort is effective. The uncertainty mentioned above could be categorised under three headings: (a) lack of information, (b) not knowing how to respond, and (c) not knowing the outcome of an action or decision. For example, Hampton (1985) found that fears of the computer and the system, based on a misconception, ensured that the system once installed was very ineffective until those fears had been allayed. The leadership in that particular situation must bear these three points in mind in assessing the company's situation because the behaviour of the leadership is a very important factor in successful introduction. At this point it is worth also mentioning the value of the change agents in assisting with not only the selection of the system, but also with its installation and the necessary organisational changes. These will be returned to shortly.

## Leadership Patterns

Back in 1952 Argyris suggested that, in particular, budgets might have dysfunctional consequences for individuals operating under budgetary constraints, as well as for the organisations in which they worked. This led to a considerable amount of research on the effects budgetary systems had on managerial attitudes, budget oriented behaviour, and leadership styles (Swieringa and Moncur, 1975; Stedry, 1960; Hopwood, 1973; Otley, 1978 are just a few of the references one can list here). In the context of this paper, it is more pertinent to look at the work concerned with impact in the opposite direction, namely have the individual personalities, who have required and perhaps designed the budgetary system, imposed their attitudes and desires upon the system that they are working in, or helped set up?

In a small business this is a very pertinent question, since for some the business is an extension of the owner and managing director's self. Thus when a computer-based financial system is introduced, its incorporation and design may bear the hallmarks of the personality attributes of the 'leader' of the company. The impact will be more visible in the general process of introducing the computerisation and in the more people-oriented process of the budgetary system when the company moves on to that stage in the use of its micro.

Early work by authors such as Christie (1952), Tannenbaum (1957) and Vroom (1960) and others found links between types of managerial behaviour and personality variables. In particular Vroom (1960), by use of a correlation study, showed that there was a definite relationship between the extent of participation and, the presence of a positive attitude to the job for those persons who were low on authoritarianism and high on need for independence.

Tannenbaum and Schmidt (1958) suggested three groups of factors that an individual should take account of, when trying to decide the best way to manage. They said that the choice of leadership pattern should take into account: the leader's own characteristics, those of his subordinates and those of the situation. Once again the direction of emphasis is adaptation of leadership to the environment. In the sort of situation under discussion this is only partially relevant because the system and the method of its introduction may have to be tailored to meet the demands of the leader, as well as the rest of the firm's environment. For example, if the leader is someone who has under-researched the magnitude of the impact of the arrival of the new computer-based system, then some of the problems already mentioned can manifest themselves, e.g. falling behind in preparation of reports, dissatisfaction amongst staff, and the like. These resulting problems, if not quickly put right, can result in staff leaving or wrong decisions being taken on incorrect information, and even rejection of the system and the return to the original approach.

A later study by Seiler and Bartlett (1982) found that the personality traits of authoritarianism, need for independence and flexibility were correlated with the individual's perception of organisational climate and with certain attitudes towards the budgetary system that the individuals were in. By use of discriminant analysis, utilising these three personality variables did have a predictive ability concerning group membership by participants of budgeting systems which exhibits high or low levels of rigidity or participativeness and thus are of interest when considering the effects of leadership patterns on the setting up of a new budgetary system.

A budgetary system is a result of combined personalities; when setting up a new system there are roles for those involved in the building up of the structure and a chance to influence the structure. A mature system is more likely to consist of self-selected persons who are compatible with its characteristics, and, if not, perhaps then will adapt to fit the system. Sudden changes in the system are likely to affect job satisfaction, budgetary motivation, and work stress. In fact Seiler and Bartlett (1982) state that:

> A significant change in budgetary systems will probably be evolutionary, and if it is revolutionary, it will necessitate shifts in attitudes and personalities of the employee population.

Unfortunately their results indicated that the three personality variables chosen had no predictive ability concerning an individual's attitudes and perceptions towards a budgetary system because these appear to be masked by their personality traits. It does indicate that it is necessary to review carefully the mix of personalities with their traits and perceptions before the introduction of a computer based system, or else its arrival could be dysfunctional. Pratt and Jiambalvo (1982), in reviewing the determinants of leadership behaviour in an audit environment, rehearsed some of the elements in the process of task introduction that are impinged upon by leadership behaviour. Firstly, they highlighted the possibility of differences in the perception of task difficulty by the leader and the subordinates, which can increase the feelings of uncertainty and ambiguity towards the task by the subordinates. Following on from this is the need to ensure a correct match by the leader of the experience and skill of the subordinates with the level of complexity of the task to be undertaken. Obviously if the perceptions differ then problems arise.

They identified six leadership behaviour patterns that were pertinent to the effectiveness of the introduction. These included the amount and timing of feed-back to the subordinates, the design of the task itself, the amount of help given during the process of the design and carrying out of the task, the amount of time pressure the group is under and its membership. It was asserted that the greater the gap between the task complexity and the quality and experience of the staff assigned to it, the greater the dominant leader should structure the innovation activities. This may seem obvious but in practice small company leaders in many cases operate by the seat of their pants and have not considered all the facets surrounding the innovation and adoption of a computerised accounting and budgeting system (see Hampton, 1985, where in one company surveyed there was a fear of negative effects on health through sitting in front of screens). All this just increases the need for effective change agents to assist in the adoption.

Also it is worth considering the evidence set forth in McKenna's study (1980) into leadership patterns in the finance function. Using Heller's power/influence continuum (Yukl, 1971), McKenna presented five decision styles with style A being "own decision without explanation" through style C "prior consultation" to style E "delegation". From observational data he noted that the directive style was more pronounced in the smaller company, allegedly because of the relatively low calibre of staff, though nonetheless the approach was informal. Thus if there is considerable dependence by subordinates on the leader in the existing tasks undertaken then all the more need for the leader to obtain good and effective advice from the change agents.

## Change Agents

The role of change agents in the adoption and diffusion of innovations is well known (Rogers, 1962; Comiskey and Groves, 1971). Because of the small size of the organisation, the external change agent takes on a much more important role since it is unlikely that there will be anyone in the organisation trained in the use and understanding of computers and computer based systems.

Seiler and Bartlett (1982) maintain that the individual who acts as change agent must adjust the speed at which the system is changed and adopted so as to be appropriate for the ability of the individuals who are controlled by the system, so that they can adapt easily to it. If these two speeds are out of line then the 'self selection process' they talk of will be triggered, i.e. people will leave because the organisation and system within which they work is no longer compatible with their personal attitudes and needs. At this stage it is easy to visualise the range of scenarios involving change agents and small companies, with little or no guidance in the purchase of the hardware or after-sales activities at the one end, to full and useful discussions with advice and training at the other end of the spectrum. These agents may be the firm of auditors, the retail organisation or a third party brought in for the job.

Whoever is engaged by the company has an important role in the switch to computerisation. Edwards (1983), from his experience, reinforces this point, as do numerous other horror stories written in the trade press.

### Other Important Aspects

Various other personal demographic attributes have a bearing on the speed and style of adoption of such a system. For example, how long have the managerial class employees been with the firm, and how long have they done the job they are presently doing? Does the 'leader' owe them some allegiance for long service? What are the ages of the company and the leader - the older, the greater likelihood of intransigence, perhaps?

Other non-sociological variables are equally important, one being the pressures on the company from the economic environment of the market place - what are the competitors doing? Is the company in a high technology industry? These pressures may bring undue haste into the development of the system which could be fatal to it.

Other questions that should be asked are how dependent has the company been on the auditors/accountants for the provision of financial information in the past? Perhaps the financial information was prepared annually in arrears, but now information is needed and could be provided quarterly with monthly cash reviews, and so on. What method of accounting is to be used? Will it ensure that the appropriate SSAPs are complied with in the annual accounts? Should full or variable costing be used? Some of these are similar questions to those needing answers when dealing with larger companies, though here the problems, results, and solutions are much closer at hand, so if mistakes are made it is more immediately obvious with perhaps more disastrous consequences.

## CONCLUSIONS

The discussion has suggested that there have been few studies investigating the organisation frameworks of small businesses, and that those studies concerned with large organisations cannot always be extended to small ones. The availability of the microcomputer gets easier daily and large sales are being made to the private buyer. Similarly the capacity and abilities of microcomputers are being increased and improved at a very rapid rate. All this will increase the pressure on the small businessman to acquire one or more for the business and this brings with it the attendant points that have been discussed above.

With the increased speed of communication and operations within business comes greater pressure for more planning and control and thus better information. The microcomputer is the tool that can help provide that information. Thus one would expect budgetary systems set up to be influenced by the personality attributes of the leader of the small business. Greater planning and more bureaucracy will probably come about and possibly increases in the administrative workforce to cope with this, even though sometimes this point is not mentioned by the hardware or software sales personnel. This is only one aspect of coping behaviour; other aspects depend on how the introduction of the computer is made. There are some individuals who fear the machine and who would leave rather than try to come to terms with it, and others who try to understand and operate it.

There are certain similarities with the situation in the 1950s and 1960s when large firms were first-time buyers of mainframe computers and computer systems. Then the specialists within and without the companies had much more time to devote to solving the problems that arose. These days, though similar problems exist, there is neither the time nor the opportunity for the first-time users to learn in detail about the computer and the computer-based systems before they are plunged into full-time use. For example, much software has now been developed external to the firm, and so perhaps needs adaptation to the needs of the present user; previously this was done internally and the 'experts' learnt as they went along or they were brought in. Today, this can mean adaptations can be attempted by persons who neither wrote the original software nor have the expertise to understand the existing system. It can also mean that the company is better if it adapts its organisation and systems to match the bought-in software requirements.

The role of the change agent is a crucial one here since clear identification of the client's needs, not just for software and hardware, but also in the system design is required. Personnel management will be crucial to the good and fast introduction and acceptance of the new technology into the company. There are many short articles in the trade press on the 'dos and don'ts' of acquiring a microcomputer and virtually all relate only to the hardware and software and do not include the change in systems and personnel required by the introduction. So to make sure the new technology is adopted successfully by small businesses there is still much to be done.

## REFERENCES

Anderson, N.B. and Pedersen, P.H. (1980) 'Computer Facilitated Changes in the Management Power Structure', Accounting Organizations and Society, 5 (2), 203-216

Argyris, C. (1952) The Impact of Budgets on People, The School of Business and Public Administration, Cornell University

Bhaskar, K. (1978) Building Financial Models: A Simulation Approach, Associated Business Programmes

Blau, P.M., McHugh-Falbe, C., McKinley, W. and Tracey, P.K. (1976) 'Technology and Organisation in Manufacturing', Administrative Science Quarterly, March, 20-40

Bruns, W.J. and Waterhouse, J.H. (1975) 'Budgeting Control and Organization Structure', Journal of Accounting Research, Autumn, 177-203

Child, J. (1972) 'Organization Structure and Strategies of Control: a Replication of the Aston Study', Administrative Science Quarterly, June, 163-177

Christie, R., (1952) 'Changes in Authoritarianism as Related to Situational Factors', American Psychologist, 307-308

Comiskey, E.E. and Groves, R.E.V. (1971) 'The Adoption and Diffusion of an Accounting Innovation', Accounting and Business Research, 5

Dyckman, T.T., Hoskin, R.E. and Swieringa, R.J. (1982) 'An Accounting Change and Information Processing Changes', Accounting, Organizations and Society, 7(1), 1-11

Eason, K.D., Damodaran, L. and Stewart, T.F.M. (1976) Report of a Survey of Man-Computer Interaction in Commercial Applications, Department of Human Sciences, Loughborough Technical University

Edwards, C. (1983) 'Developing Micro-computer Based Business Systems', Journal of Systems Management, April, 36-38

Ferris, K.R. (1982) 'Perceived Environment Uncertainty, Organizational Adaptation, and Employee Performance: A Longitudinal Study in Professional Accounting Firms', Accounting, Organizations and Society, 7(1), 13-25

Gambling, T.E. (1985) 'Expert Systems: Stone Age Rules, OK?', Accountancy, 96, 125-127

Gambling, T.E., Arnold, M.R. and Rush, D.G. (1985) 'Expert Systems: As Expert as Accountants?', Management Accounting, 63, 20-22

Ginzberg, M.J. (1980) 'An Organizational Contingencies View of Accounting and Information Systems Implementation', Accounting, Organizations and Society, 5(4), 369-382

Grinyer, P.H. and Wooller, J. (1975) Corporate Models Today, a New Tool for Financial Management, Institute of Chartered Accountants in England and Wales

Grinyer, P.H. and Wooller, J. (1980) 'An Overview of a Decade of Corporate Modelling in the UK', Accounting and Business Research, Winter, 41-49

Hampton, R. (1985) Implementation of Computer Systems in a Small Business, Unpublished M.Sc. thesis, UWIST

Heller, F.A. (1971) Managerial Decision-Making: A Study of Leadership Styles and Power-Sharing Among Senior Managers, Tavistock, London

Higgins, H.C. and Finn, R. (1977) 'Planning Models in the UK: A Survey', Omega, 133-147

Higgins, J.C. and Opdebeeck, E.J. (1984) 'The Microcomputer as a Tool in Financial Planning and Control: Some Survey Results', Accounting and Business Research, Autumn, 333-340

Ho, T.C. (1985) A Survey of the Use of Micro Computers in Small Accountancy Firms, Unpublished MBA thesis, UWIST

Hopwood, A.G. (1973) An Accounting System in Managerial Behaviour, Saxon House

Huff, A. (1978) 'Conceptual Uncertainty', Academy of Management Review, July, 651-654

Leavitt, H.J. and Whisler, T.L. (1958) 'Management in the 1980s', Harvard Business Review, Nov-Dec, 41-46

Likert, R. (1967) The Human Organization: Its Management and Value, McGraw-Hill, New York

McKenna, E.F. (1980) 'An Analysis of Leadership Patterns in the Finance Function', Accounting, Organizations and Society, 5(3), 297-310

Otley, D.T. (1978) 'Budget Use and Managerial Performance', Journal of Accounting Research, Spring, 122-149

Pratt, J. and Jiambalvo, J. (1982) 'Determinants of Leader Behaviour in an Audit Environment', Accounting, Organizations and Society, 7(4), 369-380

Rogers, E.M. (1962) Diffusion of Innovations, Free Press, New York

Sathe, V.V. (1974) Structural Adaptation to Environment: Study of Insurance Company Departments and Branch Banks, Unpublished Ph.D. Dissertation, Ohio State University

Searfoss, D.G. (1976) 'Some Behavioural Aspects of Budgeting for Control: An Empirical Study', Accounting, Organizations and Society, 1(4), 375-385

Seiler, R.E. and Bartlett, R.W. (1982) 'Personality Variables as Predictors of Budget System Characteristics', Accounting, Organizations and Society, 7(4), 381-403

Simon, H.A. (1965) The Shape of Automation for Men and Management, Prentice-Hall, Englewood Cliffs, N.J.

Stedry, A.C. (1960) Budget Control and Cost Behaviour, Prentice-Hall, Englewood Cliffs, N.J.

Stewart, R. (1976a) The Reality of Management, Pan, London

Stewart, R. (1976b) How Computers Affect Management, Pan, London

Swieringa, R. and Moncur, R.H. (1975) Some Effects of Participative Budgeting on Managerial Behaviour, National Association of Accountants, New York

Tannenbaum, A.S. (1957) 'Personality Change as a Result of an Experimental Change of Environmental Conditions', Journal of Abnormal and Social Psychology, 404-406

Tannenbaum, A.S. and Allport, F.H. (1956) 'Personality Structure and Group Structure: an Interpretive Study of their relationship through an event structured hypothesis', Journal of Abnormal and Social Psychology, 99, 272-280

Tannenbaum, R. and Schmidt, W.H. (1958) 'How to Choose a Leadership Pattern', Harvard Business Review, 36(2), 95-101

Thompson, J.D. (1968) Organizations in Action, McGraw-Hill, New York

Vroom, V.H. (1960) Some Personality Determinants of the Effects of Participation, Prentice-Hall, New York

Whisler, T.L. (1970) The Impact of Computers on Organizations, Praeger, New York

Yukl, G.C. (1971) 'Toward a behavioural theory of leadership', Organisational Behaviour and Human Performance, 414-440

# 6. Management Accounting and New Information Technology

by Christopher J Cowton

## INTRODUCTION

New information technology provides unparalleled challenges and opportunities for management accounting, as for many other organisational functions. To date, its impact on accounting has been primarily through computers (Collier, 1984) which, as they have improved in hardware, software and cost-effectiveness, have had a growing effect upon the discipline. The purpose of this chapter is to concentrate on computers in reviewing some of the implications of new information technology, focusing primarily on the technical opportunities offered and on changes in the relationship of management accountants to other organisational members.

## TECHNICAL OPPORTUNITIES

According to Mattessich (1980), the impact of electronic data processing (EDP) on the work of management accountants has been 'spectacular'. One of the most obvious and major ways in which new information technology has entered into management accounting is in the regular collection of data and routine preparation of reports. A number of factors may account for this most basic of impacts. In some ways, it can be viewed simply as a further development in the tradition of punched cards and tabulating machines. It is quite natural to first apply new tools to the performance of existing tasks (Harper, 1985), since these are the most obvious applications.

It is also easier to convince management of anticipated cost savings on current activities than of prospective benefits arising from new functions. This was of particular importance when the purchase of <u>any</u> computer system was a significant resource decision in which high capacity usage of expensive mainframes had to be confidently expected before approval would be granted. Indeed, Land (1984) suggests that, in some situations, efficiency and cost saving goals may still be paramount and overshadow any consideration of other possible benefits. Carr (1985a) documents the case of the Central Computer and Telecommunications Agency (CCTA) which, as part of the Treasury, acts as a guardian of rules on capital expenditure relating to computer-based equipment in the UK Civil Service. Only since 1983 have the rules allowed consideration of quantifiable service benefits in addition to cost-displacement in evaluating a potential investment.

Management accounting is a prime candidate for cost savings through computerisation because its basic activities such as payroll and sales accounting involve substantial volumes of arduous work and are relatively simple to automate to some degree. Anticipated savings may not be apparent at first, because of the complexities involved in introducing information technology: 'the procedures under the new system seem to be much slower than they were under the old method. However, after the new system has settled down and the operators have become accustomed to the new way of doing things, substantial time savings can be achieved' (McCosh, 1984). For example, the introduction of an electronic point of sales (EPOS) system into the department stores of the Dingles division of House of Fraser has led to a reduction in the time taken to produce computer-held group sales statistics from ten days to one (Carr, 1985a).

One consequence of the improved handling of data is that there is a much reduced need for clerks and other lower grade accounting support personnel (Reynolds, 1982). Thus, to use the distinction proposed by Menzies, it is a typical case of 'information workers' - that is, those involved in the routine entry, recording, storage and transmission of data - dwindling in number (Long, 1984). This trend is likely to continue, not only as more organisations computerise their basic accounting systems, but also as data are increasingly fed directly into the management accounting department's computer files from remote terminals or computers in locations such as warehouses, through EPOS systems in retail outlets, and even from sales representatives using small hand-held devices which can be frequently and easily linked up to the main computer through the telephone system.

Murray (1967) believed that the effectiveness of accountants' response to the IT challenge would determine whether their stature and role would grow or diminish during the remainder of the century. 'Knowledge workers' - those who analyse and utilise the output of information workers - are not likely to suffer in the same way as clerks. Indeed, a number of writers are optimistic about the implications of new information technology for qualified accountants who possess professional skills and abilities. '"Everything to gain and nothing to lose" might well be the slogan for management accountants in this electronic age,' states Banyard (1982), who at the time of writing his article was a

Vice-President of the Institute of Cost and Management Accountants. Gale and Kaye (1984) also envisage management accountants benefiting as - released from the conduct and supervision of mundane tasks - they are able to make a more valuable contribution to organisations, placing greater emphasis on interpretation and communication, 'which are the true professional skills' (Collier, 1984). Certainly, there seems to be some potential for this to occur, especially now that 'modern computer technology has helped accountants overcome many of their data storage, retrieval, manipulation and aggregation problems' (Sizer, 1981). Although many of these advances would be envisaged as occurring in large organisations, Banyard (1982) looks forward to improvements also taking place in the standard of management accounting in small companies.

The application of new quantitative techniques to management accounting, which Schoenfeld (1980) argues has tended to dominate past developments, 'will be accelerated through the availability of less expensive computer technology, because many techniques hitherto regarded as too costly will become economically feasible' (Schoenfeld, 1980). A simple example is budgetary control, which in many organisations could previously not be done cheaply and quickly enough to be effective (Sizer, 1981). Now, according to McCosh (1984), most businesses of any size have an accounting system that uses a computer to produce a statement showing the budget, the actual outcome and the resultant variance by department on a monthly or four-weekly basis.

It is also possible that some of the more sophisticated techniques long advocated by academics - for example, mathematical programming - will begin to replace the apparently crude approaches frequently observed to take place in practice. As Bhaskar puts it:

> One of the arguments for favouring 'rules of thumb' over more sophisticated solutions is that such rules are simpler to calculate. The silicon chip now means that the tediousness of long calculations can be removed. What may have been dismissed by the practitioner as being too complex can be fully utilized by today's practitioner. (Bhaskar, 1981)

Clearly, software has an important role to play. Already, for example, linear programming packages are widely available which not only discover the optimal solution but also, through the provision of dual or shadow prices and the ease of re-calculation, permit the operation of sensitivity analysis to probe the implications of different assumptions. In general, the development of deterministic models which include explicit consideration of constraints has been 'considerably aided by the development of large mainframe computers, without which the burden of calculation required would have rendered practical application infeasible' (Otley, 1983). Now, minis and micros are playing their part too.

Sensitivity analysis, which aids managers in their task of coping with uncertainty, can now occur in other areas of management accounting. 'Already budgeting is becoming the iterative exercise that the textbooks recommend it should be. Computer spreadsheet analysis packages such as VISICALC now permit the rapid exploration of the consequences of a wide range of alternatives in contrast to the static analysis that constrained much conventional budgeting' (Otley, 1983). Thus management accounting techniques, which in the past have been most suited to placid and stable environments in which, it can be argued, they are least needed (Otley, 1983), can be increasingly useful in situations characterised by considerable uncertainty. They can be used as 'learning machines' rather than simple 'answer machines' (Burchell et al, 1980).

It should be noted, however, that while the computer may help in the calculative aspects of more sophisticated techniques, 'the chip ... will not aid the information requirements of such techniques and the problem of understanding how they work' (Bhaskar, 1981). It is often very difficult to obtain reasonable surrogates for the inputs required by many formal decision models, and many line managers appear to have difficulty in understanding more than the most simple financial concepts.

New information technology can not only help the management accountant to expand the range of services he provides, but also change the way in which he supplies management with information. Using older technologies, the management accountant typically relied upon aggregation to guard against managers suffering from information overload, thus at the same time destroying much potentially useful information (Sorter, 1969). New information technology provides the opportunity to be much more selective in the reporting of information. 'Advances in computer file capabilities and data management systems, coupled with improved remote output devices and an increasing knowledge of their use, should reduce the emphasis on routine reporting in the form of comprehensive reports of what has transpired' (Sizer, 1981). Instead, the accountant can serve management on a much more flexible basis; for example, the use of spread sheet packages has become widespread in the solution of ad hoc problems (Collier, 1984).

Whether attention should be focused on managers' information needs (the 'decision models' approach) or on their wants (the 'decision makers' approach) has been a moot point in accounting in general for some time (Sterling, 1970; Cooper and Essex, 1977; Bird, 1975), but care should certainly be exercised in harnessing the abilities of the computer; there is a considerable danger of waste or even information overload when a manager, who may be interested in only a small set of key variables, is provided with more frequent and detailed analysis (Tricker and Boland, 1982).

## THE ACCOUNTANT AND OTHER INFORMATION SPECIALISTS

The potential for enhancing the scope and impact of their craft is not the only challenge for management accountants brought about by advances in information technology. Some commentators (e.g. Gale and Kaye, 1984) have pointed to the likelihood of management accounting as an identifiable organisational function disappearing or being subsumed within a very much broader management information system (see Earl, 1983). Leaving aside questions of definition, the rationale for such a view derives partly from recognising the user of information, rather than the provider, as being of prime significance. 'Management accounting is but one component in the manager's informational environment, and only by integrating its activities with other information providers will it contribute to the meaningful development of an appropriate ensemble of information resources for management' (Boland, 1980). Another argument for the integration of all databases, which has now lost much of it force owing to the economics of distributed processing, was that this was a highly efficient and effective manner of utilising large, expensive mainframe computers (Lieberman and Whinston, 1975; Colantoni, Manes and Whinston, 1981). As well as potentially leading to the disappearance of management accounting as a separate organisational phenomenon, there was the question of who would be in charge of the new, integrated information system (Beyer, 1967). Thus, in personnel terms, 'the data processing revolution of the last twenty years has confronted the management accountant with a powerful and growing cadre of professional information specialists' who constitute 'important rivalries' (Boland, 1980).

Boland, however, appears to see management accounting as still having a viable, independent existence. 'It is not a merger or a takeover that is sought here, but an active working relationship that recognizes the tools and techniques of any one specialist are inadequate in isolation, and only in concert will the information environment they provide meet the objectives of each' (Boland, 1980). Indeed, in practice, management accounting is often more closely linked, for better or worse, to the financial reporting system which is geared to the statutory rights of external parties, rather than to some recognisable management information system. Thus, while it may seem conceptually neat and reasonable to integrate the two, since 'at the macro level of definition, considering goals and objectives, management information systems (MIS) and management accounting are virtually identical', 'in practice, they are not the same' (Davis, 1980). This is not only because there are significant unique topics in each, but also because of the operation of certain educational, organisational and technical factors.

Certainly, in the educational field, there has been a tendency for MIS and management accounting curricula to develop independently (Davis, 1980). Although efforts are being made to both teach about computers and to employ them in the pedagogic process within accounting degrees (Hein, 1965; Bhaskar, 1982, 1983; Kaye, 1985), the typical text on the use of computers to perform accounting functions is focused on a relatively low level, and contains little advanced MIS material.

In the organisational context, economies of scale available in computers up to the mid 1970s, with a reliance on large mainframes, meant that enterprises desiring their own EDP facilities tended to have them centralised (Land, 1984). These facilities were usually located in a separate department, not least because early commercial computer programmers were highly paid and so sought an independent existence (Davis, 1980), which also gave them a secure power base. That they did not come to dominate the management accounting function, encompassing it within a comprehensive MIS, can be at least partially explained by their scientific, rather than accounting, background (Davis, 1980; Hein, 1965); the mysteries of the accounting craft were, to a considerable extent, left to its initiated practitioners. Another factor is that basic accounting functions such as payroll and sales have characteristics which lend themselves to computerisation and so in many organisations they became the focal point for first applications of computers. 'The legacy of this early development can still be seen in many organisations which continue to locate the computing function under the finance director or treasurer' (Carr, 1985b).

Since it was not possible to keep uptodate with organisationally-relevant EDP developments without a full-time commitment, the position of the leading members of centralised EDP departments generally appeared strong. However, for a number of reasons, the power of centralised EDP functions has tended to decrease more recently. Groups which lost power as it shifted towards those who developed and controlled computerised information systems have regained much of it more recently, with the development of on-line systems and the spread of the micro. A variety of interrelated factors have enabled the ordinary manager to take advantage of information technology developments for himself: its cheapness, which means that its purchase no longer involves a major capital account decision in many cases; significantly increased availability of commercial software packages; higher level programming languages which are considerably more user friendly; and his own familiarity with the technology, through training in school, university and the organisation itself (Gale and Kaye, 1984). All this has not led to the disappearance of EDP specialists, but it has resulted in a re-drawing of boundaries, with the role of the information technology manager becoming more complex and ambiguous (Earl, 1984). There is still a place for centralised planning and coordination, but many activities are now more advisory than directive in nature.

Management accountants should be counted amongst those non-specialists who have responded to the challenges of new information technology, not only enhancing their services and preserving their positions in large companies, but also, in the case of many small and medium-sized enterprises, being responsible for the introduction of computers (Carr, 1985b). The positive response of many management accountants is evidenced by the content of professional magazines and by surveys of attitudes and experience. According to one survey jointly funded by the Department of Trade and Industry and the Chartered Association of Certified Accountants, many accountants working in companies are keeping up with the IT challenge, although there is some criticism that the accounting bodies themselves are lagging, which may be reflected in the finding that, while most accountants recognised the importance of IT in their work, a substantial number, particularly in public practice, felt unsure of their own abilities in the area (Carr, 1986).

## MANAGERS INFORM THEMSELVES

The previous two sections have suggested that many management accountants are responding well to the technical opportunities provided by new information technology. Their craft seems likely to remain, and indeed develop, as a significant, identifiable aspect of the control of large business enterprises, at least in the manufacturing sector, for some time. There is, however, one type of challenge to their position which has not been considered so far, signs of which are now beginning to appear.

The challenge to their role as major information providers, of which management accountants have been most aware over the past two decades or so, has been from information specialists possessing computer expertise, as discussed in the previous section. However, while the 'user' of information has been much cited, if not much studied, in the context of accounting, relatively little attention has been paid to how he informs himself. Some acknowledgement has been made of the notion of 'informal' information systems and it is known that some managers maintain parallel manual systems, but the possibility of many managers being informationally self-sufficient for many of their tasks has not been a central concern in debate regarding the role of the management accountant. Now, however, 'information technology has ... provided line managers with a series of communications tools so that they do not really need management accounts to inform themselves about the performance of the segments of the enterprise which they are expected to control' (McCosh, 1984). They are thus able to maintain their own substantial databases and to manipulate these in relatively sophisticated ways.

The ability of line managers to furnish many of their own information needs does not mean that the management accountant can no longer have a role as a provider of information. First of all, in much the same way as financial accounts frequently serve to confirm information that is already known in the stock market, so management accounts may have a subordinate status in confirming information which managers have already learned from other sources (McCosh, 1984). They also portray events in monetary terms, which may be particularly important for managers with a technical bias who do not readily proceed to consider the financial consequences of their activities.

The use of money as a unit of measurement leads to what McCosh views as the 'residual advantage' of the management accountant, that is, 'that the package of management accounts is the best collectively complete description of the enterprise as a totality' (McCosh, 1984). This is of importance not only to top management concerned with the broad task of overseeing the enterprise, but also has a significant role to play in creating and sustaining common concerns and shared values within an organisation (Burchell et al, 1980).

The integrated nature of the management accounting system may make it an efficient means of dealing with information from an organisational perspective, especially when compared with the proliferation of independent databases. Even if this is not the case, the management accounting information will appear to be virtually costless to the individual manager - although he may be apportioned a share of the cost in the form of overhead, this figure will not be affected by whether he uses the information provided. Therefore, if the management accounting reports match up tolerably well with his desires, it may not be worth his while investing substantial resources in his own extensive information system, even though he may possess the capability.

It seems clear that the approach of the management accountant will have to change, especially as managers become increasingly adept in the use of information technology and as it grows more user friendly and more cost-effective. If the manager does not receive the information he wants from the management accountant he will generate it himself or seek it from other sources. Sterling (1970) argues that the 'decision makers' approach - giving the manager what he requests - can inhibit progress and be ultimately self-defeating, but, if the accountant wishes to be more prescriptive in his information provision, he will need to be much more careful in his 'education' of the user, given the manager's own informational capabilities. The accountant will also have to accept that, particularly with the advent of new manufacturing technology, the manager will be able to generate some data far more quickly and efficiently than the accountant could ever hope to do, and so the possibility of the co-operative linking of databases should be considered (Reynolds, 1982).

All this implies a more responsive, possibly advisory, role for the management accountant, paralleling what has happened to the data processing expert. McCosh (1984) suggests that, as 'internal consultants', management accountants can contribute valuably to line managers' tasks. As well as continuing to provide their own specialist information, they will be able to use their expertise in enhancing and helping to design managers' own information systems, as well as providing help in interpretation.

## SUMMARY AND CONCLUSION

The growth of new information technology has provided the management accountant with an unparalleled set of opportunities and challenges. The enormous capacity of computers for storing data and for processing them at immense speeds, together with developments in software, has made possible substantial savings in time and effort devoted to routine activities. Many such savings have already been achieved and can be expected to continue, but further opportunities also exist for the management accountant to make real technical progress in the practice of his craft. Such advances will need to be made if the management accountant is to remain a central figure in the management of information within organisations. The information technology revolution has not only brought about the significant challenge of other information specialists, but more recently has also greatly enhanced the capacity of the ordinary manager to inform himself. Unless the management accountant changes his emphasis accordingly, his role in key decision making will rapidly diminish.

## REFERENCES

Banyard, C. (1982) 'Computer Technology and Its Effect on Management Accounting', Management Accounting, 60 (8), 32-53

Beyer, R. (1967) 'Management Information Systems: Who'll Be in Charge?', Management Accounting (USA), 48 (10), 3-8

Bhaskar, K.N. (1981) 'Quantitative Aspects of Management Accounting', in M. Bromwich and A. Hopwood (eds.) Essays in British Accounting Research, Pitman, London

Bhaskar, K.N. (1982) 'Use of Computers in Accountancy Courses', Accounting & Business Research, 49, 3-10

Bhaskar, K.N. (1983) 'Computers and the Choice of Accountancy Syllabuses', Accounting & Business Research, 50, 83-93

Bird, P. (1975) 'Objectives and Methods of Financial Reporting: A Generalised Search Procedure', Accounting & Business Research, 19, 162-7

Boland, R.J., Jnr. (1980) 'Three Challenges for Management Accounting in the 1980s', in Holzer, H.P. (ed.) Management Accounting 1980, University of Illinois, Urbana-Champaign

Burchell, S., Clubb, C., Hopwood, A., Hughes, J. and Nahapiet, J. (1980) 'The Roles of Accounting in Organizations and Society', Accounting, Organizations & Society, 5 (1), 5-27

Carr, J.G. (1985a) Information Technology and the Accountant, Gower, Aldershot (on behalf of the Chartered Association of Certified Accountants)

Carr, J.G. (1985b) Information Technology and the Accountant: Summary and Conclusions, Gower, Aldershot (on behalf of the Chartered Association of Certified Accountants)

Colantoni, C.S., Manes, R.P. and Whinston, A. (1981) 'A Unified Approach to the Theory of Accounting and Information Systems', Accounting Review, 46 (1), 90-102

Collier, P.A. (1984) The Impact of Information Technology on the Management Accountant, Institute of Cost and Management Accountants, London

Cooper, D. and Essex, S., (1977) 'Accounting Information and Employee Decision Making', Accounting, Organizations & Society, 2 (3), 201-17

Davis, G.B. (1980) 'Management Information Systems and Management Accounting', in Holzer, H.P. (ed.) Management Accounting 1980, University of Illinois, Urbana-Champaign

Earl, M.J. (1983) 'Management Information Systems and Management Accounting - A MISalliance?', in D. Cooper, R. Scapens and J. Arnold (eds.) Management Accounting Research and Practice, Institute of Cost and Management Accountants, London

Earl, M. (1984) 'Emerging Trends in Managing New Information Technologies', in Piercy, N. (ed.) The Management Implications of New Information Technology, Croom Helm/Nichols, Beckenham

Gale, C. and Kaye, R. (1984) 'Information Technology: What is the Future of the Management Accountant?', Management Accounting, 62 (6), 32-3

Harper, B. (1985) 'Old Accounting Theory Slows Database Advance', Accountancy, March, 152-3

Hein, L.W. (1965) 'EDP in the Accounting Curriculum', Journal of Accountancy, 120 (2), 78-84

Holzer, H.P. (1980) (ed.) Management Accounting 1980: Proceedings of the University of Illinois Management Accounting Symposium, University of Illinois at Urbana-Champaign

Kaye, G.R. (1985) 'Teaching Strategies in Computing and Accounting', British Accounting Review, 17 (1), 22-36

Land, F. (1984) 'The Impact of Information Technology on the Work Place', in Piercy, N. (ed.) The Management Implications of New Information Technology, Croom Helm/Nichols, Beckenham

Lieberman, A.Z. and Whinston, A.B. (1975) 'A Structuring of an Events-Accounting Information System', Accounting Review, 50 (2), 246-58

Long, R.J. (1984) 'The Application of Microelectronics to the Office: Organisational and Human Implications', in Piercy, N. (ed.) The Management Implications of New Information Technology, Croom Helm/Nichols, Beckenham

McCosh, A.M. (1984) 'Management Accountancy in the I.T. Age', (Paper, dated September 1984, based on a booklet entitled 'The Management of Information Technology')

Mattessich, R. (1980) 'Management Accounting, Past, Present, and Future', in Holzer, H.P. (ed.) Management Accounting 1980, University of Illinois, Urbana-Champaign

Murray, G.L. (1967) 'Information Technology and the Professional Accountant', Management Services, 4 (6), 15-21

Otley, D.T. (1983) The Fall and Rise of Management Accounting: The Inaugural Tom Robertson Memorial Lecture, Department of Accounting and Business Method, University of Edinburgh, Edinburgh

Piercy, N. (1984) (ed.) The Management Implications of New Information Technology, Croom Helm/Nichols, Beckenham

Reynolds, R.P. (1982) 'Bookkeepers Will Bite the Dust!', Management Accounting, 60 (1), 36-9

Schoenfeld, H-M.W. (1980) 'Management Accounting: Discernable Future Directions', in Holzer, H.P. (ed.) Management Accounting 1980, University of Illinois, Urbana-Champaign

Sizer, J. (1981) Perspectives in Management Accounting, Heinemann, London (in association with the Institute of Cost and Management Accountants)

Sorter, G.H. (1969) 'An "Events" Approach to Basic Accounting Theory', Accounting Review, 44 (1), 12-19

Sterling, R.R. (1970) 'On Theory Construction and Verification', Accounting Review, 45 (3), 444-57

Tricker, R.I. and Boland, R.J. (1982) Management Information and Control Systems, 2nd ed., Wiley, Chichester

# 7. The Design of Marketing Accounting Systems*

by Timothy F Barrett

## INTRODUCTION

This paper seeks to explore the influences upon and the issues arising in the design of Marketing Accounting Systems (MAS). This area, which relates to the provision of financial information to marketing management, has been evolving since 1932 when the significance of such information in developing corporate profitability was first realised.

However, while practices in this area have shown some development, at least among the more concerned companies, the surveys which have been carried out of such practices are uniform in criticising both the accounting processes and the analytical techniques utilised in this area. Rayburn (1981), commenting on a review of such practices amongst Fortune magazine's 500 largest US firms, states 'that it is difficult to understand why so many financial controllers were not performing analyses which are thought to be important and essential for a better understanding of marketing costs'. While dissatisfaction with the practices in the area is manifest, little work has, as yet, been carried out to establish how improvements may be achieved.

This paper does not aspire to prescribe how improvements in the area can be achieved but rather seeks to explore the evolution in the practices of accounting for marketing and to make explicit at least some of the influences which likely shape the design of such accounting systems. As such the paper is in the nature of a review of the influences and issues which relate to the design of marketing accounting systems. The paper initially reviews the evolution in the practices of MAS, utilising the surveys of the area published during the fifty years between 1932 and 1982. Such surveys tend however to be of a purely descriptive

---

* The work upon which this paper is based was funded by the Development Fund of University College, Cork.

nature. While an examination of such surveys may establish emerging trends and developments in practices, it does not directly address the influences which currently shape the design of such systems of accounting, nor does it provide an explanation for the diversity of practices within the area. The second part of the paper attempts to consider these issues by drawing upon both empirical and theoretical works which place accounting systems within their organisational context and which explicitly consider diversity in accounting systems design.

A review of the surveys carried out in the area of marketing accounting over the past fifty years suggests that the development of the area has been uneven. While the functional areas of marketing have been subjected to increasingly sophisticated accounting treatment, the profitability analysis of market segments by comparison remains primitive. Thus while budgetary control and standard costing techniques are now common within the functional cost centres, the profitability analysis of market segments, e.g. products, territories, customers and mixes of these dimensions, is still relatively unsophisticated, heavy reliance continues to be placed on arbitrary allocation routines, promotional expenses are not usually lagged, market performance indices are not incorporated into reports, costs which may be viewed as investments in the market are expensed as incurred, while segment analysis is often confined to revenue or gross margin with no attempt to match costs with the revenues to which they contribute. It is perhaps not surprising, therefore, that such reports do not seem to be used in assessing market performance, or in aiding marketing decisions.

The initial work in the area of marketing accounting was Bromwell's (1932) 'Louisville Grocery Survey' carried out between 1924 and 1930 for the US Department of Commerce. Up to that point, 'post factory' costs were commonly classified by natural expense headings, and if further processing of these costs took place, they were charged to products on the basis of product revenue. Bromwell argued for a functional classification of such costs and that their allocation to products should be on the basis of the functional resources utilised by the various products. He identified six relevant functional cost categories, and their associated allocation bases, as shown in Table 7.1. The use of allocation bases which approximate resource utilisation rather than benefits generated was undoubtedly a step forward in matching costs to revenues for the purpose of profitability analysis. However the proposed treatment of promotional expenses, i.e. allocation on the basis of gross profit, remained an allocation on the basis of benefit received. The approach adopted by Bromwell was extensively refined in the literature over the following thirty years.

**Table 7.1: Cost Allocation Bases**

| Function | Allocation Bases to Products |
|---|---|
| Investment | Average inventory value |
| Storage | Floor space occupied |
| Checking | Number of orders handled |
| Handling | Number of standard units handled |
| Promotion | Gross profit |
| Reimbursement | Sales dollars |

Source: Bromwell (1932)

Thus Longman (1941), Alexander, Surface and Alderson (1953), the National Association of Accountants (1954), Sevin (1965) and Rayburn (1966 and 1967) developed the use of cost centres within the functional cost analysis and the use of budgetary control techniques within such cost centres based upon flexible budgeting and standard costing. The developments relating to flexible budgets, standard costing and statistical cost analysis were however largely confined to the responsive functions of physical distribution and personal selling rather than to the discretionary areas, or order generating activities, of advertising, promotions and customer service, and may be viewed as the application of techniques initially developed within the production process to certain cost responsive marketing functions.

The allocation routines utilised in charging functional costs to revenue segments improved with the recognition that, while some functional costs varied with product characteristics and product activity levels, other functional costs varied with customer characteristics and customer activity levels. The bases of cost variability began to be utilised as the bases of allocation of functional costs to product and customer revenue segments. In 1963 Sevin stated:

> The functional cost groups are allocated to products, customers, territories, and other segments of sales on the basis of measurable factors. These measurable factors or bases of allocation are product, customer, and territory characteristics which bear a 'causative'

relationship to the total amounts of the functional cost groups.

Sevin developed in great detail the bases of allocation which he considered appropriate for various functional cost groupings. Once the initial functional cost had been allocated to products or customers, he argued that all such should be reallocated over the other segments to yield full marketing costs by customer class, product line, etc. Thus costs initially allocated to customer grouping would be reallocated over the products sold within each such grouping to yield total product cost. Apart from the increasing sophistication of the allocation routines, Sevin's work also emphasises that it is not only product analysis which may be yielded, but also an analysis by customer class, geographic region and channel of distribution. While the above developments had emerged in the literature, the actual practices of accounting for marketing were first reviewed by Mellman in 1965, who surveyed segment profitability reporting practices in twenty-eight US companies, twenty-two of which were listed in the 1960 Fortune Magazine List of 500 largest manufacturers. He found that while twenty-six of the twenty-eight companies generated product profitability analysis, usually monthly, in all cases national aggregates of products were used i.e. product profitability by geographical area, customer type or distribution channel were not provided. In the generation of the product profitability analysis, Mellman noted that the distinction between fixed and variable costs 'were for the most part either completely lacking or else arbitrarily designed' and 'in the process of cost allocation, the writer has repeatedly witnessed the banding together of heterogenous functional costs, and consequently the allocation of those costs on somewhat arbitrary bases'.

Apart from the analysis of national aggregates of products, territorial analysis was also commonly provided, while an analysis by customer or customer class was quite rare. Territorial analysis was carried out by twenty-five of the companies and, interestingly and quite in contrast to the practices of full cost allocation to products, twenty of the companies utilised a contribution margin approach to the analysis of geographic territories, i.e. the analysis usually included only those costs which were directly traceable to the territories. Mellman noted that this difference in practice was probably due to the differing uses to which the analyses were put the territorial analyses were utilised to evaluate the performance of the territorial management and thus costs over which such management did not have control were excluded, while the product analysis was utilised to evaluate the product's contribution to organisational profit and was not associated with the evaluation of executives.

The lack of a customer orientation in the analytical reports was evidenced by the fact that only three of the twenty-eight companies generated a customer or customer class analysis. Mellman commented on this lack by stating that it 'certainly indicated a failure to orientate cost accounting analysis to markets as would be suggested by the reorientation of managerial interest'.

Apart from profitability analysis by segment, Mellman also examined practices in the area of functional cost analysis. He found that functional analyses were utilised by all companies in the survey, and the use of cost centres within functions was common. However in the evaluation of the efficiency of such functional cost centres, he found that 'cost centre expenses are judged in the aggregate in terms of a pre-defined relationship to sales volume'. While such an approach might be appropriate where sales volume causes marketing expenditure, where the expenditure is incurred to generate sales it is not appropriate. For example if sales volume declined such an approach would lead to the reduction of marketing expenditure perhaps at the very time when additional expenditure might increase sales volume. In conclusion, Mellman was somewhat less than euphoric. He stated 'practices in the analysis of marketing costs have not kept pace with needs as suggested by the changes in the marketing scene'. In effect, during the thirty years since the Louisville survey, while functional cost analysis and cost centre reporting had improved, segment profitability analysis and control of marketing expenditure remained primitive.

The potential usefulness of management accounting to improve marketing decision making was considered by both Sevin (1965) and Feder (1965) both of whom emphasise the need to integrate accounting and marketing information so as to identify the relative profitability of marketing expenditure in different market segments. By reassigning marketing resources to the more responsive segments, the productivity of such resources might be improved and profits enhanced. Sevin pointed out that while the accounting system may monitor the relative productivity of marketing expenditure in different market segments, the results of reallocating such expenditure between market segments would likely be difficult to forecast and he urged controlled experiments be carried out and carefully monitored before major policy charges are implemented. In 1967 Baumol and Sevin developed a linear programming approach which, while acknowledged to be based on limiting assumptions, e.g. linear responses, attempted to indicate 'at least the direction' in which market resources might be reassigned toward those market segments which provide greater contribution from marketing expenditure.

While both Feder and Sevin recognised the potential which marketing accounting systems provided for profit performance, Feder argued that the conventions of accounting actually inhibited the analysis of marketing performance and he instances the following three such conventions as being particularly inappropriate:

1. The expensing of marketing costs in the period in which they are incurred.

2. The use of full cost allocation.

3. The time period used in the analysis.

It was suggested by Feder that the expensing of promotional costs should be lagged by a period equal to the time lapse between consumer purchase and manufactured sales to the first point in the distribution channel. The longer it takes for the goods to pass through the distribution channel then the longer should be the lagging of the expenses. That the logic of this argument did not overcome the rubrics of the accountants can possibly be established by the fact that in 1982, some seventeen years later, Mason was still arguing for the approach to be accepted and pointing out the dangers of misinterpreting marketing accounting reports if such lagging was not introduced. The use of full cost allocation to segments may result in a distortion of the analysis since no causational relationship may exist between the revenue generated by the segment and the cost allocated to it. Sevin however suggested that allocation of full costs to segments may have an advantage in that it may indicate the amount of resources which would become available for use elsewhere should marketing effort be withdrawn from the segment. However, the desire for 'bottom-line' analysis of segments may given a spurious accuracy to the analysis.

The third difficulty mentioned by Feder, that of the time period used in the analysis, arises since the routine reporting schedule of management accounts may not correspond to the period over which the market segment responds to marketing expenditure. As Feder stated, 'An analysis performed on the basis of the results achieved in any one month would probably exclude a substantial portion of the sales revenue generated by the marketing effort expensed that period. On the other hand, considerably longer periods (say, a year) probably combine the results of many spending decisions.'

Having raised these issues, Feder outlined an approach which he classified as a 'rough beginning - a place from which to move towards refinement', but which was in effect quite a sophisticated system designed to overcome the problem caused by the application of traditional accounting rubrics to an area which requires multiperiod, long term analytical techniques. The early 1970s produced two significant surveys of actual practices in the area of accounting for marketing. Both of these surveys were carried out in the USA, the first of which, published in 1971 by the National Association of Accountants, developed a stage model of the development of MAS. Based upon a survey of twenty-five companies deliberately drawn from different industries and of differing size, the authors argued that there were three clearly identifiable stages in the development of marketing accounting systems. The three stages suggested were as follows:

| | |
|---|---|
| First stage of development : | The accounting function provided straight reporting of information from routine source documents. |
| Second stage of development: | The accounting systems combined the stage one data to yield marketing profitability reports. |
| Third stage of development : | Mathematical techniques used to redefine the stage two reporting. |

The report notes that while the 'development of a particular marketing information system seems to depend on the companies size, industrial segments, and human and physical resources, the developmental process appears to follow a rather common pattern'. (Emphasis added) Apart from the actual practices in each of the stages of development, this survey also elicited the views of marketing executives as to their unsatisfied information needs. A matching of such information needs with the stage of development of the system is provided below in Table 7.2. The report found that some two-thirds of the companies surveyed felt that they were in or entering the second stage of development, and that 'their greatest need is for reports which will provide profitability by region, customer and other variables'.

This finding is strongly supported by a far more comprehensive survey published one year later. In 1972 the American Accounting Association published the report of its committee on 'Cost and Profitability Analysis for Marketing'. As part of its work the committee issued a survey questionnaire to four hundred and thirty-two of Fortune magazines, five hundred largest firms, to which seventy-three responded. A cross-tabulation of type of task with the focal segment is shown below in Table 7.3.

This cross-tabulation indicates the various revenue generation segments which are routinely reported. By

**Table 7.2: A Stage Model of Marketing Accounting Information**

| Practices | Further Information Required |
| --- | --- |
| Stage 1 | |
| Sales volume in $ and units by product and region. | Better methods of analysis. |
| Sales by key accounts. | More exception reporting (less unnecessary detail). |
| Functional analysis of costs. | |
| Narrative competitor information. | |
| Product profitability nationwide. | |
| Stage 2 | |
| Sales forecasts. | Profitability analysis by region, product line and customer type. |
| Market share studies. | |
| Sales and marketing effort by account type, geographical area and profit potential. | Evaluation techniques for: Promotion, advertising, pricing, new products and distribution activities. |
| Incremental product profitability by period. | Analysis of reallocation of marketing effort. |
| | Competitor analysis. |
| Stage 3 | |
| Consumer behaviour. | Predictive models. |
| Research findings. | Market simulation. |
| Demand models. | |

Source: National Association of Accountants (1971)

**Table 7.3: Ranking of Market Segment by Management Task**

| Type of Task | Product | Customer | Territories | Channel | Order Size |
|---|---|---|---|---|---|
| Sales forecasting | 1 | 2 | 3 | 5 | 4 |
| Variance analysis | 1 | 2 | 2 | 5 | 4 |
| Budgeting | 1 | 3 | 2 | 4 | 5 |
| Distribution planning | 1 | 2 | 4 | 2 | 3 |
| Promotional mix planning | 1 | 2 | 3 | 5 | 4 |

Source: American Accounting Association (1972)

comparison with the Mellman survey nine years previously, customer analysis had increased in utilisation as a reporting segment with some thirty-five per cent of the companies commonly utilising both product and customer analysis. However, the level of sophistication observed in the segment analysis was poor. None of the companies lagged promotional expenditure, though nine utilised accrual techniques for special promotions and contests. Twenty-seven companies utilised a revenue analysis only, i.e. did not charge costs to the segments, fifty-eight deducted production costs, fifty deducted physical distribution expenses, and fifty deducted promotion costs. No indication is provided as to the bases of charging functional costs to the segments.

Apart from the choice of segment to utilise for planning and reporting purposes and the level of sophistication observed in the reporting of such segments, the survey also listed the type of analysis utilised in the functional analysis of costs. While all companies utilised functional analysis of costs, the use of standard costing was confined to physical distribution activities and was utilised by 50% of the companies. Standard costs were utilised primarily for functional control purposes but 30% of the firms also utilised such costs in the design of the distribution systems and 20% utilised them as the basis of charging market segments for their use of functional services. The survey did not address the question of the analysis and control of order generating costs.

Apart from its survey work the A.A.A. report developed an approach to marketing accounting which it termed 'The Modular Data Base System'. This differed significantly from the previous approach of Bromwell and Sevin outlined above, in that it sought to avoid allocation routines by developing a multidimensional, disaggregated data set of both costs and revenues, which would be capable of being aggregated along any dimension to yield a profitability analysis by required segment. To operationalise the approach, all cost and revenue items would be coded at entry utilising a multidimensional coding system, which would relate the items to their relevant function and segments. Thus revenue would be coded to all relevant segments, e.g. customer, product, geographical area, channel of distribution. Fixed costs, both discretionary and committed, would be coded to their relevant function and cost centres and if separable also coded to the segment to which they related. For variable costs the committee suggested that the standard variable cost per unit of causational activity be constituted a 'cost module' which would form the basis for charging functional costs to the revenue generating segments which benefited from the services provided by the function. As such the system attempted to avoid reliance upon allocation routines by holding all information at a high level of disaggregation and rather than allocating functional costs to the revenue segments, the costs would be coded to both function and segment at the input stage. By holding all such information within a computerised matrix, it would be possible to aggregate the information along any chosen dimension to yield segment profitability reports and also to yield multidimensional analysis. The use of standard costs as the cost modules allows expenditure and efficiency variances to be isolated within the functional cost centre. An outline of the system is provided below in Figure 7.1.

The capabilities of the system to produce multiple segment analysis is illustrated below in Table 7.4 which is based on a simple two-product two-area company position.

**Table 7.4: Two Dimensional Cost Analysis, by Product and Area**

| | Product Dimension | | Area Dimension | |
|---|---|---|---|---|
| | A | B | 1 | 2 |
| Standard Variable Cost of | | | | |
| Product A in Area 1 | X | | X | |
| Product B in Area 1 | | X | X | |
| Product A in Area 2 | X | | | X |
| Product B in Area 2 | | X | | X |
| Separable Fixed Costs | | | | |
| Product A | X | | | |
| Product B | | X | | |
| Area 1 | | | X | |
| Area 2 | | | | X |
| Discretional Costs | | | | |
| Product A | X | | | |
| Product B | | X | | |
| Area 1 | | | X | |
| Area 2 | | | | X |

Since all costs and also revenues are coded to their relevant products and areas the data may be aggregated either by product dimension or area dimension. The separable fixed costs are however coded only to those segments with which they are uniquely identified; no allocation basis is used. Thus for example the fixed costs of a warehouse which services a particular area would be coded to the area but

**Figure 7.1: Modular Data Base System Flow Diagram**

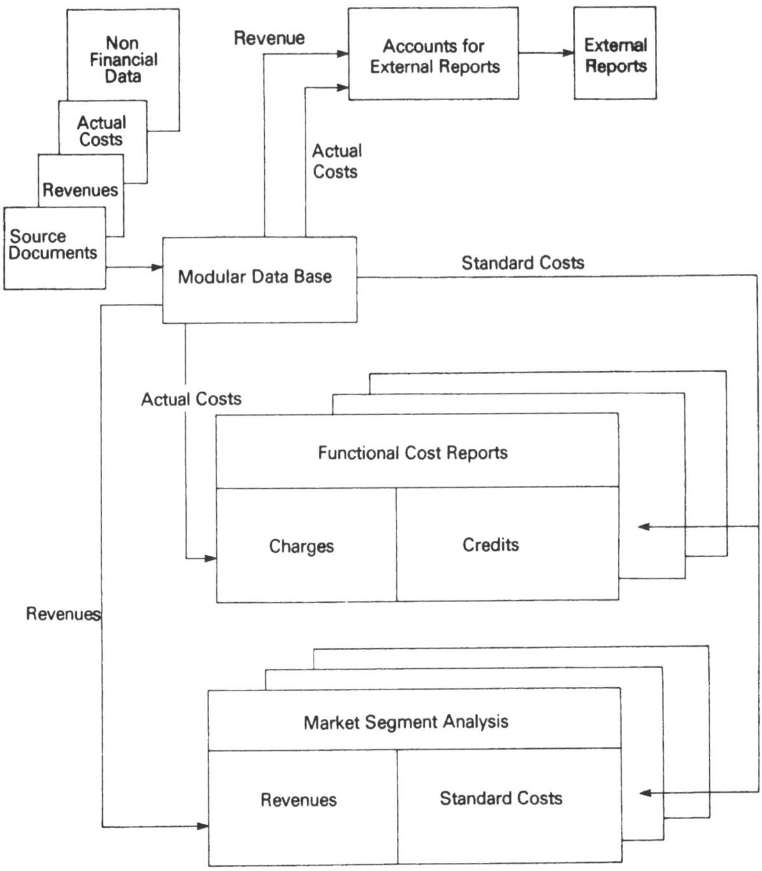


Source: Adapted by author from Crissy & Fisher, Financial Dimensions of Marketing Management, 1978

not to the products which are sold within the area. Likewise national product advertising expenditure would be coded by product but not by area.

While the potential of the system to generate multidimensional segment reports was exciting, particularly if marketing data could be included within the data base to allow integrated marketing/accounting reports to be produced, the actual uptake of the system in the form envisaged by the AAA Committee has not been impressive. The approach was however given support by the independent work of Liebermann and Whinston (1975), who point out the benefit of Mass Data Bases. If one such MDB was available for each organisation, then user-defined structures and operations could be developed which allow the utilisation of the MDB by specific units of the organisation, a major benefit being that all organisational executives would utilise a common information set contained in the MDB.

While some further work, mostly of an advocacy nature, on the Modular Data Based System was carried out by Mossman, Fischer and Crissy (1974 and 1978), the one major attempt by Lambert and Armitage (1979) to implement the approach, indicates the difficulties of operationalising the system. The Lambert and Armitage work was confined to the cost analysis of distribution, which being a responsive function was likely to be the area where standard cost modules could be generated. That their ambition for the system was high may be gauged by their stated intention of 'solving the many difficult allocation problems such as determining the transport cost by segment (customer, product) for a full truck-load shipment comprizing of multiple products for multiple customers'. Such common transport costs, while perhaps being direct costs of a territory, cannot however be disaggregated in any non-arbitrary fashion over the segments within the territories, as the work by Thomas (1969, 1974) on allocation routines shows. As such the Lambert and Armitage expectations were in direct conflict with the views of Mossman, Crissy and Fischer who pointed out that 'if costs common to multiple segments are allocated, the process is necessarily subjective and arbitrary'.

While the proposed system had the capability of handling high volumes of data, its avoidance of allocation routines meant that the more specific the segment chosen for reporting purposes, the lower the proportion of the total costs which could be identified with it, an observation which Beckett (1957) had made in relation to the use of direct costing within distribution systems; indeed he had pointed out that for highly specific segments 'the gross margin is approximately equal to the revenue'. This difficulty has probably proven to be the main reason why the system as proposed by the AAA Committee has not been taken up in practice. While Modular Data Bases are increasingly being used within marketing costing systems, they usually utilise allocation routines to yield total costs by various segments.

In 1981 Rayburn repeated the survey aspects of the AAA report. She surveyed by postal questionnaire the practices in the area of MAS within Fortune magazine's 500 largest US industrial companies, and analysed the practices in both functional and segment reporting. From the sixty-five usable responses which she received, she found that functional analysis was relatively well developed, all companies utilised budgetary control systems within the marketing functions, thirty-seven per cent used flexible budgets, and sixty-three per cent differentiated between controllable and non-controllable costs within the functional cost centres. Standard costing was commonly used, particularly within the distribution system but less so within the order generation areas of direct selling and advertising and promotion, as is shown in Table 7.5.

The analysis of segment reporting also showed that there had been some developments of practice since the AAA survey, particularly in the number of companies which were using multiple segment reporting. The choice of segment and the number of such segments utilised is shown below in Table 7.6.

In generating the segment analysis, ninety-four percent of the respondents coded expenses to the segments at point of data entry, which indicates a utilisation of some form of data base. However sixty-nine per cent of the companies expensed marketing costs in the period in which they were incurred, three per cent lagged the costs to the benefits yielded and thirty-one per cent stated that they did both.

An analysis of the practices utilised in the generation of the segment reports shows a continued heavy utilisation of allocation routines, with a surprisingly high proportion of companies not matching the marketing costs to particular segments. This is shown in Table 7.7.

By comparison with the AAA survey ten years previously, the Rayburn results show an improvement in practices among the largest US corporations. Standard costing is increasingly utilised, segment analysis is becoming more comprehensive, increasing use is being made of multi-dimensional analysis, and more companies are utilising a lagged approach to the expensing of promotional costs.

However, when Rayburn surveyed the type of analysis which was carried out on the segment performance reports she found that cost benefit relationships were usually not analysed - only 40% carried out breakeven analysis, less than 5% calculated a return on investment figures, and incremental analysis of marketing expenditure was not usually performed. She concluded that 'many firms have neglected to apply even the simplest cost tools to market activities, under the guise

**Table 7.5: Usage of Standard Costs**

| Function | Usage of Standard | | |
|---|---|---|---|
| | Standards Established | Integrated | Analysis Only |
| Warehousing & Handling | 49% | 60% | 40% |
| Transportation | 45% | 66% | 33% |
| Order Handling | 37% | 60% | 40% |
| Credit & Collections | 30% | 45% | 55% |
| Direct Selling | 27% | 22% | 78% |
| Advertising & Promotion | 22% | 26% | 74% |

Source: Rayburn (1981)

**Table 7.6: Market Segments Reported (1981)**

| | % |
|---|---|
| Product only | 43 |
| Customer only | - |
| Territory only | 7 |
| Distribution channel only | - |
| Product and customer | 5 |
| Product and territory | 15 |
| Product and channel | 10 |
| Three dimensions utilized | 7 |
| Four dimensions utilized | 13 |
| | 100% |

Source: Rayburn (1981)

that such costs were more difficult to analyse and control than product costs. Rather than isolate the cost behaviour of each element, the majority of controllers conveniently treated marketing costs as a discretionary fixed expense'.

A recent UK survey by Wilson and Bancroft (1983) into the 'application of management accounting techniques to the planning and control of marketing of consumer non-durables'

**Table 7.7: Contents of Market Segment Reports**

| | % of firms | No. |
|---|---|---|
| Revenue only | 7.7 | 5 |
| Less Variable Production Cost of Sale | 7.7 | 5 |
| Less Fixed Production Costs | 1.5 | 1 |
| Less Direct Marketing Cost of Segment | 12.3 | 8 |
| Less Allocated Marketing Cost | 66.3 | 43 |
| Return on Investment: | 4.5 | 3 |
| | 100 % | 65 |

Source: Rayburn (1981)

**Table 7.8: Market Segments Reported (1983)**

| Segment Utilized | Utilization Frequency |
|---|---|
| Brand item | 11 |
| Individual Brand | 11 |
| Product Group | 11 |
| Product Line | 9 |
| Customer Group | 7 |
| Territory | 5 |
| Order size | 4 |
| Sales person | 4 |
| Distribution Area | 1 |

Source: Wilson and Bancroft (1983)

reaches conclusions very similar to those of Rayburn. While segment analysis was carried out, usually on a brand basis, multi-dimensional segment reporting was common, as the responses from the thirteen companies given in Table 7.8 indicates.

However in the analysis of segment performance, only one company utilised variance analysis, none utilised productivity analysis and only one company developed segment budgets. Four of the thirteen companies lagged advertising expenditure while six lagged promotional expenditure. The focus of attention was not on the segment, but very much concentrated on the functional cost centres, all companies utilising budgetary control techniques in the analysis of functional cost centres. The accounting function did not appear to have any role in analysing the allocation of expenses between segments, and appeared to confine its activities to routine reporting of functional cost centre expenditure.

Based upon the above review of the published surveys of practices in the area of accounting for marketing and of some of the more normative writing in the area, it is possible to at least tentatively summarise the major changes in the practices of accounting for marketing which have occurred over the last fifty years.

1. A great deal of progress has been made in the area of functional costing. While prior to 1933 natural classifications of expenses appear to have been the only analysis carried out, it is now common to have such costs analysed by function, and by cost centres. The use of budgetary control techniques in these areas is extensive. Flexible budgeting and standard costing is common. While certain difficulties remain in this area, e.g. budget setting and control of discretionary costs, at least the MAS is providing information directly relevant to control needs in these areas.

2. Developments in generating segment analysis have also taken place. The objective of segment analysis is to match costs against the particular revenue to which they contribute to enable relative profitability, or the productivity of the cost in generating 'gain', to be established. Prior to 1933 such segmentation analysis as was carried out was achieved by allocation of costs to products on the basis of revenue generated. Over the intervening fifty years accounting practice has sought to establish the bases of cost variation, and to utilise these as a basis for charging costs to segments. Various levels of sophistication in this practice are available. Non-variable costs, either of a programmed or of a discretionary nature, may be capable of being identified with a particular segment, and charged as a direct cost. Difficulties in the area arise with expensing policies, and in dealing with non-separable fixed costs. In general, current practices in the area of segmentation have not as yet adequately dealt with these problems. Lagging of expenses is not a dominant feature, and absorption costing is extensively practiced.

3. While segment analysis has developed, and multiple segment reporting, e.g. by product and by customer type, is common, the segment report does not appear to be the focus of accounting attention. The various authors of the surveys examined are unanimous in their concern that such is the case; incremental segment reporting which would seek to

establish the impact of changes in marketing resources upon the contribution of the segment is generally not carried out, segment budgets are rarely utilised, productivity analysis is lacking. In effect, while segment reports are being generated, they are not being utilised for analytical or decision making purposes.

4. Apart from the 1972 AA Survey, none of the surveys considered have attempted to empirically establish the views of the marketing managers as to the relevancy and adequacy of the accounting reports being provided. In effect, the concern of the authors of the surveys has been either with the technical accounting sophistication of the reports, or with an evaluation of the systems against some subjective concept of appropriateness. It is almost as if the authors believe that there is a single best way of accounting for marketing, irrespective of the nature of the marketing task being undertaken. This is not to suggest that their criticisms are inappropriate, but to emphasise that while the surveys may show the evolution of accounting practice, they do not of themselves provide a criterion for evaluation, other than technical sophistication.

While it is important to appreciate the historic context in which current work in Marketing Accounting System Design is taking place, an analysis of accounting practices over time tend, to emphasise common trends and perhaps to under-emphasise diversity of practice. This may be particularly the case in MAS where the majority of the surveys have been carried out on Fortune Magazine's top five hundred, or within a particular industry as was the case with the Wilson and Bancroft (1983) study. The one notable exception is the AA Survey of 1972 which interestingly found quite distinct variations in the design of MAS. In this second part of the paper the emphasis is placed upon the organisational context of the MAS, in an attempt to render explicit why diversity in practice may exist in the area of accounting for marketing. Unfortunately the number of published studies which place MAS within an organisational context is low but inferences may be tentatively drawn from related studies.

Contingency theory as it is applied in accounting argues that the design of accounting systems is dependent upon the circumstances of the organisation. Otley (1980), when reviewing the work in the general area, points out, by way of criticism, that the underlying model assumed in much of the work is linear, i.e. environmental and technological variables are viewed as influencing organisational design which in turn influences the design of the accounting system which then in turn influences organisational effectiveness. Otley points out that such an approach is 'inappropriately simple' in that it argues for an exclusively direct relationship and does not consider for example tha the accounting system may influence the design of the organisation. As such, this linear approach is based on what Astley and Van de Ven (1983) term the 'system structural' view, and is compatible with the writings of Burns and Stalker (1961), Woodward (1965), Lawrence and Lorsch (1967) and Thompson (1967) who argue for an open systems view of organisational adaptation. While the system structural view is supportive of the argument that in differing environments differing systems may be appropriate, it emphasises that organisational behaviour is shaped by a series of impersonal mechanisms that act as external constraints. Astley and Van de Ven summarise this view as seeing 'management's basic role being to fine tune the organization according to the environment which it faces. Change takes the form of adaptation and management must perceive, process and respond to a changing environment by rearranging internal organizational structure (and process) to ensure survival or effectiveness.' As such management's role is primarily reactionary to environmental change and is environmentally determined.

The environmental deterministic view of organisations given above has been somewhat softened by the 'strategic choice' argument, which as Hambrick (1981) points out, while viewing organisations as being embedded in their environments argues that they may be loosely so embedded and that they may have leeway in which to navigate. Thus while environments may impose constraints upon organisations, various strategies may be successfully pursued within the same environment. This view, which rests upon the concept of environment niches, defined by Aldrich (1979) as distinct combinations of environmental resources and other constraints that are sufficient to support an organisation, argues that within a general environment sufficient variation may exist to allow differing strategies to be equally successfully pursued, provided that the particular niches with which the strategy interfaces are sufficiently rich in resources to allow the organisation to continue. What is significant in this view is that the choice of strategy to pursue within a general market environment is discretionary, or at least discretionary to some ill-defined degree.

Not only does the strategic choice view thus argue against environmental determinism but further suggests that the strategy chosen may itself influence the environment. Porter (1980) suggests that the competitive strategy of the organisation may for example be used to erect barriers to entry against potential competitors. Thus a low price, low margin mass market strategy might be utilised to prevent competition from entering the market. Management as such may play a proactive role in shaping its own environment, rather than being (merely) adaptive to environmental change. Furthermore within this voluntaristic orientation, organisations may be viewed as forming symbiotic relationships and the emergency of 'institutions' may, as suggested by Emery and Trist (1965), be further viewed as co-operative attempts to protect or engineer the environment against threatened hostility. This collective action approach emphasises an interactive role for the management of such organisations. An acceptance of a voluntaristic orientation to the analysis of organisations does however raise the issue of how strategy is formulated within organisations, and the role of accounting systems within such strategic choice. If, as Manghan (1978) points out, it is individuals who are appropriately viewed as sources of actions and strategies, it is those individuals and coalitions of executives who have gained access to organisational power who will control the process by which strategic choice is made. Child (1972) argues along similar lines when he points out that the choice of strategy is determined by the interaction of the environment and the internal process of decision making, which is dominated by organisational executives, each of whom plays a role in the decision process. In this view, strategic choice is the discretionary outcome of management decision process and not determined by environmental factors. These environmental factors may however provide the occasion, or the excuse, for strategic choice.

A major difference between the voluntaristic and deterministic views of organisation occurs in the view which is adopted to the role which process plays within organisations. In the deterministic systems orientation it is assumed that organisational processes are functional and that it is the individual's executive role rather than the individual which is important. In the voluntaristic analysis it is the individuals themselves and in coalitions, rather than in their functional role, which are the pivotal influence. The voluntaristic view of organisations does not necessitate an assumption that organisational processes of which accounting is one are necessarily efficient, rational or functional for the organisation. Indeed such processes may be viewed as a mechanism by which organisational actors gain a sectional advantage, necessarily at the expense of other such organisational actors. By suggesting self interest, and the desire for access to organisational resources via position in the organisational hierarchy, as a motivation force for executive action, 'process' may be viewed as both resulting from and contributing towards the particular power distribution within organisations. Accounting systems may be expected to be particularly susceptible to such influences since within capitalist organisations financial criteria will likely possess a legitimising role. This is not to suggest that such criteria are in fact utilised, but rather that they are likely to provide a justification for actions, the results of which are in the interests of those who utilise them. Thus Feldman and March (1981) emphasise the symbolic use of information while Pettigrew (1972) argues that information control is a power resource available to executives within organisations.

However, while the power structure of organisations is likely to be reflected in the design of the accounting system, the actual hierarchy within particular organisations will itself reflect the interaction between environment and strategy. Both the voluntaristic and deterministic schools accept this. Thus Thompson (1967), an advocate of open systems theory, argues that individuals whose role equips them to deal successfully with environmental uncertainty tend to become powerful within the organisation he states, 'To the extent that he (the executive) can contain contingencies and to the extent that the contingencies are important to the organization, the individual is powerful in the (internal) bargaining process.' Such powerful executives will in turn be in a position to influence the choice of strategy for the organisation.

Much the same approach is adopted by Hickson et al (1971), Hinings et al (1974) and Hambrick (1981), who develop the approach into what is now known as the 'strategic contingency theory of the firm'. This theory is attractive in that it allows a synthesis of the environmental and strategic schools of thought. Accepting the Thompson argument that successful coping with uncertainty enhances the power of the organisational actor, Hambrick points out that the contingent arises from the interaction of the external environment with the organisational strategy and, following Hinings, he emphasises the temporal dimension of power distribution within organisations. He states, 'Current strategy is a reflection of earlier power patterns just as current hierarchial position may be considered "fossilized" reflections of earlier power patterns. Similarly current power patterns effect future strategy and hierarchical arrangements.' The attraction of this argument is that it allows or enables the four sets of variables, environmental, strategic, structural/power, and process, to be examined interactively and suggests that such interactive analysis is necessary, rather than the original linear approach criticised by Otley (1980).

Having briefly reviewed the area of organisational contingency theory, the validity of Otley's criticism of the 'linear' approach to accounting studies appears to be unchallenged. The difficulty which arises with a rejection of the linear approach is that the major variables must be interactively studied. Thus the design of MAS is viewed as being interactively determined in conjunction with the environment, strategy, and organisational structure of the organisation. However, for ease of exposition, the studies which may have a relevance for the design of MAS will be reviewed under the separate heading of environment, strategy and structure.

## ENVIRONMENT AND MAS

Insofar as the environment lies outside the administrative control of the organisation, it represents an area of uncertainty, and, following the argument given above, certain environmental variables may prove significant for the accounting system provided that they interact with the organisational strategy to create strategic contingencies. A number of studies have sought to establish the direct impact of environmental variables upon the design of accounting systems. Unfortunately, as Otley (1980) points out, these studies have examined different environmental characteristics and there appears to be no consensus upon the characteristics which are appropriate to utilise. As such, the accounting literature suffers from the same defect as does the literature of organisational theory which has been criticised for the same failure by both Child (1972) and Schoorhoven (1981).

Duncan (1972), following the argument that environmental uncertainty is the major contingency, found that perceived uncertainty results from the interaction of two basic environmental dimensions, a simple/complex dimension and a static/dynamic dimension. His empirical findings are strongly supportive of the argument that it is dynamism rather than complexity which contributes most to environmental uncertainty.

Khandwalla (1972a, 1972b) examined the impact of competition upon the sophistication of management accounting control techniques. While his findings show a positive correlation between the overall level of competition and sophistication of accounting control systems, price competition had little or no effect, market competition had a modest positive effect and product competition had by far the most significant correlation.

Gordon and Miller (1976) examined the significance of three environmental variables for accounting systems, and argued the following: dynamism leads to forecasting difficulties and the need for frequent feedback; hostility leads to sophistication in accounting control systems and high frequency of feedback; and complexity leads to multiple focusing by the accounting system, i.e. multiple segment reporting.

Hayes (1977) using path analysis of a twenty-three company survey found that the performance of the marketing departments was dependent upon the external environment. He emphasised that, if such is the case, then budgetary control techniques which are surrogates for the factors which influence performance are not an appropriate method of assessing the performance of marketing departments.

Waterhouse and Tiessen (1978) argue that in uncertain environments decentralised structures will predominate, and within such the control emphasis will be placed more on resource allocation, output monitoring and socialisation rather than on standard costing, task specification and technical sophistication.

Thus the market environment appears to have certain consequences for accounting systems design. Certain characteristics of the environment directly impact upon MAS, others increase the uncertainty in which the marketing function operates, and this in turn poses contingencies for the design of management accounting systems. However, apart from such direct relationships between the environment and the design of MAS, indirect relationships also likely exist, since the environment strategy structure and accounting process may be interactively determined.

## STRATEGY AND MAS

Porter (1980) when considering the competitive strategy which an organisation may adopt states that 'the essence of formulating competitive strategy is relating a company to its environment'. Simmonds (1981) likewise emphasises the role of environment in strategic choice, defining market strategy as the 'core of actions through which position in a market, relative to competitors, is manipulated over time to maximise the firm's objective'. Porter provides a two-dimensional analysis of competitive strategy, relating to focus - generalist, specialist or segmented - and mode of competition - price, product, promotion or customer service - and suggests that variations of these strategies are suitable in varying marketing environments and in influencing such environments.

The significance of marketing strategy for the design of MAS is considered by Simmonds, who points out that in accounting reports 'sales and profitability are shown as coming from the physical asset with frequently no mention of competitive market position'. He claims that 'the truth is much different. Sustained profit comes from the competitive market position. New product investment to expand sales must imply a change in competitive postion and it is this change that should be the focus of the investment review.' He further argues that as strategic thinking filters through the management accounting system 'calculations of return from changes in competitive position will replace the return on investment'. To monitor such competitive position, he suggests that competitor monitoring and segment incremental analysis are necessary. However his prime argument is that the MAS should focus upon marketing strategy as this is the key determinant of profitability. Tilles (1966) likewise argued that organisations may be expected to adopt differing focuses in their analysis of the allocation of marketing investment funding and that the accounting system in seeking to monitor and control such investment will reflect the strategic focus. Thus we would expect that, in organisations which are pursuing geographic expansion by building regional sale forces and distribution channels, regional analysis may have a high priority rating among the accounting reports, while for organisations which are focusing upon penetration of major accounts, for example in the retail food markets, customer account profitability analysis may be a priority accounting information report. Interestingly and partially supporting this argument, Wills and Kennedy (1982) point out that organisations which are pursuing such penetration strategies tend to exclude price discounts from the marketing budgets and to show such in the sales budgets. Likewise they argue that, depending upon whether the organisation is pursuing a brand or a customer strategy, retail promotional costs will be assigned either to brand budgets or sales budgets. As such the marketing strategy will likely be reflected in both the focus of the accounting reports and in the expenditures included in such reports.

## ORGANISATIONAL STRUCTURE AND MAS

The organisational design of the marketing function appears to be related to both the strategy and the environment in which the strategy is executed. Thus Kotler (1980) states that 'the organization's performance in the market place is a matter of degree of alignment between the organization's environmental opportunities, objectives, marketing strategy, organizational structure and management systems'. Likewise, McDougall and Tookey (1969) emphasised the impact of both marketing strategy and marketing environment upon the organisational structure of the marketing department, while Keith (1960) pointed out the organisational structural significance of the 'marketing revolution' in which companies move from a production orientation via a sales orientation to a marketing orientation. There is now an acceptance in the marketing literature that there is no 'one best way' of organising the marketing function and the major structural stereotypes are seen as offering particular advantages or disadvantages depending upon the competitive environment and strategy of the organisation. Comparative analyses of these stereotypes are provided by Kotler (1980), Hayhurst and Wills (1972), Buell (1966) and Corey and Star (1971). The consensus may be summarised as follows.

The strictly functional marketing organisation type structure is considered appropriate where the organisation is dealing with low diversity, i.e. where the number of market/ product mixes are such that individual members of the marketing department can adequately deal with each such combination. Thus a single product company or a company with a limited range of products and/or few customer types is thought likely to benefit from a functional organized structure. While Kotler points out that this type of organisational structure is the most common, Corey and Star found that of a 397 firm sample drawn from the 1,000 largest US manufacturing companies in 1968, 23% had such a functionally organised marketing structure, and while the larger businesses were less likely to have such a structure, slightly less than half of the smaller businesses (those with annual sales or less than fifty million dollars) had functional structures. Hayhurst and Wills note that the number of layers in the hierarchy of such companies is affected by the span of control of the executives, and that additional layers may be deliberately introduced to free the chief marketing executive to concentrate on developing strategic market plans. As diversity increases, additional layers are also likely to be added.

Product orientated marketing structures, in which individual product managers have a staff function and have responsibilty for the competitive strategy of individual brands or products (brand groups), may be viewed as an adaptive response to product heterogeneity, where the marketing strategy is product or brand orientated. In this structure, the chief marketing executive delegates the planning of the product strategy to an individual executive, or specially constituted group of executives. The concept was introduced by Proctor and Gamble in 1927, and in 1962 Schiff and Mellman found that 75% of the companies included in their survey were utilising this type of organisational structure. Corey and Star, whose survey has been mentioned above, found that 32% of the companies examined had product-orientated structures. Within such organisational structure, the product manager may not have operational responsibility with regard to any of the marketing functions, but seeks, by liaison with the functional managers, to ensure that the strategic plan for the product, once approved by the chief marketing executive, is implemented.

Where the customer/product mix is dominated by greater customer type variety than by product diversity, e.g. a homogeneous range of products being sold into many different markets, then the organisation may adopt a market based strategy and develop an organisational structure based around markets rather than around products. In effect the heterogeneity of the environment is homogenised by market rather than by product. In this type of structure a staff executive who has responsibility for the development of strategic plans relating to individual markets replaces the product manager. Ames (1963) points out that while the product manager approach is most appropriate for companies with a number of different products which have to be produced and marketed through the same manufacturing, marketing or sales divisions, where a company has an essentially homogeneous or closely related line of products which appeal to different segments of the market, then the market manager approach may be more appropriate since it may put appropriate focus on each of the marketing opportunities. Morein (1975) points out that brand or product multiplicity does not give economies of scale in promotion and advertising and that a market orientation may be a more 'effective' way of organising the marketing function. Likewise, Hanan (1975) suggests that a market orientation is more customer orientated and allows a more effective focusing of marketing strategy. Corey and Star found that, of the companies included in their survey, 8% had such a market orientated structure.

These three stereotypes appear to be the dominant structural formats utilised within competitive marketing organisations. Within these types geographical sub-organisation may take place where the company operates in geographically diverse markets. While all of these structures are capable of being implemented either in unitary form organisations, or within the divisions of multiform organisations, where divisionalisation has taken place, an additional structural complexity is added. This arises where the corporate head office has a marketing specialism attached to it. In these circumstances, the role of the head office marketing staff vis-à-vis the divisional marketing staff may be pivotal to the marketing strategy and organisational structure adopted within the division. While it may be argued that the very concept of divisionalisation necessitates that discretion be afforded the divisions, the need to integrate the operations of the divisions within the overall corporate strategy may be facilitated by a corporate or head office marketing function. Such integration of divisionalised operations is considered by Greiner (1972) and the argument for 'strategy centres' is also supportive of this view.

The three stereotypes of marketing organisational structures, i.e. functional, product and marketing, may be viewed as attempted matching of the organisational structure to the diversity of the environment so as to more effectively develop and focus the marketing strategy of the organisation. The main argument as to the appropriateness of the various types of structure can be summarised within a two-way matrix of product and market diversity, as shown in Figure 7.2.

Companies which find themselves within cell one of the matrix may be expected to have functionally organised marketing departments. Those within cell two with high product heterogeneity and low market heterogeneity may be expected to adopt a product orientated marketing structure, while companies within cell three which have low product but

**Figure 7.2: Marketing Organisational Structure Matrix**

| | | Product Diversity | |
|---|---|---|---|
| | | Low | High |
| Market Diversity | Low | 1 | 2 |
| | High | 3 | 4 |

high market heterogeneity may be more likely to adopt a market orientated structure. The focus of marketing strategy for companies within cells two and three would also be quite likely to differ. For companies within cell four which face high heterogeneity in both products and markets, a three-way matrix organisation form may be appropriate, i.e. by product, by market and by function. Corey and Star found that such structures were utilised within 38% of the companies surveyed, being more often utilised by 'larger businesses which presumably can more easily afford highly elaborated program structures'.

As such the literature on organisational structure of the marketing function suggests that the structure is influenced by the interaction of the environment and the strategy being pursued within that environment. The significance of the organisational structure for the design of the marketing accounting system will likely be high. Thus in functional marketing structures where profit responsibility is not delegated to brand or market managers it may be expected that the accounting reports will adopt a cost by responsibility area orientation, while in product orientated structures product profitability analysis and product reporting may be routinely focused upon by the accounting system. Likewise in market orientated structures customer analysis may feature routinely. In effect, if the accounting system seeks to create a visibility upon the performance of the various marketing executives, we would expect their tasks to be reflected in the accounting systems. The differing organisational structures assign marketing tasks in different ways and as such we would expect differing focuses to the accounting reports within differing organisational structures.

## INTERACTIVE ANALYSIS

Above we have briefly reviewed some of the likely relationships between MAS on the one hand and the individual areas of environment, strategy, and organisational structure on the other. However it has been emphasised that the relationships between these four sets of variables are not likely to be either linear or independent. As such, more complete understanding of the issues and influences involved in the area likely necessitates an interactive analysis of the four areas of accounting on process, structure, strategy and environment. While a theoretical model for such an analysis may be provided by the work of Hambrick (1981), Hinings et al (1974), and Hickson et al (1971) under the general title of strategic contingency theory, no empirical work using interactive analysis is as yet available in the area of marketing accounting. The difficulties of empirical work of such a nature are undoubtably significant, given the lack of consensus upon classification systems of environments and strategies. Interestingly, however, the work of Miles and Snow (1978) and Miles et al (1978), though not directly relevant to marketing accounting, does seem to support the argument of the significance of the interactions between the set of variables.

Thus the 'defender organizations' in the Miles and Snow study are characterised by combinations of the four sets of variables, i.e. a narrow environment, a price competitive strategy, a functional form of organisational structure and a sophisticated cost control system.

The organisational power dimension is also encompassed in this analysis, since the accounting function is viewed as being relatively powerful within the organisation, by means of its control of the cost system when cost effectiveness is of strategic importance. Miles and Snow were of course concerned with analysing the total organisation, and whether a similar approach would yield as satisfactory an understanding when confined to accounting for marketing must await empirical finding. The general approach does however offer hope that a more complete understanding may be achieved by interactive analysis.

## SUMMARY AND CONCLUSIONS

The paper has examined both the evolution in the practice of accounting for marketing during the fifty years to 1983 and the major variables which influence the design of such accounting systems. Utilising the published surveys of practices, it has been argued that increased sophistication in accounting practices has occurred particularly in the functional areas of marketing. Thus budgetary control and standard costing techniques are now common. However, in the profitability analysis of markets, while practices have developed in sophistication, heavy reliance continues to be placed upon arbitrary allocation routines, expenditure is not usually lagged and costs which have multiperiod benefits are expensed as incurred. The advent of data based systems has allowed routine reporting of multiple market segments but such systems continue to utilise arbitrary allocation routines. Perhaps for this reason such segment reports do not appear to be the focus of management attention.

The major variables which affect the design of marketing accounting systems have been considered in the second part of the paper. These variables, which were initially individually considered, are the environment in which the marketing plan is executed, the marketing strategy and the organisational structure of the marketing department. It has however been emphasised that such individual consideration of the variables is probably incomplete as they are likely to interactively influence and be influenced by the marketing accounting system. In support of this view, strategic contingency theory has been utilised and the work of Miles and Snow has been instanced as an approach which allows interactive analysis of the variables and which might be usefully adopted in the analysis of the issues and influences in the area of accounting for marketing. As such, it would currently appear that we can at least tentatively identify the major sets of variables which relate to the design of marketing accounting systems but must await further analysis to clarify the interaction between the variables and to advance our understanding of the area of accounting for marketing.

## REFERENCES

Aldrich, H.E. (1979) Organizations and Environments, Prentice Hall, Englewood Cliffs, N.J.

Alexander, R.S., Surface, F.M. and Alderson, N. (1953) Marketing, 3rd ed., Gunn and Company, New York.

American Accounting Association (1972) 'Report of the Committee on Cost and Profitability Analysis for Marketing', American Accounting Review, Supplement.

Ames, B.C. (1963) 'Payoff from Product Management', Harvard Business Review, November/December, 66–70.

Astley, W.G. and Van de Ven, A.H. (1983) 'Central Perspectives in Debates and Organizational Theory', Administrative Science Quarterly, (28), June, 245-273.

Baumol, W.J. and Sevin, C.H. (1967) 'Marketing Costs and Mathematical Programming', in T. Williams and C Griffin (eds.) Management Information: A Quantitative Account, Richard D Irwin, Homewood, Ill.

Beckett, V.A. (1981) 'The Art and Science of Distribution Costing', National Association of Cost Accountants Bulletin, April.

Bromwell, J.R. (1932) 'Wholesale Grocery Operations', Part IV, Louisville Grocery Survey, Distribution Cost Studies No. 14, US Department of Commerce.

Buell, V.P. (1966) Marketing Management in Action, McGraw Hill, New York.

Burns, T. and Stalker, G.M. (1961) The Management of Innovation, Tavistock, London.

Chandler, A. (1962) Strategy and Structure, Harvard University Press, Cambridge, Mass.

Chandler, A. (1977) The Visible Hand, Harvard University Press, Cambridge, Mass.

Child, J. (1972) 'Organizational Structure, Environment and Performance: The Role of Strategic Choice', Sociology, January, 2-22.

Corey, E.R. and Star, H.S. (1971) Organization Strategy: A Marketing Approach, Division of Research, Harvard University, Boston, Mass.

Duncan, R.B. (1972) 'Characteristics of Organizational Environments and Perceived Environmental Uncertainty', Administrative Science Quarterly, September, 313-237.

Emery, F.E. and Trist, E.L. (1965) 'The Causal Textures of Organizational Environments', Human Relations, (18), February, 21-32.

Feder, R.A. (1965) 'How to Measure Marketing Performance', Harvard Business Review, May/June, 132-142.

Feldman, M.S. and March, J.G. (1981) 'Information in Organizations as Signal and Symbol', Administrative Science Quarterly, (26), June, 171-186.

Gordon, L.A. and Miller, D. (1976) 'A Contingency Framework for the Design of Accounting Information Systems', Accounting Organizations and Society, (1)1, 59-70.

Greiner, L.E. (1972) 'Evolution and Revolution as Organizations Grow', Harvard Business Review, July/August, 37-46.

Hambrick, D.C. (1981) 'Environment, Strategy and Power Within Top Management Teams', Administrative Science Quarterly, June, 253-276.

Hanan, M. (1975) 'Re-organize your Company Around its Markets', Harvard Business Review, September/October, 56-64.

Hayes, D. (1977) 'The Contingency Theory of Management Accounting', Accounting Review, January, 22-39.

Hayhurst, R. and Wills, G. (1972) Organizational Design for Marketing Futures, George Allen and Unwin, London.

Hickson, D.J., Hinings, C.R., Lee, C.A., Schneck, R.E. and Pennings, J.M. (1971) 'A Strategic Contingencies Theory of Intraorganizational Power', Administrative Science Quarterly, 16, 216-229.

Hinings, C.R., Hickson, D.J., Pennings, J.M. and Schneck, R.E. (1974) 'Structural Conditions of Intraorganizational Power', Administrative Science Quarterly, 19, 22-44.

Keith, R.J. (1960) 'The Marketing Revolution', Journal of Marketing, January, 35-38.

Khandwalla, P.N. (1972a) 'The Effect of Different types of Competition On the Use of Management Controls', Journal of Accounting Research, Autumn, 275-285.

Khandwalla, P.N. (1972b) 'Environment and its Impact on Organisations', International Studies of Management and Organisation, Fall, 297-313.

Kotler, P. (1980) Marketing Management, 4th ed., Prentice-Hall, London.

Lambert, D.M. and Armitage, H.M. (1979) 'Distribution Costs: The Challenge', Management Accounting, May, 35-45.

Lawrence, P.R. and Lorsch, J. (1967) Organization and Environment, Harvard University Press, Cambridge, Mass.

Liebermann, A.Z. and Whinston, A.B. (1975) 'A Structuring of an Event-Accounting Information System', Accounting Review, April, 246-258.

Longman, D.R. (1941) Distribution Cost Analysis, Harper, New York.

McDougall, C. and Tookey, D. (1969) Marketing Organization Structure, 2nd Marketing Theory Seminar, Ashridge Management College, April.

Manghan, I.L. (1978) Interactions and Interventions in Organizations, John Wiley and Sons, New York.

Mason, R.S. (1982) 'Distributed Lag Effects on Sales Accounting', Management Accounting, December, 20-21.

Mellman, M. (1965) 'Marketing cost analysis, development and current practice', Accounting Review, January, 118-123.

Miles, R.E. and Snow, C.C. (1978) Organizational Strategy, Structure and Process, McGraw Hill, New York.

Miles, R.E., Snow, C.C., Meyer, A.D. and Coleman, H.J. (1978) 'Organizational Strategy, Structure and Process', Academy of Management Review, (3) 3, July.

Morein, J.A. (1975) 'Shift from Brand to Product Line Marketing', Harvard Business Review, September/October, 56-64.

Mossman, F.H., Crissy, W.J.E. and Fischer, P.M. (1978) Financial Dimensions of Marketing Management, John Wiley and Sons, New York.

Mossman, F.H., Fischer, P.M. and Crissy, W.J.E. (1974) 'New Approaches to Analysing Marketing Profitability', Journal of Marketing, (38), April, 43-48.

National Association of Accountants (1954) Cost Control for Marketing Operations, Research Series, Nos. 25,26,27, New York.

National Association of Accountants (1971) Information for Marketing Management, New York.

Otley, D.T. (1980) 'The Contingency Theory of Management Accounting: Achievement and Prognosis', Accounting Organizations and Society, (5) 4, 413-428.

Pettigrew, A. (1972) 'Information Control as a Power Resource', Sociology, (6), May, 187-204.

Porter, M.E. (1980) Competitive Strategy, Free Press, New York.

Rayburn, L.G. (1966) Control of Distribution Costs through the use of standards, Ph.D Thesis, Department of Economics, Commerce and Business, Louisiana State University.

Rayburn, L.G. (1967) 'Setting Standards for Distribution Costs', Management Services, March/April, 42-52.

Rayburn, L.G. (1981) 'Marketing Costs: Accountants to the Rescue', Management Accounting, January, pp. 32-41.

Schiff, M. and Mellman, M. (1962) Financial Management of the Marketing Function, Financial Executions Research Foundation, New York.

Schoorhoven, C.B. (1981) 'Problems with Contingency Theory: Testing assumptions hidden within the language of Contingency Theory', Administrative Science Quarterly, 26, 349-377.

Sevin, C. (1965) Marketing Productivity Analysis, McGraw Hill

Simmonds, K. (1981) Strategic Management Accounting, Institute of Cost and Management Accountants, Technical Symposium, Oxford.

Thomas, A.A. (1969, 1974) The Allocation Problem in Financial Accounting Theory, American Accounting Association, Studies in Accounting Research No. 3 and No. 9.

Thompson, C. (1967) Organizations in Action, McGraw-Hill

Tilles, S. (1966) 'Strategies for Allocating Funds', Harvard Business Review, January/February, pp. 72-80.

Waterhouse, J.H. and Tiessen, P. (1978) 'A Contingency Framework for Management Accounting Systems Research', Accounting, Organizations and Society, (3)1, 65-76.

Wills, G. and Kennedy, S. (1982) 'How to Budget Marketing', Management Today, February, 58-61.

Wilson, R.M.S. and Bancroft, A. (1983) The Application of Management Accounting Techniques to the Planning and Control of Marketing of Consumer Non-durables, Institute of Cost and Management Accountants, London, July.

Woodward, J. (1965) Industrial Organization: Theory and Practice, Oxford University Press, London.

# 8. Marketing Information and New Technology

by Deborah A Martell

## INTRODUCTION

A new division has been created in the marketing sphere by the impact of NIT which has provoked this present discussion, highlighting the ensuing changes in the marketing field as applications of NIT spread to both operational and strategic decision making.

It is intended that several issues will be studied in this discussion: (a) observable effects: NIT changes the marketing scenario; (b) invisible effects: NIT changes marketing organisation; and (c) information effects: NIT encourages the development of a marketing information system (MKIS) to handle the increased information. A set of recommendations and an agenda for marketing management's approach to information systems will conclude the analysis.

## OBSERVABLE EFFECTS: HOW NIT HAS CHANGED THE MARKETING SCENARIO

It was Davidson (1980) who noted: 'Marketing has not fulfilled its golden prophecies - more through misapplication than lack of utility' and he maintains marketing management needs to be 'successfully pumped into the bloodstream of the organisation'.

At its simplest, the advent of NIT encourages such effective dissemination of marketing expertise through improving marketing analysis, inquiry handling, product planning and so on.

Other writers have noted how this 'galloping technological change in information gathering and dissemination' (Schultz and Dewar, 1984) will threaten what have become the traditional marketing approaches of the past few decades.

The familiar marketing mix, which outlines the basic activities of the marketing sphere, is shown in Figure 8.1 as part of the overall managerial marketing process.

If one looks specifically at the marketing mix, despite its familiarity and over-simplicity, it forms a clear,

**Figure 8.1: The Managerial Marketing Process**

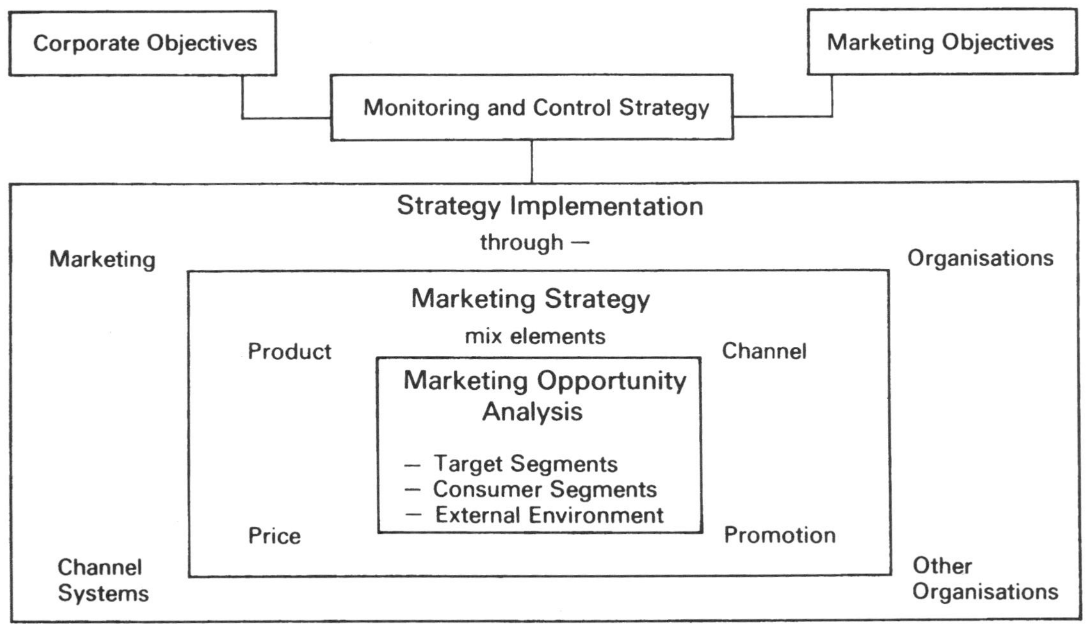

categorical point of departure from which to discuss the NIT impact.

Firstly, price - a change here triggers effects on other elements within the mix. It can generate income to cover the cost of activities concerning other elements. Indeed, price is closely analysed by competitors, as responses to any change frequently need to be rapid and NIT increases the potential for more accurate tracking of competitive prices. Likewise, costings of products through all stages of the life-cycle will be assisted, with the future having suppliers and retailers sharing information, being accessed remotely by terminals. Indeed, a body exists which advocates such sharing of information: the Article Numbering Association has established a central clearing house to receive, process and distribute data from scanning stores. However, very few stores initially chose to cooperate in this venture (Connell et al, 1982), and opinion is divided as to the benefits of sharing information with suppliers. However, price manipulation to penetrate new marketing areas, and relating to new images, will be more effective through NIT.

Secondly, an accelerating, shift towards more complex products is observable in today's marketplace. Therefore, the more sophisticated products and services become so 'new types of marketing, from new forms of marketing organisation, staffed by new breed of marketer' (Schultz and Dewar, 1984) will be demanded.

Indeed, the collection of information to guide marketing and product decisions is of utmost importance for efficient operations, e.g. telemarketing can provide a quick and effective way to gather research data, either on an ad hoc or a continuous basis. This method affords greater control over research activities, by eliminating the outside agencies, and provides a cost effective way to gather data from present and future markets (Vorhees and Coppett, 1983). Accurate survey research is of utmost importance in marketing evaluations and NIT is improving this accuracy all the time. This has be shown by Rowley et al in their description of the Questionic Project at the University of Sheffield. The first commercialised product to evolve from this is the Ferranti Market Research Terminal (MRT). The MRT is a battery-operated, hand-held, data-capture terminal, which is an electronic replacement for the clipboard and pencil used for gathering information from consumers. This innovation offers real advantages for survey research, due to easier processing, since data is stored electronically it is already in a form which can be directly entered into a computer. Likewise, the elimination of the data preparation stage decreases the errors created by human processing. More importantly survey results can be more topical since the MRT decreases the time delay in data preparation. Other benefits accrue from decreased handling and stationery costs and increased interviewer productivity.

Indeed, the Questionic MRT procedures, with their instant processing abilities, allow more specific monitoring of TV advertising effects. A particular attraction is the removal of the traditional 'bottleneck' at the data preparation stage for input into the computer.

Successful companies will, in future, emphasise even more the matching of a product to consumer requirements. Consequently, the old Henry Ford adage, 'you can have any color you want as long as its black', will be gone forever. Voorhees and Coppett (1983) speculated that the creation of more complex products and services would force standardisation to decrease. Figure 8.2 shows how product research will be affected by NIT developments - in this case through telemarketing.

The environment created by using telemarketing in the distribution channel will be one of greater cost effectiveness, as can be seen in Figure 8.2, through direct submission of information to interested parties. Other examples of NIT in this area are to monitor stock turnover efficiently in retail outlets and the use of laser scanners in supermarkets.

Typically, this relates to the electronic point-of-sale systems (EPOS), which give retailers access to sales data, which can be used to improve retail efficiency. EPOS potentially gives retailers: (a) the ability to record and store sales data, and print a receipt with an abbreviated description of each item purchased; (b) access to a library of price/product data; a code entered at checkout is matched with the correct price; (c) the ability to record and update stock movements as products are sold; (d) access to the timing of particular product sales; and (e) a reduction in human error.

Over and above operational advantages, EPOS potentially enhances the power position which retailers command in the structure of the channel MIS, enabling them to exert pressure on manufacturers to meet changing distribution demands (Lewis, 1984).

Thirdly, the channel concept preempted above must be analysed. The ensuing NIT changes have widened manufacturers' search for supplies to that of global proportions (Schultz and Dewar, 1984); designers, engineers and even purchasing agents increasingly use the computer to aid their material searches and screenings, thus showing how this important decision process has moved into the hands of machines.

One can go on to outline the potential changing relationship between buyers and sellers, caused by NIT, with both parties being equal in terms of product knowledge and application. But further interaction between NIT and marketing information will accentuate the erosion of the manufacturer position and elevate retailer power, e.g.

**Figure 8.2: Marketing and Product Research**

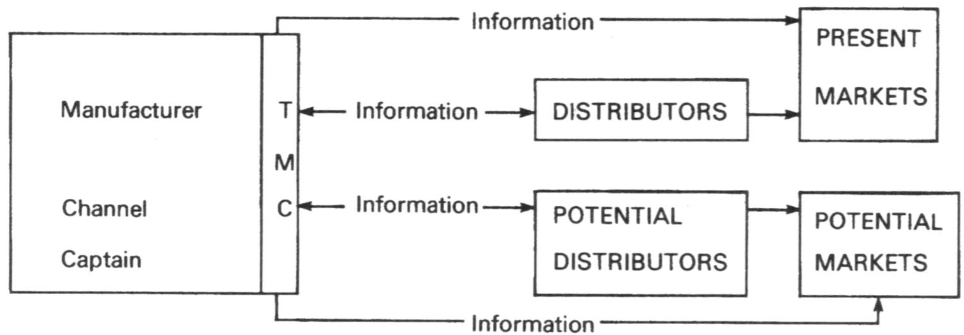


Source : Voorhees and Coppett (1983)

possibly Marks and Spencer being prototypical here.

Returning to the extensive discussion by Vorhees and Coppett (1983), this has shown how telemarketing can benefit distribution channels, by governing the volume of product flows, controlling their speed, minimising their costs, and in the case of information, improving the accuracy of the data.

For example, the 3M Company uses telemarketing to assist customers with equipment trouble. The customer calls the company and describes his problem to a skilled technician, who has access to an on-line computer system. 3M has found more than 30% of the calls can be solved without dispatching an engineer. Taking the increasing trade concentration in most industries, which gives sellers more power, one stage further, NIT advances this change by making distribution middlemen a redundant species in the purchasing process.

Finally, promotion - this being an element of varying importance in the mix, the extent of which depends on the particular product characteristics: whether it is of a mass consumption or high repeat-purchase nature. The greater the number of target consumers, the more likely the enterprise will view this component as significant. In this area NIT has affected the ability to segment markets with more precision, attaining greater accuracy in reaching specialist markets. It is postulated, by Schultz and Dewar (1984), that market research will become even more vital as a function; greater data manipulation will be required to provide the essential knowledge of markets and customers, needed by dealers and distributors. This update is essential, as too often important marketing decisions are based on inadequate or out-of-date information. NIT in this area takes large, geographically organised databases, e.g. census statistics, and links them to other sets of marketing data. This results in new marketing insights, producing better targeted advertising (Whitehead, 1986), promotional and merchandising activity.

Already many organisations use the ACORN system (A Classification Of Residential Neighbourhoods) and its contemporaries for market research purposes. New advances have been made in this area of linking such demographic data to lists of retailers, postcodes and travel information, thereby producing promotional material of a new product aimed at target consumers within specific travelling distances from certain outlets. Such accuracy will truly revolutionise marketing promotions, e.g. some large grocery multiples reckon they have the ability to predict new store performance with a high confidence level.

Inevitably, one will see an increase in non-personal sales contact, as more consumers use electronic databases. Likewise, new methods of monitoring and evaluating promotional response with greater objectivity can be achieved

**Table 8.1: Telemarketing Functions**

| | |
|---|---|
| Advertising | Physical Distribution |
| - inquiries per advertisement | - consumers orders |
| - profiles of respondents | - distributor's orders |
| - sales conversion rates/ad. | - tracing and dispatching shipment requirements |
| Market Management | - inventory requirements |
| - segment analyses | - product return needs |
| - marginal account identification | - customer service needs |
| Marketing Research | Product Management |
| - demographic data | - sales per product |
| - image and attitude studies | - questions and complaints |
| - forecasting data | - consumer profiles |
| Sales Management | |
| - lead qualification | |
| - marginal account status | |

Source: Voorhees and Coppett, 1983

(see Figure 8.1). Indeed, sales force efforts can benefit from a computerised scheduling system, capable of producing the optimum sequence for the representative's calls (Shaw, 1986).

However, queries have been raised as to the appropriateness of such intensive segmentation through NIT for frequently-bought goods (Ehrenberg and Goodhart, 1977). They postulate a relatively high duplication between brands of similar, or identical, product formulation. Summarising, they view the mass market as consisting of consumers with highly varied needs, overlapping to some extent. They postulate the consistent preferences required for efficient segmentation usually relate to a general product characteristic, rather than the particular brand characteristic, upon which most marketing is based. Therefore, intensive segmentation becomes a fruitless waste of resources.

So far this analysis of NIT effects on the marketing mix only scratches the surface of the varied, observable effects the technological revolution is having on the marketing world, and would seem to advocate that drastic scenario changes are in order to keep pace with the developing marketplace.

However, such a drastic change of marketing fundamentals may not be the answer. Why not simply be more thorough in existing marketing applications? This strategy is adopted by the Japanese, with their interactive marketing strategies (Turnbull and Yamada, 1984). The Japanese have gleaned success by following 'team approaches' as opposed to the 'individual approaches' adopted by the UK companies. However, Japan is characterised by a great number of small trading companies, with export and import trade being dominated by the 'Big Six' general trading firms, collectively known as 'Sogoshosha', who account for a half of the Japanese total export and import volume. Therefore the differing economic structures must be taken into account.

Yet the problem persists in the conflict of traditional techniques with new marketing approaches/innovations, e.g. telemarketing/teleshopping. The usefulness of telemarketing can be seen in Table 8.1.

Indeed, NIT goes further to affect even the mass communications of marketing media, e.g. with satellite broadcasting, cable television and videotex, the applications of which can be seen in Table 8.2. Following this, advertising is seen as increasing its sources, but this has raised much speculation of higher costs being incurred only to reach thinner audiences (Piercy, 1984b). Increasingly, advertising is becoming more image directed, to create and reinforce trust in the chaotic process of multiple product choice.

**Table 8.2: Private Business Videotex Applications**

| | |
|---|---|
| Internal Benefits to Marketing: | (One Company) |
| - ordering samples | - sales quotes |
| - checking customer sales history | - mailing lists |
| - checking credit | - call reports |
| - product direction | - sales expense reports |
| - order entry | - price lists |
| - sales forecast | - sales presentation |
| External Benefits to Marketing: | (Customer, Distribution, Supplies, etc) |
| - direct order inquiry | - ordering from: :customers' office :sales reps' homes :remote telephone |
| - product applications | - selling tips for distribution |
| - monitoring distribution sales | - related product-line directory |
| - market surveys | |
| - industrial product-line directory | |

Source: N Wiener, 1984

This supports the traditional axiom that marketing is most important in businesses where technology changes rapidly, competition is fierce and products are bought frequently by a large number of consumers, and least important in monopoly situations (Davidson, 1980).

## INVISIBLE EFFECTS: HOW NIT CHANGES MARKETING ORGANISATION

As has become apparent, the whole scenario in which marketing acts is rapidly changing with NIT developments. Undoubtedly, to accommodate the external changes in the marketplace, the internal organisation must also adapt.

Institutions are no longer discrete collections of individuals meeting in some physical location, but are complex information systems which connect people in a myriad of economic and social relationships.

Information forms invisible links which bind the organisations together, its output producing more accuracy, wider knowledge, increased power, broader choices and heightened awareness.

These fundamental changes are indicative of modern economics having entered an era of unusually complex, difficult and constantly changing relationships, which cannot be mastered using the traditional structures.

> The existing organisational infrastructure was built on the old foundations of the assembly-line and now computerised information systems are beginning to create an upheaval in the economic order which will alter the structure, behaviour and texture of society as a whole (Halal, 1986)

The required marketing adaptations centre on the structural, but also tend towards the political.

The newly evolved structural form must provide quick, flexible, strategic responses to the constant changes in the market place. Perhaps such demands warrant the application of 'organic networks and multi-dimensional matrices, combining rigorous accountability with autonomous operations' (Halal, 1982) in the organisation as a whole.

Many writers have noted the implications of NIT to the traditional hierarchal structure; it becomes flatter, with more integrative functions than its predecessor. This NIT - caused flattening of the hierarchy is speculated to have several implications for the internal organisation, with regards to computer literacy, decentralisation of decision making and retraining of personnel. One can implicitly assume the same related problems to affect the individuals in the marketing sphere as well. NIT is reducing the size of the marketing department and its coordinative and informational roles. It is this which creates the power change.

The decrease in human input to the marketing function could be the start of a replacement of whole management levels; e.g. in a retail setting, the automation of stockholding and scanning to collate sales data may remove the need for the general area management (Piercy, 1984a). The flatter structure adopted will depend in part on the degree of change in communications from paper to electronic mail. Ultimately the organisation will be structured around the technology adopted. This implies a change in the power of the marketing department; as NIT increases so dependency on the latter will decrease. Consequently, marketing needs an information strategy to determine how NIT is to be used in an organisation.

Returning to the Schultz and Dewar (1984) analysis of these effects, one finds, firstly, mastery of basic computer-handling skills will need to become commonplace, both with subordinates and management. Unequal skill development in this area leads to problems in itself; people possessing the skills will tend to threaten the power/role of the other group. However, joint development in computer knowledge will increase participative management decision-making, along with the developing horizontal communications. Likewise, the usage of rules and procedures will tend to decline.

Secondly, individuals will be able to handle more complex information and process it much quicker. Therefore, decision-making will be decentralised. In the case of the marketing department, more ideas will be generated and checked at the lower levels with faults being more easily spotted. Indeed NIT will enable market data to be reanalysed at lower levels, thus airing viewpoints previously unavailable. In short, the possibility exists that increasing NIT may be the source of idea rejuvenation within the marketing field.

Leading on from this, the easier access to data means groups/committees will become more popular in the decision-making process. The individual with the computing knowledge will become much sought after.

Hence the implication for marketing is clear; if market information becomes more accessible to other departments, marketers must be aware of the possible power shift (Piercy, 1984c) and revision of their work to an extent not previously experienced. It can be suggested with the advent of NIT that, market information can be processed at many points in the organisation, regardless of formal marketing department existence. However, one must not push the marketing role too much into insignificance. Yet, NIT may result in a sacrifice of decision-making discretion, through having to, share information and decision-making on a wider basis.

> The scope of much of marketing's conventional organisational points of reference will crumble. However, the points of contact with finance and research and development will lead to a wide variety of new organisational forms for marketing to attempt to enhance effectiveness in rapidly changing circumstances (Hayhurst and Wills, 1972).

Finally, the cumulative effect of NIT demands personnel to be retrained, often completely. One expects a sales force decline as computers take over much of the initial inquiry-handling (Benecin, 1984) and, indeed, much of the inquiry-tracking role of the salesman. One notes how the selling aspect of marketing will demand less human effort.

Of course, these assumptions all point to a decline in the middle management role and the restructuring of the organisation. But marketers must be aware of these potential changes as they apply both in a macro and a micro sense. Marketing is advised to strive for formal corporate positioning and structuring, which will enable them to handle the conflicts on the 'corporate battleground' (Piercy, 1983b), between technical and marketing management. Each department will fight for dominance, with the former advocating its advanced computer knowledge as the basis for its superiority. The immediate implication is that the organisation design problem in marketing is that of matching marketing structure with the environment. Therefore, one needs a contingency view, based on the relationship between the environment and the implied need for informationprocessing in the structure. This analysis of the environment in terms of the information-processing concept would seem to be at the heart of the question of organisation analysis and design for marketing. On this basis it would seem reasonable that organisation forms should be regarded as short-term and temporary, adjusting in response to the frequent alterations of the contingencies which created them.

However, the opportunity still exists for marketing to retain its central importance as "the hub around which the wheel of the firm revolves" (Kotler, 1967). The NIT impact can provide more data, faster and cheaper for example, advanced test marketing through television advertising, with direct advertising to consumers through media networks, and companies supplying data using interactive television sets and electronic questionnaires. A recent example is W H Smith, who are testing a consumer-channel, cable concept in Windsor, with 15 minute 'infomercials' (Financial Times, April 1986). However, present experience suggests there are too few subscribers to interest UK sponsors in cable T.V. advertising (D Wood - media director, Ogilvy and Mather, 1986). Other examples of NIT affecting the marketing world are laser scanning and bar coding in retail outlets, to measure sales etc. Many marketing functions, e.g. stock handling, sales ordering and logistics, market reseach, product planning, lend themselves easily to automation. Therefore, it is the marketing future to adapt and capitalise on these technological advances and appropriate them in their field, to retain their corporate positioning.

At this juncture it is essential to note the political pitfalls which could hamper NIT and marketing interaction.

> Differentiation within the organisation is one important source of disagreements on goals and beliefs about technology. (Pfeffer, 1981)

Political influence can be described as the

> organisational design outcomes as both causes and consequences of underlying forces operating in, and between, organisations. (Pfeffer, 1981)

An important consideration is what new power and political system will be created by the emerging structure; the more centralised the structure, the less likely political interference will arise in other parts of the organisation.

> Reorganisation may be a rational necessity in modern times, but it often appears to be a political near-impossibility. (Child, 1984)

The reorganisation costs must be balanced with the political adversity. Child suggests a process of proposal, implementation, review and further proposal in order to gain the political support of organisation members.

The advancement of NIT and its associated 'freedom of information' may, in reality, prove to be puerile fantasy. Information in the organisation is rarely neutral - generally it gives the holder some degree of influence, status and power. The main question is, will the individuals privy to the increased information access it freely, will true information permeation in the organisation ever exist?

One must remember power can be increased by control of such information (Piercy and Evans, 1983). Therefore, the esoterical problems will be reinforced. Whereas information processing is thought to expedite the marketing function, in actual fact it may prove ineffective in rapidly changing conditions, with marketing power being reduced if political games are played.

Keen (1980) called this 'social inertia'; counter-implementation games by those who are threatened by the NIT. This takes the form of diverting resources, deflecting its goals, and dissipating its energies.

Without constant monitoring of the changing structures,

power will tend to flow to those who control the technologies. The suggestion is for a life-cycle of the marketing department; as the variety in the environment increases, so a more complex, decentralised marketing department will evolve.

One must consider the impact of NIT on the marketing organisation and adapt a contingency view of marketing, based on environmental analysis, management choices and marketing policies.

The newly evolved strategy must accommodate NIT, the consequent availability of new organisational design choices and the entry into new product/service markets. Marketing needs both an organisation and information - strategy to answer such questions as:

- Should there be a marketing department?
- If so, positioned where and what role should it have?
- What degree of centralisation/decentralisation is applicable?
- What structure should be adopted?

It follows that the organisation and information strategy will respond to the invisible effects of NIT, and the contingency strategy will respond to the visible effects. Appropriately, this brings us to a discussion of the Marketing Information System (MKIS).

## INFORMATION EFFECTS: MKIS AS A NIT MEDIATOR

By definition, NIT increases the amount of information available. Therefore, as well as changing the inherent strategy adopted by the organisation, a management information system (MIS) is required to handle the extra information created. Hand-in-hand with this MIS development is that of a marketing information system (MKIS), which deals specifically with marketing strategy and operations.

In real terms, the MKIS is the MIS, or indeed the decision support system (DSS), which relates to marketing activities and marketing information. A more formal definition is supplied by Buzzell et al (1969) as,

> A set of procedures and methods for the regular, planned analysis and presentation of information for use in making marketing decisions.

Various writers have analysed this phenomenon (Uhl, 1974; Graf, 1979) and in summary they have shown how the MKIS can be used for:

- data storage and retrieval, simplifying the accessibility of information;

- monitoring systems, checking progress and variations in, for example, sales or market share data.
- analytical information systems - a facility for options as to the results of various competitive actions e.g. price cuts, merchandising policies, etc.

All this provides an in-depth crisis information system along with current-awareness and incidental-information systems.

Formal recognition of MKIS is needed because of the increasing information derived from NIT adoption. The basic research information collected in this way can be used to develop cause and effect models of responses to marketing actions. It follows that, as NIT increases and suggests new marketing approaches, an efficient MKIS is essential for efficient information management.

However, this is the ideal. In reality, Piercy (1981) has shown how such attention to system creation is sadly lacking in many companies.

MKIS development tends to be hampered by the ability of managers to process the information produced by computer systems and to cope with NIT itself. Indeed, the question is raised whether such management is able to choose the actual information sources so as to compile the MKIS in the first place.

It has been postulated that the MKIS concept can be both micro and macro, as relating to the company or to the channel of distribution or product market respectively.

The micro theory is expanded by treating the whole of the marketing function as an information-processing structure. Following this logic, organisation structures exist purely to permit flows of authority and the communication of information (Farley et al, 1971).

It was Piercy (1983a) who developed the macro position of the MKIS concept. Specifically here one is referring to the channel of distribution as being a source of marketing information. Special attention is warranted here, as it is the macro MKIS which feels the true force of the NIT explosion. This is exemplified by the aforementioned laserscanning devices at point-of-sale, which read the bar codes and relate product, price, stock level information, etc., to a central computer and ultimately effect retailer/ manufacturer power.

A C Neilsen, the research agency, estimates that 1000 stores will have some form of scanner between 1987 and 1990. Many UK stores advocate the use of such methods, realising considerable savings in terms of retailing efficiency (Walters, 1980). Such data, the collation of which is made possible by NIT, can be used variously: to adjust promotional mixes in accordance with purchasing patterns, to allocate performance, e.g. bar codes used in conjuction with advertisements in the press, coupons or in-store displays, to monitor any changes in consumption.

Piercy (1983a) suggests that laser-scanning at the checkout, plus scanning of coded cartons in the warehouse, could replace the traditional retail audit. In combination with consumer interviews, observations and testing, this in turn may replace the established consumer panel.

However, one is forced to note, along with other writers on the subject (Fletcher, 1982; Jobber, 1977; Amstutz, 1969; Piercy, 1981), that MKIS is limited in its development, and even more so in its adoption as an entity, which is added to corporate functions as NIT increases the informational levels within a company.

Perhaps a more acceptable view is of MKIS as the ultimate stage in the development of information-processing; as the volume of information increases, so a function will evolve to manage it. This is purely a natural evolution of business strategy, following the same path as other functions, in emerging from the corporate mass according to company requirements. An example of this evolutionary trend is advertising - originally integral to particular companies, progressing over the years to a generalised, external, consultative function. Advertising agencies have developed which are no longer encapsulated within an individual company, but are accepted as managing this company function from an independent stance.

Therefore the MKIS evolves in, rather than is added to, the organisation. With all these aspects taken into account, the advanced marketing environment created by NIT will be one with direct information networks between buyers, distributors and suppliers, improved advertising and promotional effiency through the cable and advanced monitoring systems aforementioned, with a general deterioration of the traditional, organisational hierarchy and power structure.

## RECOMMENDATIONS

The issue is of the need for strategic planning to cope with NIT changes and for thorough integration of the marketing function. Without such adaption the chances of commercial failure are heightened. Examples proliferate to highlight this, as in Prestel's limited market penetration through a lack of market information. Likewise there are doubts previously raised by D Wood (1986) of too few subscribers to cable television. The changes in the mix foundations will demand a response from the marketing departments. Schultz and Dewar (1984) recommend a total organisational re-evaluation, with a changing management style and a repositioning of the marketing function within the organisation. They suggest manufacturing and market research will be of more importance. Postulations are made that the organisation will need fewer people, but all will be conversant with current computing techniques and less skilled in other areas. Indeed, pressure will rise for marketing and manufacturing to integrate - possibly to the extent of matrix formulation.

Also, a revamped mix will be demanded, with more tailored products and exploitation of the efficiency accrued by NIT adoption. Indeed, the communications function of the marketing department will be emphasised, detracting from the sales department - its previous controller. Taking the implications further, Piercy (1984c) advocates a more strategic and long-term approach to the NIT impact, because its effects are widespread on the control of the business, its management style, its structural changes and its supplier/consumer/competitor relationships. The new ways of operating will tie the organisation into technological innovation and therefore become intrinsically a long term issue. Also proposed is more corporate and strategic planning; NIT development should be integrated with all parts of the business, not marketing alone, and aim to accept new systems to handle the changes.

Inevitably, the new genre of marketing will raise many questions as to which NIT packages to adopt. A few critical points have been raised by Maher (1984), in choosing the appropriate marketing decision-support system (DSS) -

- What decisions do different managements make?
- Which can be automated?
- What sales and marketing data will be necessary?
- What analytical tools will be necessary?
- Should data processing, manufacturing and finance departments be involved in the DSS decision?
- Are individual microcomputers enough, or are more powerful microsystems required?
- Should marketers engage consultants to provide customised hardware?

All such questions are very important to the marketing world, in its assessment of the impact of NIT on its functions. Consideration of the above is vital in order to retain central importance in a changing contextual environment. Therefore, a process of selection, adaptation and exploitation is the key.

## CONCLUSION

This chapter has shown how NIT can be seen as having visible and invisible effects on the marketing process. The visible effects concentrate on the external marketing scenario and mix formulation, whereas the invisible focus on the structural and strategic response of the internal organisation.

It has been shown how the individual elements of the mix experience the NIT impact in real terms, and how a general strategic response is called for to ensure that marketing holds its position in a business world, where 'information is destined to hold the place that energy once held in yesterday's industrial society' (Sevan-Schreiber, 1980), and how MKIS should be viewed with an open mind as the possible evolutionary result of increasing information.

The suggestion is for a transfer of marketing power to the retailer and a relocation of formal marketing organisation. The emerging NIT scenario, corporate needs and business approach must be analysed in order to make suitable marketing choices in the future (Piercy, 1984c). Such extensive adaptation is especially warranted in the marketing of service industries (Foxall, 1985), although not to the exclusion of marketing in other areas.

## REFERENCES

Amstutz, A. (1969) 'Market Oriented Management Systems: The Current Status', Journal of Marketing Research, 6, 481-96

Benecin, R.L. (1984) 'Why you should close the advertising loop electronically' Business Marketing, March

Buzzell, R.D., Cox, D.F. and Brown, R.V. (1969) Marketing Research and Information Systems: Text and Cases, McGraw-Hill, New York

Child, J. (1984) Organization: A Guide to Principles and Practices, 2nd ed., Harper and Row, London

Connell, S., Morris, A. and Whitten, P. (1982) 'The Challenge of Change', Journal of Marketing Research Society, 24(3)

Davidson, J.H. (1980) Offensive Marketing, Pelican, Sulfolk

Earl, M. (1984) 'Emerging trends in Managing New Information Technologies', in Piercy, N. (ed.) The Management Implications of New Information Technology, Croom Helm, Beckenham

Ehrenberg, A.S.C. and Goodhart, G.J. (1977) 'Understanding Buyer Behaviour', published jointly by J. Walter Thomspon Co and Marketing Research Corporation of America

Farley, H.U., Howard, J.A. and Hulbert, J. (1971) 'An Organisational Approach to the Industrial Marketing Information System', Sloan Management Review, 13

Fletcher, K.P. (1982) 'Marketing Information Systems: A Cost Opportunity', in M.J. Thomas (ed.) Marketing: Bridging the gap between theory and practice, Proceedings: Marketing Education Group Conference, Lancaster

Foxall, G. (1984) 'Marketing in the Service Industries', The Service Industries Journal, 4 (3)

Graf, F. (1979) 'Information Systems for Marketing', Marketing Trends, 2

Halal, W. E. (1986) 'Organisational Networks: The Structural Imperative of the Information Age', Chapter 12 (below)

Halal, W.E. (1982) 'Information Technology and the Flowering of Enterprise', European Journal of Management, 1(2)

Handy, C. (1980) 'Through the Organisational Looking Glass', Harvard Business Review, January/February

Hayhurst, R. and Wills, G. (1972) Organisational Design for Marketing Futures, Allen and Unwin, London

Hedberg, B. (1980) 'The Design and Impact of Real-time Computer Systems' in Bjorn-Anderson, N., Hedberg, B., Mercer, D., Mumford, E. and Sole, A. (eds.) The Impact of Systems Change in Organisations, Sijtoff and Noorddhoff, Alphen

Jobber, D. (1977) 'Marketing Information Systems in US and British Industry', Management Decisions, 15(2)

Keen, P.G.W. (1980) 'Information Systems and Organisation Change', Working Paper, Centre for Information Systems Research, Massachusetts Institute of Technology

Kotler, P. (1967) Marketing Management: Analysis, Planning and Control, Prentice-Hall, Englewood Cliffs, N.J.

Land, F. (1984) 'The Impact of Information Technology and the Workplace', in Piercy, N. (ed.) The Management Implications of New Information Technology, Croom Helm, Beckenham

Lewis, D.J. (1984) 'EPOS: Will the Benefits be Realised?', unpublished dissertation

Maher, P. (1984) 'The Road to Marketing Decision Support: How to Get on it', in Business Marketing, March

Nonaka, I. and Nicosia, F.M. (1979) 'Marketing Management, its Environment and Information Processing: A Problem of Organisation Design', Journal of Business Research, 7 (9)

Pfeffer, J. (1981) Power in Organisations, Pitman, Marshfield, Ma.

Piercy, N. (1981) 'Marketing Information: Bridging the Quicksand Between Technology and Decision-Making', Quarterly Review of Marketing, Autumn

Piercy, N. (1983a) 'A Social Psychology of Marketing Information - Learning to cope with the corporate battleground', Journal of the Market Research Society, 25 (2) April

Piercy, N. (1983b) 'Retailer Information Power - The Channel Marketing Information System', Marketing Intelligence and Planning, 1 (1)

Piercy, N. (1984a) Marketing Organisation - An Information Processing Perspective, Allen and Unwin, London

Piercy, N. (1984b) 'Marketing Information Systems: Theory vs. Practice', Quarterly Review of Marketing, 6 (1)

Piercy, N. (1984c) 'Retailer Marketing - International Strategies, European Journal of Marketing, 17 (6)

Piercy, N. and Evans, M. (1983) Managing Marketing Information, Croom Helm, Beckenham

Rowley, G., Barker, K. and Callaghan, V. (1986) 'The Marketing Research Terminal and Developments in Survey Research', European Journal of Marketing, 20 (2)

Schultz, D.E. and Dewar, R.D. (1984) 'Technology's Challenge to Marketing Management', in Business Marketing, March

Sevan-Schreiber, J. (1980) The World Challenge, Simon and Schuster, New York

Shaw, M. (1986) 'Keeping to a strict schedule' in Marketing, 6 March

Turnbull, P. and Yamada, T. (1984) 'Interactive Marketing - The Japanese Approach', Management Research News

Uhl, K.P. (1974) 'Marketing Information Systems', in R. Ferber (ed.) Handbook of Marketing Research, McGraw-Hill, New York

Vorhees, R. and Coppett, J. (1983) 'Telemarketing in Distribution Channels', Industrial Marketing Management, 12

Walters, R. (1980) The New Technology as an Environmental Factor: Its Impact in Retailing Operations, unpublished MBA dissertation, Bradford University

Whitehead, J. (1986) 'Keying in to New Data', Marketing, 6 March

Wiener, N. (1984) 'Should you invest in private videotex?' Business Marketing, March 1984

Wood, D. (1986) Marketing, April

# III APPLICATIONS IN PRACTICE

# 9. Management Information Systems: Some Reflections and Evidence

by Stephen Hill

## INTRODUCTION

This paper reports certain of the results of a recent survey carried out in South Wales into the decision making processes employed by a sample of twenty seven engineering firms. The survey casts considerable doubt on the hypothesis that modern firms utilise sophisticated systems of information collection, processing and retrieval for decision making purposes. Moreover, the survey allows some consideration of the reasons *why* information systems have yet to gain widespread acceptance in the small to medium sized firm.

Before considering the survey it is useful to examine the nature of information systems, at least as seen by academics. According to Morden, a Management Information System (MIS) is 'a formal system which enables organisation members to access and transform stored data so as to provide information that will support and assist the management process of planning, organising, directing and controlling the activities of the business. An MIS uses existing data to provide information which should assist policy "formulation and decision-making"' (Morden, 1985).

Given this framework, an information system is identifiable by the characteristics of:

(a) stored data;
(b) direct data access by decision makers;
(c) transformation of data for decision making purposes; and
(d) use of transformed data for planning and policy formulation.

Although the use of an information system is not dependent on the existence and utilisation of computerised information processing hardware, the development of low cost computer facilities has, supposedly, put information systems within the capacity of all but the very smallest organisation. Speaking in the late 60s, R. Newman of General Electric suggested that 'Within ten years, decision theory, conversational computers and library programs should occupy the same role for the manager as calculators, slide rules and mathematical tables do for the engineer today' (quoted in Brown (1970)).

Within the organisation, decisions are taken on many different levels. The usual categorisation is in terms of:

(a) strategic planning;
(b) management control; and
(c) operational control.

This structure is described for example, in Anthony (1965) or Higgins (1980). It is at the strategic level that information systems have attracted most attention. However at least one authority (Claret, 1985) sees information systems as percolating throughout the entire decision hierarchy, becoming increasingly prevalent at the management and operational control levels (and in fact regards them as 'potentially Armageddon for middle and lower managements'). Forecasts of doom in relation to the introduction of information technology are not uncommon.

However, there is as yet relatively little evidence on how widespread information systems have become and little evaluation of the perceived benefits information systems bring to performance.

For example, Fletcher (1983) reports a survey of 200 of THE TIMES Top 500 firms, with a questionnaire response rate of 58%, two-thirds of which claimed to have some form of Marketing Information System in current use. However, Fletcher states that the 'evidence suggests that companies are slow to adopt information systems, and when they do so the system is relatively unsophisticated'. Moreover, Moynihan (1985) suggests that, far from bringing about radical change, computer based systems are most commonly used to reinforce the organisational philosophy which preceded their introduction.

There is an obvious need for close examination of the actual decision making processes employed in organisations of a variety of sizes and activity ranges. If information systems are not widely utilised, then, given their potential relevance to decision making (at least as seen by Governments, professions and academic authorities), early consideration needs to be given to the obstacles preventing implementation. An integrated information system, with the rapid assimilation and analysis of informational inputs and an output suitable for decision making purposes, offers considerable advantages to the organisation concerned about performance in a changing environment. There is a clear expectation that the quality of decision making will improve with the quality of available information. Moreover the use of an information system offers the opportunity to provide decision information in a brief and relevant format which can preclude the inverted U-shaped function between judgemental accuracy and information supply found in empirical studies (for example Shields, 1983).

## THE SURVEY

The detailed characteristics of the survey, together with survey results, are outlined in Hill et al (1984), whilst the implications for decision analysis are considered in Hill and Blyton (1985).

Interviews were conducted with the managing directors of twenty-seven South Wales engineering firms, ranging in turnover from just under £1m to over £50m, and employing some 9000 people in total. Questions were asked about the decision processes employed in the areas of output, employment, pricing and investment decisions. The survey looked in detail at the organisational relationship between the planning process and the decision areas outlined above.

The general conclusion drawn was that the decision processes employed in practice owed very little to the text-book exponents of decision analysis. Major decisions were taken on ad hoc pragmatic lines, with more concern for survival than with the search for long run optimal solutions. For example, most firms went through the motions of drawing up a three or five year corporate plan, but a typical comment was that the plan was developed 'more in hope than expectation', with little regard for its operational and management implications.

Yet twenty-five of the twenty seven firms employed some form of computer, most often used for routine tasks such as stock control or wage accounting. Less than a quarter of firms used their computer facilities for production control, despite the prevalence and favour of such high technology equipment as computer numerically controlled machinery. Yet much of the hardware was used routinely to collect information that was of some relevance to decision making. For example, stock control information can be used relatively easily as a method for demand estimation (Scherer, 1970). The one firm that did mention information systems stated that it would be 'too expensive to buy a computer based information system'. Yet the same firm, with a turnover of some £5m, already enjoyed an impressive array of computer hardware for stock control, sales ledgers and wage payments. In this case at least, a management information system was seen as somehow independent of the facilities and information currently available, when very little effort (and software) would have been required to transform their present arrangements into a decision support system. In one (relatively large) firm the managing director had himself written the software to transform basic engineering cost information into a pricing information system, but this was used independently of the planning and control systems in operation.

Overall the evidence clearly suggested that the majority of firms possessed the hardware associated with information systems, but that its potential to assist decision making was vastly underutilised, even when relevant information was already being collected and processed. In terms of the characteristics of an information system discussed earlier, it appears that characteristics (a) and (b) were fully satisfied, but that there is a gap preventing the leap to characteristics (c) and (d), i.e. that the collection of, and access to, relevant data is a necessary but not sufficient condition for the use of that data for decision making purposes. The major academic achievements of carefully formulated rates for optimality in pricing, stock control, investment analysis, and so on, remain irrelevant until information presently collected can be expanded and transformed into a format suitable for decision making.

This is not to imply that the quality of information presently collected was sufficient for a fully fledged decision support system. The sample firms exhibited a marked reluctance to collect and process information that was relatively easy to obtain and which could have become crucial inputs into the decision making process. For example half of the sample firms were content to base market forecasts solely on the opinions of present sales staff. Only four of the twenty-seven firms took advantage of the information services available externally and these were the firms which expressed greatest contentment with the adopted forecasting methods.

## THE OBSTACLES TO INFORMATION SYSTEMS

The distinction between data collection and decision use can be regarded as a credibility gap, in that the theory of information systems was perceived as irrelevant to the management needs of the firms under study. At the seminar to present the survey results to participants, managers suggested strongly that the use of information within a scientific framework for decision making purposes needs to be packaged in a more digestible form, if it is to be implemented by those actually involved in business decision processes. The major obstacle to implementation remains the absence of perceived relevance, in the form of a lack of clearly demonstrated advantages. Given the levels of hardware utilisation that existed, the benefits of an integrated information system need not be enormous to cover the relatively small costs involved in money terms.

More problematic is the presence of organisational

obstacles to implementation. The structure of decision making in the firms under study was generally decentralised, with firms generally having considerable autonomy from the parent company. Within the firms studied, a high proportion employed some form of group decision making for major items (such as capital investment). There is a danger that integrated information systems may be seen as a force for centralisation. For example, considering supermarket chains, Piercy (1984) suggests that:

> The networking effect of making ... information instantly available at the centre, together with greater ability to process that information, may lead to the removal of a whole tier of middle management ..., as well as reducing the management role in the store itself.

Such implications are clearly not lost on existing management, and are likely to colour attitudes towards MIS implementation.

A further obstacle to the implementation of information systems is the problem of individual competence. Efficient managers must already possess considerable skills of leadership, organisational ability, administrative and financial qualities, etc. To acquire expertise in the design and use of information systems is undoubtably asking a great deal of the already busy manager. And yet the design of the information system must be influenced by the experiences of existing management, if it is to have relevance to their informational needs. At the same time sole design reliance on existing management is liable to ensure that the information system does not disrupt current management practices so that the information system is already superfluous as soon as installed. Clearly there is a tightrope to be walked between the experience of current management and improving management practice that can only be navigated with considerable balance and skill.

The final hurdle for the information system is in the treatment of uncertainty. The range of possibilities for the decision environment requires careful monitoring of events and outcomes. The tendency to develop satisficing rules of thumb can only be avoided by 'softening' the system to allow for the creative interpretation of information outputs.

## OVERCOMING THE OBSTACLES - SOME THOUGHTS AND CONCLUSIONS

The basic conclusion that emerges from the survey is that the sample firms were possibly missing the opportunities both to improve their productive facilities and to expand their product and market bases, because of a lack of careful consideration in the collection and processing of information. It may be that the use of sophisticated decision support systems would be inappropriate to some of the smaller firms, because the costs may outweigh the advantages. However, as we have seen, most of the firms already had the technology associated with information systems, and many already collected and processed information of potential relevance to decision making. This information was not being used for decision purposes because the mental connection had not been made between the quality of information inputs and judgemental accuracy.

One of the major roles of management education is in reinforcing this connection. However, the conclusion that managers simply need more education would be too simplistic. Considerably greater attention needs to be given to the problem of 'marketing' information systems in terms that are seen as relevant to the informational needs of managers, laying greatest emphasis on the potential for performance improvement that information systems facilitate. At the same time the proponents of the information system approach could benefit from exposure to the realities and pressures of business practice.

The organisational obstacles to system implementaton can be overcome by the careful design of systems. Wilkinson (1983) demonstrates that information technology is basically neutral towards organisations. It is management attitudes and preferences that determine whether information technology leads to the centralisation or diffusion of decision making powers.

## REFERENCES

Anthony, R.N. (1965) Planning and Control Systems: A Framework for Analysis, Harvard Business School, Boston, Mass.

Brown, R.V. (1970) 'Do managers find decision theory useful?', Harvard Business Review, 48, (May), 78-89

Claret, J. (1985) 'Computers for Efficient Utilisation of Resources', Management Accounting, February, 24-27

Fletcher, K.P. (1983) 'Information Systems in British Industry', Management Decision, 21,(2), 25-36

Higgins, J.C. (1980) Strategic and Operational Planning Systems, Prentice Hall, London

Hill, S. and Blyton, P. (1985) 'The Practice of Decision-Making: Some Evidence', Managerial and Decision Economics, December

Hill, S., Blyton, P., Patrick, C. and Peregine, J. (1984) Decision-Making in the South Wales Engineering Industry: A Survey, UWIST Discussion Papers in Business and Economics, Cardiff

Morden, A.R. (1985) 'Management Information Systems; Role and Policy in an Organisational Context', Management Decision, 23,(2), 52-64

Moynihan, T. (1985) 'Computers, Decision-Making and Centralisation', Management Decision, 23, (2), 28-32

Piercy, N. (1984) 'How to Manage IT', Management Today, March, 72

Scherer, F.M. (1970) Industrial Pricing: Theory and Evidence, Rand McNally, Chicago

Shields, M.D. (1983) 'Effects of Information Supply and Demand on Judgement Accuracy: Evidence from Corporate Managers', Accounting Review, LVIII, (April), 284-303

Wilkinson, B. (1983) The Shop Floor Politics of New Technology, Heinemann, London.

# 10. Recent Developments in Management Information Systems in the UK Motor Industry

by Richard N Ingram

## INTRODUCTION

The motor industry throughout the Western World has experienced hard times during the last ten years. Even the giants of General Motors, Ford and Chrysler have suffered severe financial losses whilst transforming their product range to more compact and fuel-efficient cars. None of the European producers are generating commercially sound profits and cashflows. However, remarkable progress has been made and in the UK-owned car producers productivity and efficiency levels now match the best of the competition.

This chapter describes some of the investments planned in information technology and being introduced in the Austin Rover Group of BL and in the newly privatised Jaguar Cars Ltd., to provide the advanced management information systems (MIS) necessary to achieve competition levels of efficiency.

Motor manufacturing is an increasingly complex business to manage and this trend is likely to continue over the next few years. On the one hand the product comprises many thousands of separate components and assemblies, which need to be designed and brought together in manufacturing to produce a reliable and high quality consumer product at a competitive price. On the other hand there is an ever-increasing range of regulations and legislation covering not only safety factors, exhaust emissions and crash impact tests, but also other features, and performance standards such as fuel economy, instrumentation layouts and the positioning of external fittings.

Worldwide over-capacity and the much increased range of model derivatives, paint colours and accessories now expected by the marketplace have increased the pressures on management for high levels of efficiency and plant utilisation but with much greater flexibility to respond to consumer demand than ever previously envisaged.

MIS in the motor industry are concerned with all stages in the life of the product from initial design through to after-sales service, and with all levels of business activity from shop floor operations management through to long-term strategic planning.

The case studies presented in this chapter describe the developments in MIS for production control, covering all aspects of manufacturing operations, and for office automation, covering the commercial, administrative and planning functions of the business. The third broad area for MIS development in the motor industry is in product design and development.

The application of computer aided design techniques is already making a major impact in improving the quality of design and in reducing the lead times needed to bring new cars to the market. However, emphasis is now being given to the development of systems which will support the optimisation of component design. Although such MIS applications are still at an early stage in implementation they probably represent the next major breakthrough in the contribution of MIS to business efficiency.

The creation of a formal data base of design knowledge, incorporating not only the experience of the design engineering department, but also manufacturing and in-service information on process capability, tolerances, quality, costs and problems, should enable the highest possible level of 'design right first time' to be achieved.

This area of development is probably the greatest challenge now facing MIS professionals in manufacturing industry. Successful implementation involves the handling of masses of data, much of it qualitative and descriptive in form, the analysis and presentation of this data using new information technologies such as Expert Systems and, probably the greatest challenge of all, the organisational integration of the traditionally separated specialisms of the product designer, the process planner and the manufacturing facilities engineer.

The case studies described have been presented as far as possible to illustrate the principles and approach followed and technical details have been kept to a minimum. Both projects help underline the technology challenge if MIS is to make its full contribution to the management of the business. The MIS professional is becoming more closely identified with the performance of the business and the successful design and implementation of relevant MIS is no longer an optional extra but the only route open to future commercial success.

## MIS IN PRODUCTION CONTROL

### Background to the Project

MIS applied to the scheduling and control of production in the motor industry can be considered as falling into two broad groupings.

Firstly, there are those systems which involve large batch processing applied to central data bases for the calculation of vehicle assembly programmes and material requirements schedules. These systems also update work-in-progress stock records with the results of production achievement exploded through the bill of material specification, which extends to many thousands of components and sub-assemblies.

These batch systems were some of the earliest developments of MIS during the 1960s and are usually characterised by a lack of integration between systems, a multiplicity of overlapping data files and by a lack of flexibility to provide management reports and analyses to assist with planning and control.

Jaguar Cars, like most companies in the motor industry world-wide, is now giving considerable effort to the implementation of an integrated data base strategy which will, for example, ensure that the product specifications applied to vehicle costing and stock accounting are fully consistent with the bills-of-material used to calculate supplier schedules and internal manufacturing programmes.

The second group of systems used in production consists of those systems which are usually processed on dedicated (single application) mini-computers and which are concerned with the online capture of shopfloor transactions and with the realtime control and monitoring of production facilities.

This group of systems was largely developed from the mid-1970s onwards when relatively inexpensive and reliable mini-computer equipment became commercially available in a form suitable for installation on the shop floor. Examples of such systems in Jaguar Cars include: the recording of component stocks through detailed machining shops; the 'mapping' of painted car bodies in a multi-level automated store; and the control of the conveyors and lifts to select the bodies required to meet the scheduled assembly sequence.

These mini-computer systems (there are 15 such applications currently installed) have in general been introduced on a piecemeal basis, according to operational needs, as new production facilities have been installed. Connections between this second level of MIS and those applications running on central mainframes is normally limited to the passing-up of transaction batches at the end of each shift, and the passing-down of the latest production schedules and order banks for the next shift. Figure 10.1 illustrates the relationship between these levels.

Over the last few years the development of MIS in production control has been largely concerned with improving and extending applications in both groups of systems.

The main focus has been on the expansion of mini-computer systems to assist production control staff in coping

**Figure 10.1: Levels of MIS and DP in Production Management**

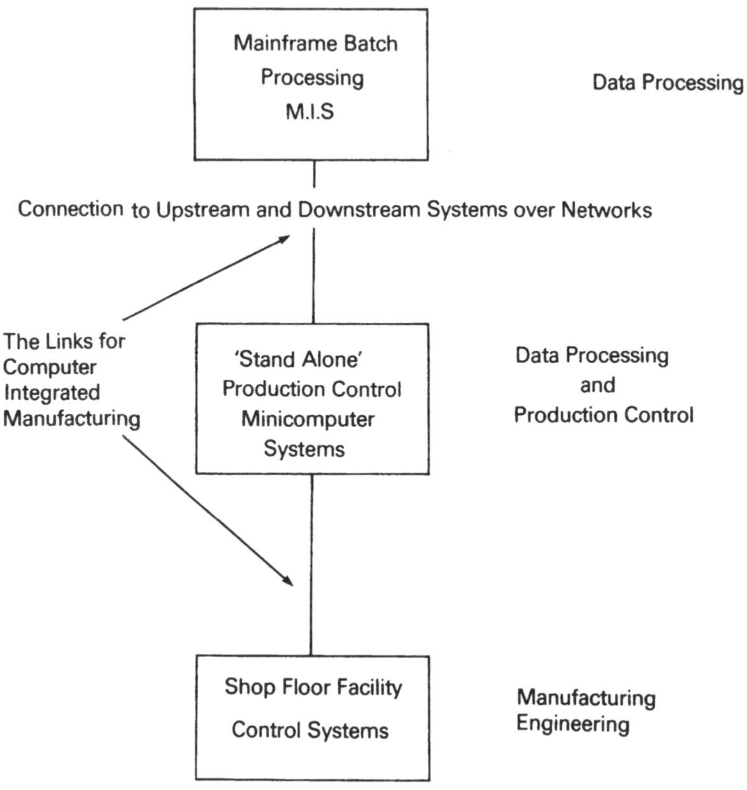

with the growing complexities of production scheduling and inventory management. In addition, mini-computer systems have been introduced to automate some aspects of quality control and testing in order to achieve a greater degree of objectivity and to cope with the complexity of, for example, vehicle electrical systems.

A further factor in considering the development of MIS in production control has been the increasing use of more powerful Programmable Logic Controllers (PLCs), supplied and installed by the vendors of manufacturing facilities in order to control switches and to activate electric motors and valves within the particular piece of equipment.

These PLC devices are also able to monitor the status of facilities through sensors and transducers and a recently introduced system at Jaguar engine and transmission plant provides an MIS which gives the realtime status of all items of equipment used in the machining of cylinder blocks, cylinder heads and crankshafts.

This information system, which is collecting data from several hundred points, provides signals to the maintenance crew on the incidence of machine breakdowns and malfunctions as they occur, and at the same time provides summary status information on an exceptions basis to senior plant management - for example, any breakdown which has not been repaired within one hour is displayed on a VDU screen to the Plant Director.

This capability for realtime data capture on the status of production facilities throughout the factory brings a new dimension to the potential for MIS in production control.

Of equal significance is the recently developed so called 'intelligent tag' device which enables identification and status data to be carried through production by major units such as body shells, engines, axles and gearboxes. These devices, which are of the size and weight of a litre of oil, can be programmed and scanned using radio waves as they pass within about 1 metre of a transmitter/receiver pad.

The potential therefore exists for a transformation in MIS in production control. The infrastructure of mainframe batch systems, micro-computer recording and control systems and shopfloor realtime data capture is proven. The objective in Jaguar Cars is to integrate the data bases and applications so that the full benefits of MIS can be realised across all areas of manufacturing.

## The Computer Integrated Manufacturing (CIM) Strategy in Jaguar Cars and the Implications for the Development of MIS

Computer integrated manufacturing is a philosophy now being widely explored in manufacturing industry particularly where batch production processes are involved.

The last part of this chapter described the developments under way for the closer integration of the product design functions with manufacturing engineering and process planning. In this section, the concepts of CIM are further developed to explain how they are being implemented for the scheduling and control of production and what impact they will have on the traditional approach to production management and MIS.

In November 1983 senior Jaguar management attended a seminar at which the philosophy of CIM was adopted as the way forward to achieve the growth objectives for the company in output volume, productivity and profitability.

The CIM philosophy within manufacturing was described as having three main strands:

(a) a move away from batch production towards 'real time' scheduling and control techniques for all major assembly (i.e. labour intensive) activities;

(b) the vertical integration of data and information systems, from shopfloor facilities control and production status monitoring through to production management systems and company data base maintenance; and

(c) the selective introduction of automation technology wherever beneficial and the parallel installation of appropriate levels of MIS to match the requirements of automation and ensure that flexibility was retained.

In mid-1984 a team of senior managers in manufacturing was formed to further develop these concepts into implementation plans and to identify the priorities and guidelines which should govern investment decisions in new production facilities, automation and MIS.

It was recognised from the beginning that the closer integration of manufacturing operations did not necessarily require high levels of automation.

With the relatively very low volumes of production in Jaguar, compared with the mainstream volume car producers, the opportunities for cost-justifiable automation are somewhat limited.

The CIM study team in manufacturing approached its task from a top-down viewpoint starting with the strategic business objectives for the company and assessing how manufacturing would be able to achieve these objectives, which in summary were defined as follows:

a substantial growth in the volume of production using existing plants, with a wider model range and product variety (customer choice) but without significantly increasing production labour or inventory.

Four areas of investigation were identified and management involved from other functions, particularly quality, sales, systems and personnel, and these four sub-teams were each given the task of preparing policy guidelines and implementation plans which could be applied to the major investment projects under development in order to bring about the objectives and benefits of the CIM philosophy.

These four teams completed their initial planning work in six months and covered the following aspects.

**Assembly automation opportunities.** An analysis of the structure of production costs showed that some 50% of labour and 50% of inventory value was incurred in the trim and assembly of the vehicle at the main assembly plant. Although considerable progress has been made in introducing automated methods for body welding and for the machining of components, where the technologies available are already well proven, few opportunities had so far been identified for the cost effective use of robotics and other automation techniques in vehicle assembly.

The philosophy of CIM requires that the development of MIS (i.e. the systemisation) is matched to the level of mechanisation (i.e. automation). Development plans for MIS in the vehicle assembly plant therefore need to be based on a well-defined plan for future assembly methods and facilities. Figure 10.2 illustrates the need for compatibility between the levels of automation and MIS for efficient manufacturing.

Furthermore, the achievement of the company's business objectives for productivity and inventory turnover requires that substantial improvements are made at the vehicle assembly plant.

This study team illustrated the point at an early stage of its work by demonstrating that if existing methods of assembly and levels of efficiency continued, then the achievement of the company's business objectives could only be brought about through 'unmanned factories' for body manufacture and paint, component machining, engine and axle assembly!

The results of the work of this team indicate that MIS would need to be developed in the assembly areas to support:

(a) selective automation of certain processes with traditional assembly tracks being replaced by layouts which allow for flexibility in the routing of vehicles through certain single-station shared facilities (to provide the volume throughout necessary to give investment justification);

(b) 'on-line' auditing of quality and diagnosis and rectification of problems to maintain the continuous flow of assembly build and thus avoid the labour cost

**Figure 10.2: The Matching of MIS to Methods of Production**

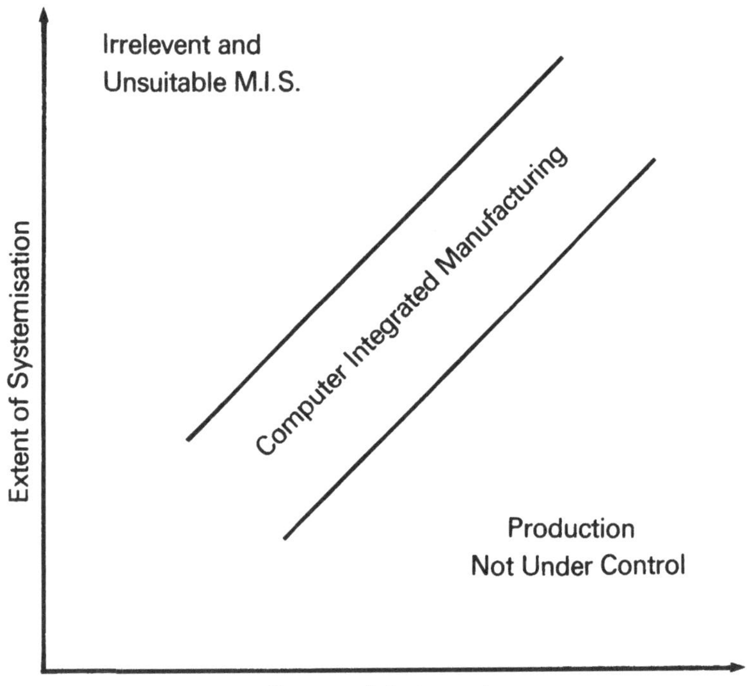

and inventory penalties of the traditional approach of 'off-track' rectification of faults; and

(c) the 'tracking' of vehicle sub-assemblies which may require to be assembled in parallel with the body, in order to facilitate automation techniques, but which will need to be brought together as a matched set at the appropriate point in the assembly process. A prime example of this approach will be the separate assembly of the doors to enable robot access to the body interior for fitting trim, electrics and other components.

The work of this team has confirmed the significance of MIS in production to the achievement of the output and productivity objectives of the business. Projects which are now at an advanced planning stage show that the investment required in computer hardware and software, and in communication and control systems will represent some 10% to 15% of the investment costs in new manufacturing facilities and automation equipment.

This poses new problems of resources and responsibilities concerning the traditional roles of the DP department, manufacturing and the vendors of production facilities, many of whom are now developing closer collaboration and commercial relationships with computer software houses and hardware suppliers.

**Production scheduling and control.** Traditional systems for scheduling production are based on the definition of batch machining and assembly schedules for several days ahead, with very limited flexibility to adjust these to reflect changes of circumstances and priorities.

The effects of breakdowns, material supply shortages and other uncertainties are accommodated by the holding of buffer stocks between major stages in production, and by leaving the allocation of particular order specifications to bodies, until the last possible moment in the manufacturing sequence - usually at the start of the trim and final assembly tracks.

Where major deviations occur to plan, or buffer stock levels prove inadequate, then production operations can quickly revert to a disorderly situation of 'build to shortage' whereby all considerations of manufacturing efficiency are subsumed in the overriding objective of keeping the assembly track going.

Such situations, although not frequent, are not unknown to most motor manufacturers and the structure of the MIS available usually proves of value in the 'crisis' decision making with which production management are faced.

Not only are traditional MIS seen to be irrelevant to such situations but management often face an additional task in helping to reinstate such systems once the crisis is over; files have become out of date, schedules no longer feasible and the 'credibility' of the whole approach has been further called into question.

The study team on production scheduling and control identified the need to make a complete break with the traditional approach to MIS, if such systems were to be relevant and beneficial to the management of production under a philosophy of CIM. The main conclusions of this work, which are now being incorporated into the design objectives for MIS, were as follows:

(a) Achievement of the productivity and inventory-turn efficiency objectives requires that sales orders are associated with major production components much earlier in the production sequence than at the start of the final assembly. This concept of 'triggering' all major assembly processes from the point of order association requires a realtime approach to assembly sequencing, and an efficient and reliable communications network within and between plants.

(b) This approach in which a 'vehicle set' of all major components is sequenced to meet at the appropriate points in the assembly process 'just-in-time' should also be extended to the suppliers of all expensive or bulky major components. There should therefore be much closer involvement in the development of compatible MIS and on-line communications systems between Jaguar and its suppliers. Figure 10.3 illustrates the 'just-in-time' approach.

(c) Whilst the adoption of a 'just-in-time' philosophy would provide substantial gains in efficiency, it introduces a much more immediate sensitivity and seriousness in the event of a facility breakdown or failure of material supply. The elimination of safety buffer stocks between major production processes and between plants requires that urgent production resequencing decisions are made centrally, if chaos is not to ensue from which orderly recovery will be very difficult to achieve. MIS will therefore need to be developed to provide realtime 'decision support' services to central production control staffs to enable the appropriate response to be made to such situations. This is a new and relatively unexplored area of MIS which is recognised by the growing interest of Expert Systems and AI Technology, and it is interesting to note that even in the process control industry, with its high levels of automation and investments in MIS, there has been a collaboration development project, initiated under

**Figure 10.3: Production Scheduling Philosophy**

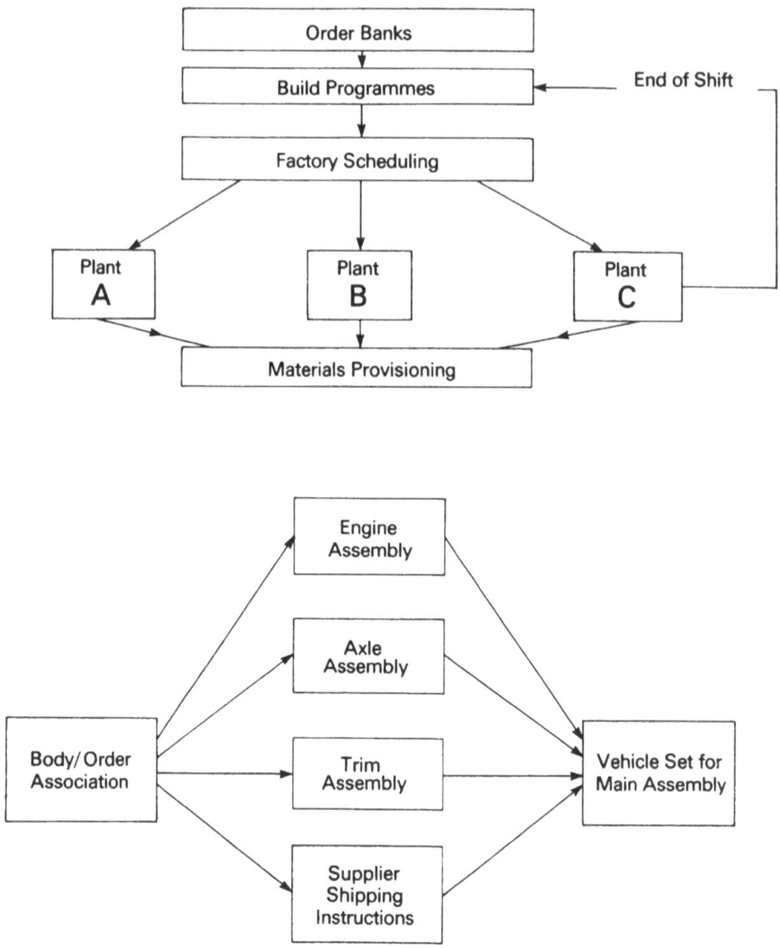

the auspices of the Alvey awareness programme, to explore the practical application of these latest techniques to the realtime control of complex production processes, in which a combination of data processing and human judgement is needed to cope with the results of uncertainty.

The successful development of such MIS is very dependent on the design of systems which are reliable and robust in the different situations which may arise. This CIM study team is making extensive use of computer simulation techniques to 'model' the alternative production scheduling and sequencing rules, and to explore the effects on output and inventory performance of variations in approach.

A much closer working relationship is being developed between production control staff, manufacturing facilities engineers and production line management to ensure the compatibility of the production methods and facilities with the MIS to be used to manage production in both normal and abnormal circumstances.

The recent availability of simulation techniques using interactive colour displays has enabled a major breakthrough to be achieved in a collaborative approach to the design of MIS, with a much greater degree of confidence that the resulting systems will be relevant, usable and, perhaps most important of all, able to adapt to and cope with the variety of situations which can occur during the normal course of a day in the life of a production manager in vehicle manufacture.

Technical Strategies for MIS. The third study team established to develop implementation plans for CIM was required to define the technical strategies and standards necessary to enable the MIS required at different levels and across all areas of manufacturing activity to exchange data and to interact in a realtime production control environment.

It was recognised that these technical strategies were required to enable the application systems to be installed and they should therefore be regarded as the essential infrastructure on which future developments could be built.

At its most basic level this team was concerned with standardisation of hardware and communications interfaces to provide for the physical compatibility of different systems and to minimise the need for a wide diversity of technical support skills, spare parts and maintenance contracts.

However, the more fundamental task of the team was to define the strategies and implementation plans for three areas of systems technology:

(a) data bases and the integration of data resources to

ensure greater consistency and reduce processing and maintenance costs;

(b) distributed processing to provide for the allocation of computer processing capacity at different levels in the organisation structure and across all areas of production activity in accordance with the operational objectives of the area concerned and also to ensure that with the increasing dependence of production on computers the necessary levels of reliability and resilience were designed in from the outset; and

(c) communications networks both within plants and across the company linking all three sites together so that data can be exchanged as required between systems which are interdependent and so that central production control management can make decisions based on the latest status information across all areas. This approach was designated as FM/PM/QM (Facilities Monitoring, Production Monitoring and Quality Monitoring), which taken together with materials movements and stock status information defines the four main inputs to the preparation of production schedules to meet sales order priorities and shipping dates.

As these three technical strategies were identified as an essential precondition for the new generation of MIS in manufacturing, they have been receiving priority for implementation.

Extensive detailed analysis of data structures was carried out during 1984 and early 1985 and a data base management system selected and installed. Implementation of fully integrated data bases will take several years to achieve, since many existing systems applications will need to be rewritten or 'bridged' to be able to access and update company databases in place of the limited local files currently in use.

As a further benefit to users, an enquiry language has also been installed which will provide much improved facilities for interrogating data base files to obtain selected information, processed and presented in the most appropriate way to help with ad hoc studies and in the formulation of plans.

The distributed processing strategy has also now been defined and is being applied to all major new systems projects. This strategy has proved to be quite problematic to resolve, since it was required to define much more precisely the operational responsibilities and working relationship between the data processing department and the users in manufacturing.

Whereas the responsibility for installing and operating

mainframe computers and batch processing systems was recognised as a long standing responsibility of the DP department and involving specialist technical skills such as systems programming, responsibilities for the middle ground of mini-computer systems had never been properly resolved.

Some such systems had been installed in central data centres and were under the control of DP even though any failure in hardware or software could rapidly lead to a shut-down in production in the area concerned. Other such mini-computer systems had been installed on the shopfloor in an office adjacent to the production facilities concerned, and were operated by production control staff but with technical assistance when required from the central DP department.

Policy guidelines and design rules have now been defined and agreed between DP and Manufacturing, governing the configuration and design of major new computer systems, including consideration of the location of, and responsibility for, computer processors and attached devices on which particular applications reside.

These guidelines support the objective of the full accountability of manufacturing management for all aspects of production performance during a shift, whilst recognising dependence on specialist technical personnel and central DP staff during abnormal situations and in order to carry out, between - shift functions, particularly those requiring access to, and involving the updating of, central company data bases.

In defining these working relationships the analogy had been drawn with other specialist skills and support services required for example to carry out preventative maintenance programmes and to validate process capability against quality standards and tolerances.

It has been recognised that many existing systems do not conform to the distributed processing strategy and the design guidelines now established, since they do not allow for the distribution of processing functions and data which technology has now made possible and which the principle of organisational accountability makes necessary. It will therefore be necessary to replace these systems progressively as opportunities arise and resources become available although this is likely to take several years to complete.

Installation of communications networks is also now proceeding and is expected to be completed by the end of 1985. These networks, which are based on broad band coaxial cable technology, introduce much greater flexibility for the design of all forms of MIS, from shop floor process control, to production planning and scheduling.

By installing such networks to cover all areas of the Plant, it becomes possible to link systems together and to access systems through VDU terminals, from any point to any point, as if the devices concerned were directly connected and in the same location.

This flexibility and adaptability of the communications network, together with the integration of company data bases and the distribution of computer processors, is transforming the scope for MIS applications in manufacturing. The costs of providing the infrastructure and of designing standard interfaces into systems applications has been estimated in Jaguar Cars as more than 5% of the total capital investment requirements in new production facilities and systems. The benefits are seen very simply as making feasible and operationally manageable the performance objectives necessary for growth in output, productivity and profitability.

Human Factors and Organisation. The fourth study team on the development plans for CIM was concerned with the organisational and personnel issues arising from both the automation of production processes and from the introduction of much more comprehensive computer-based information systems for managing production.

This team recognised that the closer integration of information systems and the development of company data bases would require adjustments to traditional boundaries of responsibility and more formal definition of procedures, to ensure that vital data were recognised as a company asset or resource, and were not owned by any one particular department or function.

The introduction of more integrated operations, with sequential stages of manufacturing more tightly coupled, will require the automation of much of the routine decision making, which is currently carried out by local production management and production control staff within each area of the plant.

The automation of the routine, together with the availability of the full range of status information to central production control staffs and plant management, raises a number of questions about the hierarchical structure of traditional organisations, and about the inter-relationships different functions, such as production control, materials control, quality control, production line management, maintenance, process engineering and data processing.

It is too early yet to draw a firm conclusion on the new structures and working relationships which will emerge, but it seems likely that greater attention will need to be given to fostering team working, since operational performance and optimisation will become more and more dependent on the quality of design and maintenance support for all aspects of the manufacturing process.

The advent of new specialisations and technical skills to support advanced manufacturing technologies and information systems will need to be managed carefully to avoid the creation of small elite groupings of specialist staff on whom the continuity of production becomes increasingly dependent.

The implementation plans being developed recognise the fundamental nature of the changes which will need to be brought about, but also the need to manage these changes as a controlled transition, whether it be in the redeployment and retraining of production operators as automation technology is introduced, or in the introduction of disciplined data base management and administration methods to ensure the integrity and security of this vital company asset.

## The Group Technology Machining Project

The first major multi-million pound project under development which will implement the philosophy of CIM concerns the introduction of advanced manufacturing facilities for the machining of detailed components at the Jaguar Cars Power Train Plant located in Coventry.

There are some 1,200 different small and medium-sized steel and aluminium components currently used in the assembly of a number of versions of engines and axles excluding the large components of cylinder blocks, cylinder heads, crankshafts and camshafts, which are machined on dedicated flowline facilities.

The traditional approach to the manufacture of such detailed components in a machining shop is to group like machines together (turning lathes, drills, milling machines), and to process batches of components through the various operations as a series of discrete production stages.

Since each component has a need for a different number and sequence of operations (which can range from a few to around 40 to 50 separate operations) each component needs to be controlled as a work batch through the shop with the consequent problems of controlling work-in-progress inventory and of balancing capacity and workloads for each of the machine tools groups and its labour.

Traditional MIS supporting machining shop production control have provided build programmes and delivery schedules based on forecast demand by the downstream engine and axle assembly activities. It has not been practical to introduce effective MIS on the shopfloor to monitor and control the progress and sequencing of work batches through the shop.

Over the next 3 or 4 years it is planned to radically change the approach to component machining through a philosophy of group technology. This approach will involve the introduction of some 20 machining-centre cells each of which will have a cluster of machine tools capable of carrying out all the machining operations required by a group of like parts.

For example, one particular cell will be concerned with the machining of turned aluminium parts and may involve a numerically controlled lathe, drill and robotic material handling device.

This quite different approach to the production of machined components will both bring a requirement for advanced management control systems locally and also provide an opportunity for much greater optimisation in production scheduling and inventory control across all areas which feed the subsequent assembly activities.

Figure 10.4 illustrates schematically the differences between the traditional approach and that based on group technology. The main features which will need to be incorporated into the design of the MIS have been identified as follows:

(a) flexibility to enable components to be produced in small batches and to effect a changeover in the tools and settings of a cell to minimise the non-productive time between batches;

(b) component identification to facilitate the down-loading of the appropriate part programmes from a locally-stored library so that numerically controlled machine tools can be loaded with the correct instruction set;

(c) in-process gauging to ensure that dimensional accuracy is achieved within design tolerances and that trends in process output can be detected and corrective action taken;

(d) facility status monitoring to ensure that breakdowns and malfunctions can be quickly detected and diagnosed, and corrective repair and maintenance action taken;

(e) tool management to provide for the recording of tool usage and the replacement of tools at the appropriate time and prior to excessive tool wear; and

(f) material movements scheduling and control to ensure that raw materials are supplied to each machining cell in accordance with planned production and that finished components are delivered to the downstream assembly/build schedules.

Such systems applications, to the extent they have previously been technically feasible, have been regarded as shopfloor control systems quite separate from the processes of management.

The need for realtime production decision making and the optimisation of manufacturing operations across all areas of production requires this traditional view to be disgarded. If buffer stocks are to be reduced to the minimum levels

**Figure 10.4: Group Technology for Machining Operations**

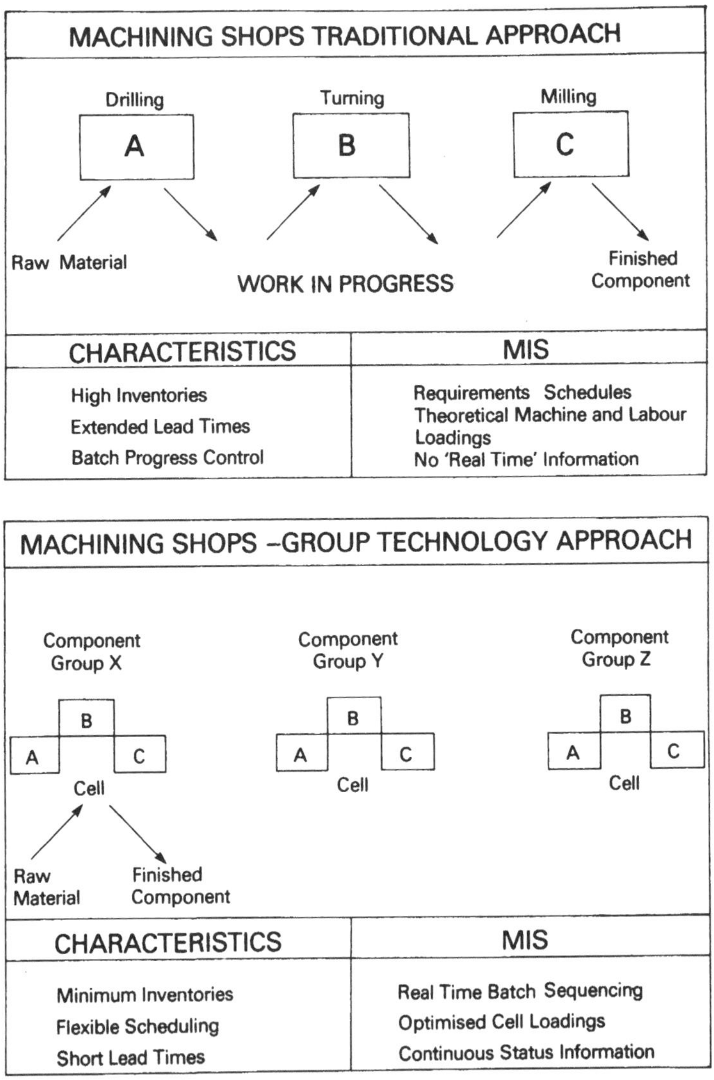

necessary for economic batch quantities, and to provide for a reasonable level of safety insurance whilst breakdowns are repaired - then central production control decision making will require access to production and facility status data from the shop floor and in real time.

The design team established to plan and implement the group technology project for machining components has fully recognised this challenge. The structure of the various elements of the control systems is illustrated in Figure 10.5.

The central theme is that of flowline production with centrally determined scheduling and sequencing decisions in response to predetermined build schedules but modified to take account of the latest status of achievement and production capability across all areas.

It is intended to implement this project in manageable stages with the first three machining centre cells being commissioned towards the end of 1986 and covering in total the manufacture of some 50 different components.

In recognition of the significance of the MIS aspects of the whole project it is intended to give overall responsibility for all aspects of information processing and systems integration to a prime contractor systems house - but with the close involvement of Jaguar systems personnel at every stage and with formal approval of design specifications and acceptance tests.

Through these arrangements, the machine tool vendors will be required to supply computer hardware and software which not only conforms to company technical standards but which provides for data and communication interfaces determined by the prime systems contractor.

This approach represents a fundamental change from the traditional arrangements for shopfloor control systems, whereby facilities vendors were allowed to design and supply their own local control hardware and software which, while suited to the facilities concerned, paid little or no regard to the longer term objectives of integration between systems across the shopfloor and, eventually, across all areas of production.

There are of course widespread systems already installed in manufacturing industry involving the use of terminals by shop floor production personnel, and it is essential that local control functions remain local and that the skills and responsibility remain where the accountability for output performance rests.

However, the approach being developed by Jaguar Cars through its group technology machining project will extend the scope and significance of MIS well beyond today's applications and in particular in the following ways:

**Figure 10.5: MIS in Production Control**

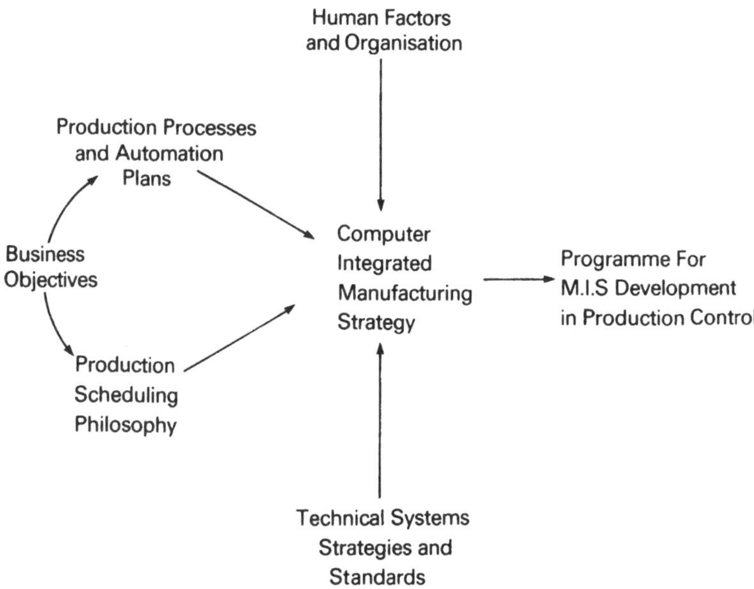

(a) Shop floor control systems and operators will be required to be much more responsive to changes in priorities and build schedules in order to optimise manufacturing performance across the company. The production facilities they use will have the capability to adapt quickly and semi-automatically to these changing requirements.

(b) Local production line management will be provided with a comprehensive range of status monitoring information on all aspects of performance, including output achievement, quality levels, facility status, materials supply, on a realtime basis. There will be a requirement for 'decision support' MIS to provide an analytical basis for local decision making to correct out-of-balance situations or deviations from schedules.

(c) Central production control management will need to be strengthened to take across-company decisions based on realtime status information derived from all areas of production.

Such decisions will often be complex and require the exercise of considerable judgement and consultation, but they will also need to be made and communicated quickly. Expert Systems and Artificial Intelligence techniques will undoubtedly be required when the extent of the new approach becomes widespread.

The group technology project is the first vehicle for introducing and proving out the philosophy of CIM and the new approaches it requires to MIS which have now become practical through recent advances in information technology.

Seven other major development programmes have been identified for implementation over the next few years to complete the transformation and to enable the ambitious growth and efficiency objectives of the company to be achieved. These seven projects together span all major areas of manufacturing from body pressing and body welding through to final vehicle assembly, test and dispatch.

In order to prove the new approach to MIS, a project is also in hand to install by the end of 1985 a pre-production proving area for computer and communications systems.

This facility, which is analogous to the extensive prototype proving used in developing new vehicles, will enable applications software and new systems techniques to be thoroughly tested not only for their performance, capacity and conformity to design specifications prior to installation in live operation. It will also provide an opportunity to confirm user acceptance and to involve users actively in influencing systems design through simulation and emulation techniques and thus minimise the risks of systems failure.

## Summary

The traditional approach to MIS can no longer cope with the complexities of production control with extensive product variety, the need for much shorter customer lead times and the growth in the introduction of automation technologies and the flexibility they bring to shop floor operations.

The need for a radically different approach is just as relevant to the medium-sized manufacturing company as it is to the high volume mass producer.

MIS technologies now make possible a realtime approach to production control but this will only be achieved if the traditionally separate 'worlds' of data processing and manufacturing engineering are brought together to work in partnership, as illustrated schematically in Figure 10.5.

The high levels of investment required in MIS to bring about this transformation need to be planned to support a well defined strategy for computer integrated manufacturing and to conform to a range of technical standards for computer and communications hardware and software. The advanced project to introduce group technology into the machine shops in Jaguar Cars will prove out the validity of the company's recently defined policies in these areas.

## MIS AND OFFICE AUTOMATION

### Background to the Project

In December 1981 a study was initiated in Austin Rover to review the status of office systems and to identify the opportunities for the introduction of advanced information technology.

This study was carried out by a small project team with representatives from each of the head office commercial and administrative departments and resulted in a concept paper being presented to and approved by the Senior Management Operating Committee in April 1982.

At the time of the study Austin Rover had identified the application of advanced technology as a central plank of its strategy to achieve a fully competitive level of efficiency and a comprehensive product range to match those of its higher volume competitors in the UK and Europe.

The strategic commitment to technology was by this time already well established for shopfloor automation with the introduction of the production facilities for the Metro at Longbridge which had transformed the 'cars per man' output to levels as good as the best of the volume producers.

At the same time, a major investment programme had been developed for the extensive use of computer aided design, computer aided engineering and product testing techniques to be introduced progressively over the following three to five years.

It was recognised by top management that a comprehensive strategy for technology must also include the third broad area of business activity - the administrative and commercial functions of finance, personnel, product planning, market research, and business planning. Although these functions only comprise some 10% of total employees, nevertheless they had a major contribution to make to effective planning and efficient administration. It is these functions which were responsible for analysing, preparing and presenting the information with which management made decisions and controlled the business.

Figure 10.6 was used in the concept proposal presentation made to management to illustrate the relationship of information technology to the other technology programmes in production and design and development.

Figure 10.7 was used to illustrate the need for a consistent strategy for MIS in the office and to support planning and decision making as the operational base of the company became more automated and efficient and thereby more capable of a flexible response to market conditions and opportunities.

Management at all levels were well aware of the increasing pressures on them to make rapid decisions based on a thorough analysis and understanding of the alternatives and the information available. These pressures on management had increased substantially with the advent of quarterly price adjustments in response to the (at the time) high levels of UK cost inflation.

Subsequently, as pricing decisions have returned to a more orderly scene, the effects of worldwide over-capacity in the car industry and the greatly expanded range of product derivatives and options have introduced a new decision making dimension into marketing and promotional campaigns in a volatile and highly competitive market place.

In the early months of 1983 an employee communications programme was carried out across all areas of the company to explain the commitment to technology and to emphasise the responsibility of all employees to ensure that the maximum benefits were obtained from the investments - whether in shop floor facilities, computer aided design or office automation.

Particular mention was made of the historical lack of investment in information systems and computer technology for office and managerial staff and reference was made to the origins of current office technology.

As part of the study carried out from December 1981 to April 1982, an analysis was made of the flows and consumption of paperwork. It came as a major surprise to all concerned in the study, and to senior management in particular, when it

**Figure 10.6: Integration of Data and MIS Between Functions**

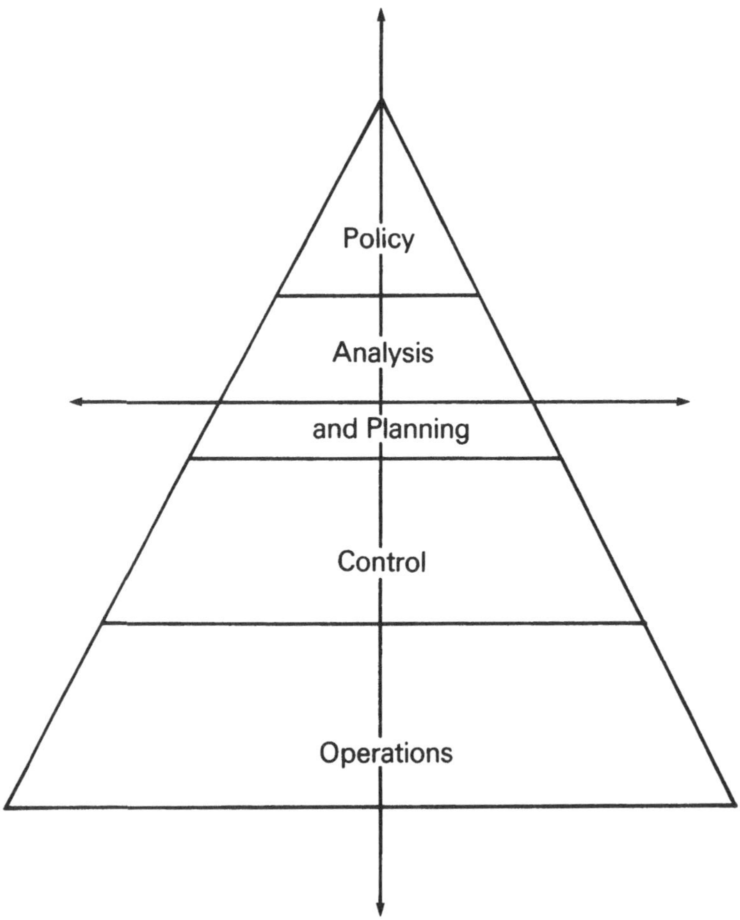

**Figure 10.7: Aspects of Office Automation**

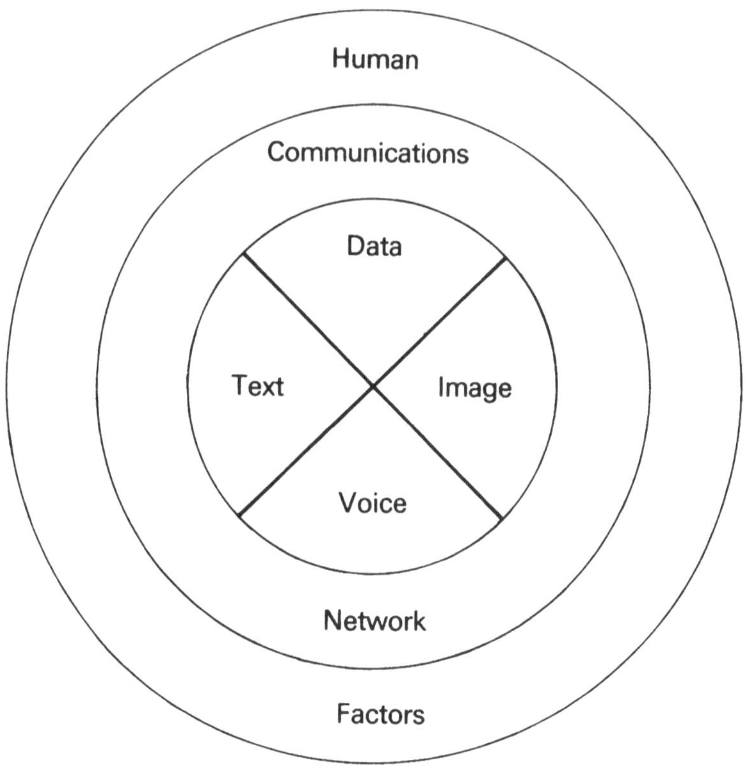

in the study, and to senior management in particular, when it was identified that the usage of photocopying paper amounted to some 50 million sheets per annum.

The conclusion was drawn in the study team's report that the two major recent advances in office technology, the word processor and the photocopier, were of doubtful value in contributing to the overall efficiency of the business - certainly when used to generate an avalanche of paper - a problem with which management found it easy to identify.

The concept paper adopted by top management in April 1982 marked the starting point of a coordinated and progressive investment programme in MIS and office automation.

Particular emphasis was given to the need to create an infrastructure which could provide the services required by management to develop the longer term plans and policies which were crucial to the survival of the business in an ever more complex and unpredictable environment, whilst at the same time being prepared to make short term tactical decisions in response to competitive pressures and to take advantage of market opportunities.

A further factor which emerged from the study concerned the growth in office micro-computers and stand-alone word processors. In common with most large industrial organisations, Austin Rover managers had responded enthusiasically to the advent of relatively low cost 'personal' micro-computers which had become available in commercial form over the preceding 2 to 3 years. Financial control procedures and conventional data processing organisations have traditionally ensured that the development of MIS and the acquisition of computer equipment has been centrally coordinated. However, the availability of personal micro-computers and word processors, including applications software, at prices well below £ 5,000 effectively opened the gates to local procurement decisions - with the added attraction of rapid availability and early implementation of simple MIS.

An audit of the micro-computer and word processing equipment installed during the preceding 3 years showed that over £0.5m of investment had been made and that inevitably, with the pace of product development and the rapid improvements in the price performance of equipment, there was little standardisation and a profusion of different makes - a situation which if allowed to continue would be likely to prove a major constraint to the integration of MIS in the future.

## Development Concepts and Implementation Experiences

**Word Processing Standardisation.** Implementation of the programme to develop integrated MIS in the office was planned in three stages for the period late-1982 to 1986.

The first stage started in December 1982 with the introduction of powerful word processing facilities for all head office secretarial staff located on the headquarters site in Coventry. The equipment was installed over a period of six months and provided work stations for some 50 secretaries and typists located in three office complexes located on the same site but about 1 km apart.

The concept proposal identified text as one of the major sources of information for the management of the business and particular attention was given at this stage to define standard document layouts, type formats and labelling conventions, to facilitate the interchange of documents electronically during the later stages of development.

During this initial stage of implementation, trials were carried out to test the capability to transmit documents between the Coventry headquarters of Austin Rover and BL headquarters in London, and also to Austin Rover management offices in Longbridge and Cowley.

Although it had always been intended to keep these trials low-key it soon became apparent that the ability to transfer short reports and management papers (up to 10 pages) in about 5 minutes over the public telephone network was seen by senior management as a significant breakthrough.

In the volatile environment in which the company operated and with the need to respond to competitor actions and operational problems on an urgent basis, there was an almost daily need to despatch personnel to drive up to a 200 miles round trip simply to deliver papers to a meeting deadline.

Not only did electronic transmission save the inconvenience and cost of this form of internal post but it also extended deadlines, giving much needed additional time for analysis and briefings in near-crisis situations.

This early use of electronic document transmission was, however, seriously limited in capacity and flexibility since it required direct operator attendance during the whole of the transmission time and could only handle one session from a single source to a single destination at a time. It did however prove very useful in opening the eyes of senior management to the potential benefits of office automation to their own needs and problems, thus justifying their act of faith in supporting the initial investment decision. A full-scale electronic mail service was planned for introduction during later stages of the programme and will be described in further detail below.

**Forms of Management Information.** Although the main focus of the first stage of implementation was on the provision of word processing services and the generation of text to a company standard, the concept proposal emphasised that management information essentially exists in four forms

- text, data, voice and image (pictures and graphics). Considerable emphasis was given to the need for the strategy for MIS to support the planning and policy-making activities of the business to be capable of handling management information in all of the above forms in an integrated way.

Although, in early 1982, the technologies to achieve this objective did not exist as commercially available and cost effective products - it was clear that such products would become available over the next 3 to 5 years. Some information technology suppliers were at that time already able to demonstrate applications software which was at an advanced stage of development.

Figure 10.7 is an illustration from the presentation of the concept proposal to senior management to emphasise the point that the successful development of MIS for management would require strategies to be defined and resources allocated to the six main aspects:

(a) the generation, analysis and processing of information in its four forms: data, text, voice, and image;

(b) the provision of a communications network to enable such information to be accessed from, or transmitted to, the point where it was needed; and

(c) human factors concerned with the man/machine interfaces, and the presentation of information in a relevant and usable form.

**Human Factors.** Particular emphasis was given at the earliest stages of implementation to the need for a continuous education and training support programme. 'Opinion leaders' were identified and appointed in each main office area, to act as office automation coordinators to ensure that help and support was always available and that outside assistance was called in quickly whenever required.

One of the central themes of the education and training programme was to recognise that the investment in powerful word processing facilities could not possibly be justified simply as a replacement for the typewriter - particularly as the full cost of providing such facilities was of the order of £5,000 per work station. Word processing had to be seen essentially as the method of capturing the data which would later be further processed, analysed and distributed throughout the system to meet management needs for information.

This theme was further developed to support the need for the changed methods of working which would become necessary if the benefits of the investment were to be achieved. The concept proposal recognised that the choice of the form (data, text, voice, image) in which management information was communicated would vary according to the circumstances, place and people involved.

It would also change over time as more efficient and easier-to-use facilities become available, and as the users become more fully aware of the possibilities and started to modify the habits of a working lifetime to take advantage of the technology available.

The first experiences of changes in working relationships and the implications for organisation structures and responsibilities came during the second stage of implementation from Autumn 1983 through to mid 1984.

**Personal Computing and Management Terminals.** During the second stage of implementation a communications network was installed on the headquarters site in Coventry to link together the several office complexes where the headquarters functions of personnel, finance, marketing and administration were located.

There were two main objectives of the investment in Stage 2. Firstly, to provide a limited number of standardised personnel computing services to professional staff, particularly those in finance and similar areas using spread sheet analysis in the preparation of profit and cost forecasts and sales volume plans.

These developments were directed towards improving the analysis and preparation of management information in the form of data, and some initial trials were also carried out in the use of graphical presentation methods (generated electronically through software packages) to replace or augment the conventional presentation of tables of numbers - easily absorbed by the experienced finance director but less easy for his managerment colleagues to absorb and comprehend.

A further benefit expected from this approach was to improve the response to particular analysis exercises and management requests by automating some of the analysis calculations and by allowing for a wider range of alternatives to be explored in greater depth in the time available.

Again considerable attention was given to the need for standardisation of those aspects of the system which would facilitate integration and electronic communications during subsequent stages.

The second main objective of Stage 2 was to provide low-cost terminals to first-line management in the administrative functions and to introduce an electronic mail and information management service. This development provided for a central computer storage and distribution system capable of handling both text files, produced from word processing, and data files, produced from personal computers, with access rights to any single file or document controlled by the originator.

With confidential information now being transmitted

electronically over a network and stored centrally, considerable attention was given to security and a system of password protection was introduced (using the proprietary software) to ensure that unauthorised access to information was prevented.

**Transfers of Function.** This second stage of implementation provided valuable insights into the way in which advanced technology in the office would lead to changes in the way people have traditionally worked and in particular in their relationships and job functions. Two particular aspects illustrate this trend.

Traditionally secretaries/typists produce draft reports and papers based on dictated or handwritten script; managers amend and check and the changes are incorporated by the secretary, reprinted for signature and issued to a circulation list. With the facilities now provided it became possible for draft documents to be sent electronically by the secretary from the word processing screen to be available for the manager to check and amend (using limited editing functions) on his own low-cost desk top terminal. Furthermore, these functions could be carried out from any office with access to the system thus giving much more flexibility and helping to reduce the paperwork bottleneck.

The electronic mail service also enables the user to release the document concerned for circulation to the addressees, each of whom then received an electronic copy in their mailbox accessible through a desk-top terminal - or through a locally sited on-line printer if they do not yet have access to the system or have not yet received the necessary training.

It is envisaged that this change in the secretary/manager roles will give more emphasis to the 'information resource management' responsibilities of the secretary as administrative assistant to the department concerned and with a new set of skills and responsibilities which go far beyond the tedious maintenance of a row of filing cabinets in which everything is neatly filed - but from which it is often difficult to extract all the relevant references to a particular issue under review.

The second area of progressively changing roles identified during this stage concerned the relationships and responsibilities of managers and their analytical and professional staff, particularly for example in the financial analysis department.

The provision of more powerful MIS software which is easy to use and which presents the results of analysis in an easy-to-understand form enables the manager to become more directly involved in the analysis of the detailed information. This can easily be seen as an intrusion by the professional management accounting staff since it puts added pressure on the need for accurate and reliable sources of data, whilst detracting to some extent from his ability to exercise judgement in making recommendations to his superiors.

Properly managed, these developments should lead to a better quality of planning and analysis and therefore to better decisions. Such an outcome will require an awareness of the changes required at all levels in the structure and sensitivity in introducing the revisions needed to working procedures and relationships, to ensure that professional and administrative staff do not become demotivated by a progressive deskilling of their jobs to the point where they become essentially data gatherers with little opportunity to exercise their judgement and professional skills.

**Current Developments.** At the time of writing in June 1985 the third stage of implementation of the Austin Rover office automation programme has received approval for introduction over the next six months.

This third stage is essentially concerned with consolidating the developments and new services installed so far, and with the extension of these same facilities across the company to make them available to the administrative functions located at Longbridge (Birmingham) and Cowley (Oxford).

This development will involve the installation of a company-wide communications network linking local site networks together, thus providing for information access and electronic mail transfer of text and data files between users wherever they are located.

With the completion of this company network and the information processing and management services available through terminals connected to it, it will become possible to start to introduce further integration of information files and administrative procedures.

Much of the routine flow of information in a large organisation is characterised by a wide circulation of planning information and management reports to ensure that all who have any possible interest in the subject concerned are appraised of the situation. It is this approach which is a major contributing factor to the paperwork avalanche which by itself is not only costly and time consuming, but is a major constraint to efficient communications.

**Company Document Libraries.** The sheer volume of paper passing across most managers' desks prevents an efficient transfer of information. Papers are scanned rather than understood, delays occur in the internal post and 'in-trays', and important information can be easily passed over.

Examples have been identified in Austin Rover where the MIS in operation require the primary circulation of over 130 copies of certain key planning proposals and reports. The only possible way of handling such a need is to provide a common standard package to everyone and to let them extract the items of relevance to their own responsibilities.

The company-wide communications network and electronic mail services now being installed will enable a quite different approach to be taken. Firstly, information will be authorised for access by all those in the organisation with a need to know - thus ensuring that the same version (the latest) is available at the same time to all recipients. Figure 10.8 illustrates schematically the structure of the system.

Secondly, information can be distributed on a selective basis so that the information relevant to a particular user can be extracted from the document or file electronically, using advanced information retrieval software - thus avoiding the expense of transmitting unwanted information. This approach, which designates the central text files as company document libraries, whilst reinforcing the responsibility of the originators of documents and reports to control access authorisation (the electronic equivalent of circulation lists), will at the same time transfer responsibility to the users of information to exercise more discipline in defining their needs, and in keeping themselves up-to-date by regularly accessing their mailboxes and files through VDU screens to determine what has changed.

The full implementation of these changes will take several years but the impact on the management of the business will be far reaching. By transferring the 'costs' of distributing information to the user there will be a new motivation to exercise greater discipline and to avoid the squandering of information resources. The availability of online access to document libraries, reports and files will give added incentive to the originators to ensure the accuracy, up-to-dateness and security of information.

This theme was characterised in the employee communications programme as formally recognising the need for 'information management' as an essential component of the jobs of all administrative, professional and managerial staff to be added on an equal standing to the long established accountabilities for man management and task management. This requirement suggests a further dimension to the traditional view of MIS - an aspect which will require its own information resources if the company is to be properly organised, managed and developed to keep pace with the changing needs of the business.

Figure 10.9 was used in the employee communications presentation to illustrate the significance of information to business efficiency.

**Figure 10.8: Structure of MIS**

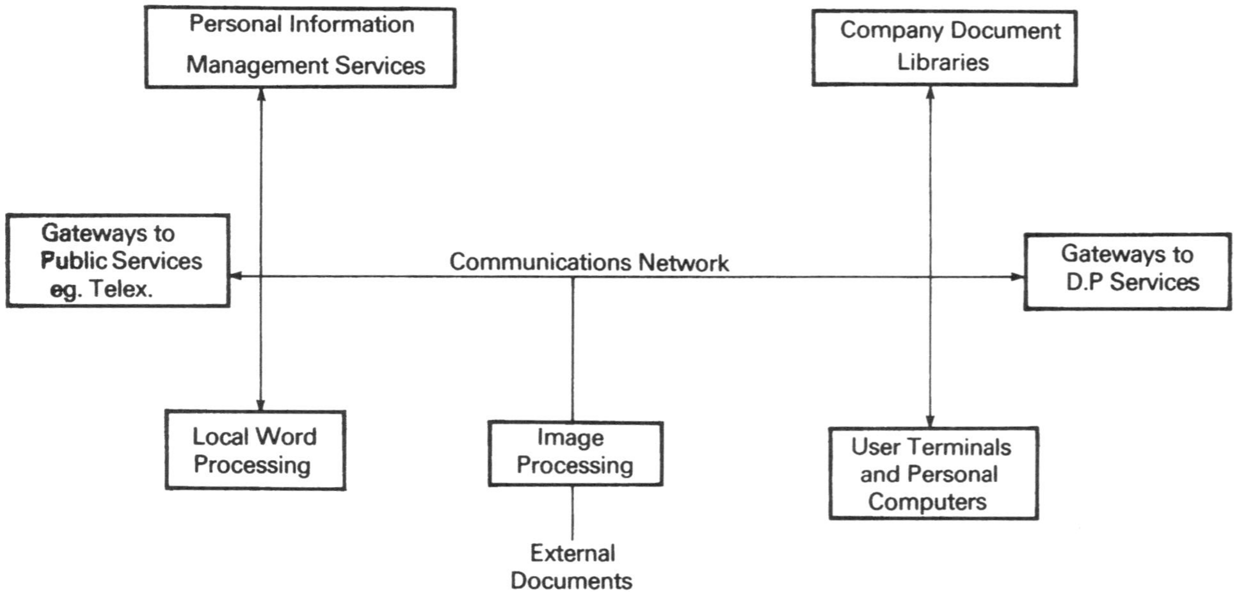

**Figure 10.9: Information Resources**

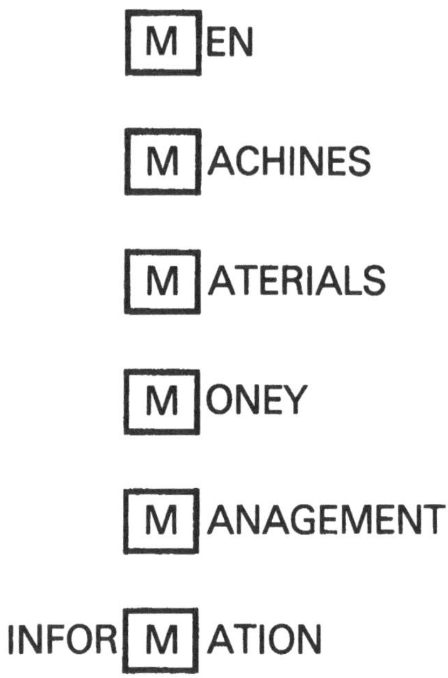

## Future Developments and Summary

The three stage initial phase of the programme will be completed during 1986, although the full benefits will only be realised as users become familiar with the services available and the capabilities of the system and understand how to use these to their fullest effect. Changing the long established traditions of office work will take several years and the pace of change will depend on the level of training support and management commitment.

MIS in the planning and managerial functions of the business have long been based on paperwork for formal communications, and voice, either by meetings or telephone, for less structured communications.

The advent of easy-to-use data analysis software packages, graphics presentation methods and on-line information retrieval services will provide the opportunity for a more flexible and more responsive information service to management, in many cases usable directly through computer terminals, with the ability to ensure that the information obtained is the most up-to-date, duly authorised, relevant to the issue at hand, and presented in a form most easy to comprehend.

The next phase of development has not yet been planned in detail - however it will centre on the application of several very recent advances in information technology. Among these the three most significant are likely to be voice storage and transmission; image processing and information retrieval packages.

There are now hardware and software packages available which enable voice messages to be digitised and transmitted electronically for storage and retrieval when required without loss of original quality. Such packages not only enable voice messages to be given a circulation equivalent to that already available for text, but more significantly it enables voice annotation to be used to comment on and modify text with the resulting mixed file of voice and text to be processed as a single 'document'.

Thus within the next phase it is envisaged that users will be able to circulate draft reports for example to a number of recipients for comment. The text will be scanned using VDU screens and voice commentary will be annotated and electronically fixed to particular points in the text and returned to the sender without the necessity to produce a single piece of paper. The recipient will only need to carry out the simplest keyboard functions probably involving a selection of keyboard symbols in response to screen image prompts.

The paperless office is an unattainable ideal since there are many situation in which the printed document will continue to have overriding advantages. However, these developments will have a substantial effect in reducing paperwork and thereby in making office workers more productive.

Thirty-three steps were identified in the life cycle of a piece of paper distributed through the internal company postal system. The full costs of processing, distributing and filing information in this way are substantial and major improvements are needed if the productivity of office workers is to keep pace with the advances made in shopfloor productivity, and more recently in the use of computer aid design techniques.

More significantly, with the volatile market environment in which most manufacturing industry now has to exist, with decisions needing to be made against tighter deadlines and reviewed more frequently, the services of the office worker in preparing, analysing and presenting management information will be increasingly vital to the quality of management plans and decisions, and therefore to the commercial profitability of the enterprise.

Developments in image processing will add the fourth dimension to MIS in the office, bringing the ability to digitise pictures at a very fine level of resolution and to incorporate such images within the electronic file for onward transmission and review.

Developments in electronic information retrieval methods are providing much more powerful tools to search extensive information files and retrieve all potentially relevant information based on certain key words defining the topic of interest. No longer will it be necessary to condense the richness and breadth of information on file by the classification of documents and files into an over-simplified coding structure, which is so necessary for manual filing systems.

These advances in the technology available for MIS in the office are of course associated with risks. The availability of a much-enlarged base of information and the flexibility to process and present information in a variety of ways require that new disciplines are established.

The successful firm of the late 1980s will have concerned itself with the management of its information resources and not just with investment in the technology.

This strategy for success was identified at an early stage in the Austin Rover programme for office automation, when three factors were identified as essential to the achievement of the challenging objects. These factors were defined as:

(a) technology - investment in the hardware, software and application systems necessary to provide the services required;

(b) methods - requiring a critical and continuing

re-examination of traditional methods of working, organisational relationships and procedures; and

(c) people - recognising that there is a need to cater for variety in the way problems can be tackled and work organised, as well as the vital need for standardisation in the underlying sytems and the way in which information is defined and stored.

Austin Rover is one of the leading UK manufacturing companies in its investment in MIS to support policy making and decisions. This is a fundamental strategy for future growth and profitability and considerable progress has been made over the last three years in investment in new MIS systems and services and in bringing this investment to bear on the daily work of administrative, professional and managerial staff at all levels in the company.

# IV STRATEGIC IMPLICATIONS

# 11. Developing Strategic Business Advantage from Information Technology

by William R King

## INTRODUCTION

The notion of a knowledge-based society has captured the fancy of many futurists during the past several decades. Drucker (1965), Bell (1973) and others have predicted that knowledge will become the 'central capital' and the crucial resource of the future economy.

Some would argue that the continuing trend to a service-oriented economy reflects this is indeed indirectly occurring. It is probably true that the service segment is built, in some sense, more directly on information and knowledge than is the production segment.

The direct transfer and sale of knowledge and information has also increased dramatically over the past few decades. The marketing of knowledge and information as commodities is commonplace today, whereas it was an anomaly only a decade or so ago (King and Zaltman, 1981). For instance, the sale of computer software involves a direct transfer of 'knowledge' since computer programs can perform their function repeatedly under various circumstances and conditions. The direct sale of scientific, technical and other data from data bases represents the direct transfer of 'information', i.e. data that have been evaluated to be useful for some purpose.

However, the information, or knowledge, 'revolution' is only beginning to be felt on a widespread basis throughout the economy. The advent of new technology and the integration of that technology into effective systems is about to enter the rapid growth phase of its life cycle. With that explosive growth will come changes that will affect the future of virtually every business, whether it is now knowlege-based or not, and whether it is service-oriented or production-oriented.

## THE CHANGING ROLE OF INFORMATION AND TECHNOLOGY IN BUSINESS

The computer is the primary mechanism for processing data in modern organisations. Although the state of the art in artificial intelligence is still not to the point where meaningful 'knowledge' is being effectively developed and used within the computer itself (Davis and Lenat, 1982) most futurists agree that computers have been, are, and will be essential to the creation of a knowledge society. Computers process data and, through the execution of decision rules that have been programmed by humans, they create new information that is of greater value. Moreover, through such devices as decision analysis models, simulation and optimisation programs, computers store and use knowledge, although they do not really create it.

While computers have already created substantial societal changes through the creation of new computer and information-related businesses (King and Zaltman, 1981) and through their application in myriad everyday contexts such as credit billing and traffic signal control (Coleman and Riley, 1972), they have not had the comprehensive revolutionary impact that has so often been predicted. Indeed, various studies of the actual 'impact of the computer' have shown that impact to be substantially less in many respects than many had anticipated (Whisler, 1970; Westin and Baker, 1972; USDHEW, 1973; Laurie, 1979).

Even in business, which depends so much on computers, one might characterise the overall role and impact of the computer to be a rather modest one. The computer has been used to automate many clerical functions to the degree that the business is dependent on computers in much the same way as we all depend on them in our daily lives. The 'nuts and bolts' of the business - billing, payments, paycheques, etc. - would quickly halt if computers were to stop functioning, just as would the telephone system and many of the other commonplace aspects of daily life.

However, many businesses are dependent on computers only in these mechanistic operational ways. The computer and its attendant information systems provide support to operations and to management that is faster, more accurate and more efficient than was previously provided, or which could be now provided by other means. But, in most instances, the computer system and the information that it processes does not yet serve as a resource that is integral and critical to business success.

The introduction and use of computers has been a low risk, and consequentially low payoff, activity for most business firms over the past several decades. They have invested an amount equivalent to perhaps 1% of sales (Kaiser and King, 1982) into a service function that has generally more than 'paid for itself', but which has not radically changed the business or the way in which it is managed. They are mechanically dependent on it, just as they are dependent on heat, light and water systems, but computer systems have little more to do with the core of the business than those other systems - i.e. they have little to do with the critical strategic resources that make the business what it is and which determine the strategies that it will follow.

Moreover, the literature of management information systems (MIS) makes it clear that computer systems have not really intruded into the daily lives of most managers to any great extent (King and Cleland, 1971). In many firms, only a relatively few computer technicians directly interact with the computer on a day-to-day basis. Only a few professionals, and managers who are so inclined, tend to be directly involved with computer systems in such firms. As an advertisement of Wang Laboratories Inc. eloquently states: 'For 25 years, the most powerful tool of the 20th century was kept in the back room.'

Thus, the principal mechanism through which the vision of a knowledge society will be achieved has not been effectively used as an instrument of strategy by most business firms. Rather, it has been used primarily as a tactical tool for achieving cost savings and greater efficiency.

Indeed, even the newly-emerging computer systems concept of 'information resource management' (IRM) merely 'upgrades' the computer system and its attendant information to the position of a resource that is to be husbanded and administered, much as are other organisational resources such as raw materials and labour. For instance, a course recommended by the Data Processing Management Association as part of a new and innovative Computer Information Systems Curriculum describes IRM as 'information systems management with emphasis on planning, organizing, and controlling user services and managing the systems development process' (DPMA, 1981).

Even Nolan's (1979) notion of evolutionary stages in the life cycle of integrating data processing into an organisation does not deal with the realisation of the real potential of computers. In his 'last' stage (VI) - 'Maturity' - he speaks of 'data resources management' in terms of 'the applications portfolio being complete' with its structure 'mirroring' the organisation and the information flows in the company. Thus, even in the most advanced stage of development in Nolan's model, the computer resource is still treated as a service function rather than a strategic resource.

Such notions as IRM and a maturity state at which the computer system is operating synchronously with the organisation have clear merit. During the era when the computer was relegated to the back-room, it was not subjected to the same levels of 'hard-nosed' management as was virtually every other element of the business firm. A basic management techniques, such as performance quotas, which are common in areas as diverse as production and sales, have been only recently instituted in the computer area. Thus, better management of the computer system and its development is a clear need that has begun to be understood and implemented.

However, the potential for information management is much greater than that which is the province of IRM. There is a stage of development, only beginning to be perceived and realised, that goes beyond Nolan's notion of 'maturity'. The role of computer systems in organisations is beginning to change dramatically. With this changing role will come the potential for vast change in the impact of computers and for the realisation of a knowledge society.

This emerging role of computer technology in business is easy to envision. One need only view a major business firm to see that new computer-based technology is being introduced in quantity at many locations - word processing systems, electronic mail and filing, electronic communications networks, desk top computers, etc. Moreover, these technologies are rapidly being linked together into more comprehensive systems. For instance, the concept of a decision support system (DSS) reflects the integration of a number of technologies that have existed for some time (Keen and Scott-Morton, 1978).

A major implication of this explosion of technology is that far more people - from clerks to executives - will be directly involved with the computer system than ever were before. Computers and appurtenant technology will no longer be relegated to the 'back-room' as a specialised service function that has little to do with the day-to-day activities of most people in the firm. They will be 'out in front' in virtually every office, workstation and production line.

In the past, only a small number of computer specialists were in direct contact with, and were direct 'users' of, the computer system. In many organisations, one member of each department or unit has been specifically identified to perform this role (Kaiser and King, 1982).

With the technological revolution that is occurring, virtually everyone will be a 'user' of the computer system. This widespread 'intrusion' of computers into the lives of so many will have profound impact, and while it will not be without problems, it will tend to increase understanding, reduce apprehensions, and enable many more people to better envision the widespread potential for computer applications. Heretofore, many such applications have been envisioned only by computer specialists, who often had difficulty selling their ideas to management, or have gone unseen because computer specialists lacked the requisite business knowledge and experience to relate computer capabilities to business needs (King and Cleland, 1971).

This pervasiveness of computers and the increasing

familiarity of people at all levels of the organisation with them will, inevitably lead to a wide variety of new computer applications. More importantly, however, it will lead to the amplification and acceleration of a phenomenon that is already beginning to be experienced - the creation of a comparative business advantage through information.

## INFORMATION-BASED COMPARATIVE BUSINESS ADVANTAGE

The concept of a comparative business advantage is now new (Grant and King, 1982). However, the notion of an information-based comparative business advantage is neither well developed nor understood. For instance, Porter (1981) describes three 'generic business strategies' - 'overall cost leadership,' 'differentiation,' and 'focus' - which may be used to achieve a comparative business advantage. Two of these generic strategies represent ways of achieving a 'competitive edge' using traditional business factors that are not generally highly information intensive. For instance, 'overall cost leadership' usually reflects a comparative advantage in pricing or profitability that is based on a product cost advantage, which may, in turn, be derived from experience curve effects or lower-than-average wage rates. Similarly, 'differentiation' is often achieved based on a quality advantage that may be derived from superior design or technology. Neither are information-intensive comparative advantages (although if such advantages are well-conceived, they are certainly derived, in part, from information and knowledge).

However, there are firms that have achieved information-based comparative advantages - i.e. the development of a relative advantage in the competitive marketplace on the basis of superior information or knowledge rather than by the more traditional business means for directly creating comparative advantage (such as a price advantage based on a cost advantage or a quality advantage based on a technology advantage).

For instance, Porter's third generic strategy - 'focus' may readily be achieved or implemented primarily on the basis of superior information. This strategy is one in which a firm concentrates on some particular product sub-line, group of customers, geographic area, or set of distribution channels to obtain a 'local comparative advantage' rather than a global one. Clearly, such a strategy can be the result of careful analytical market segmentation (Abell and Hammond, 1979). If so, it would be knowledge or information-based.

Illustrations of information-intensive competitive advantages that have been achieved by firms are not difficult to find. For instance, one firm that has developed its cost information system has, to a fine degree used this information to advantage in developing a pricing strategy, a promotional strategy, and an integrated sales incentives programme that give it a significant advantage relative to competitors. The firm's superior knowledge of the 'real' costs associated with each product in a large product line has enabled it to concentrate its sales and promotional resources to maximum advantage and profit.

Another firm has used competitive information directly through the development of a sophisticated competitor information system that allows it to infer competitor reactions and to anticipate them (Dutta and King, 1980). Yet another firm has made use of its sophisticated information on technology to develop product enhancements on a planned timely basis, giving it a continuing competitive edge.

However, the fact that such information-based comparative advantages have, or can be, created is not in itself sufficient. For this to be done on the massive scale that is required for the notion of information as an important strategic resource to be realised would require that such comparative advantages be systematically sought and created.

## THE INSTITUTIONALISATION OF MANAGEMENT FUNCTIONS

Information-based comparative advantage must be based on the systematic achievement of collection and analysis of information and its use in the creation of knowledge. The knowledge created is of the variety that was previously primarily the province of the individual manager or of a small group of executives or planners. Now, the advent of widely-distributed computer technology creates the opportunity for greater amounts of information to be collected and analysed for the purpose of identifying opportunities for salient comparative advantages rather than merely for purposes of conducting on-going business operations more efficiently.

The management function of developing insight into salient competitive advantages that might be achieved, which was formerly the province of the individual, thus becomes an institutionalised organisation process. This transformation of an individual's skill and prerogative into an organisational process is an on-going organisational phenomenon and is not restricted to the computer area or to the identification and assessment of comparative advantage. For instance, the 'planning' function was once thought of merely as one of the several major parts of the job of every manager. Now, strategic, long-range, project and other planning processes and systems exist in most organisations for performing organisational planning. These systems involve organisational activities that go well beyond the scope or responsibility of individual managers.

Indeed, even the logic and intuitive processes that we think of as the ultimate skill and prerogative of the individual are slowly being eroded by the ubiquitous computer. The science of artificial intelligence is inexorably challenging our concepts of those things that have been performed solely in the minds of individuals and which, in the traditional thinking, can 'never' be computerised.

## OPERATIONALISING THE CONCEPT OF INFORMATION AS A STRATEGIC RESOURCE

Figure 11.1 shows the generic processes that may be used to institutionalise the identification and implementation of information as a strategic resource.

Two such processes for doing this are identified by the horizontal arrows in Figure 11.1, which is derived from King (1978) and King and Zmud (1981). They are identified as 'Strategic Planning for Information Resources' and 'Information Resource Assessment'.

These two general methods represent organisational processes, each of which is essential to the creation of information as a strategic organisational resource. Although the two processes will not necessarily be separate and distinct in all organisations, collectively, the implementation of both processes will serve to ensure that the potential for making information a strategic organisational resource exists on something other than a fortuitous basis.

### Strategic Planning for Information Resources

The notion of 'strategic planning for information systems' is relatively new (King and Cleland, 1975). Many firms plan for the hardware and software that are the easily-recognised computer resource, but they do not plan for information as a resource as well. Indeed, many do not even perform the hardware and software planning in a fashion that is directly tied into business plans and strategic organisational plans (McClean and Soden, 1977).

The author (1978) has presented a notion of strategic planning for information systems that has been adopted by IBM (IBM, 1981) and which is readily broadened to the scope of information as a strategic resource.

That extension, here termed 'strategic planning for information resources', is described by the top arrow in Figure 11.1. This arrow represents the process of translating the Organisational Strategy Set, consisting of organisational mission, objectives, strategies, and other strategic attributes, into the IR Strategy Set, consisting of a defined role for information and information systems in the organisation, and IR Mission, a set of IR objectives, inform

**Figure 11.1: Operationalising Information as a Strategic Resource**

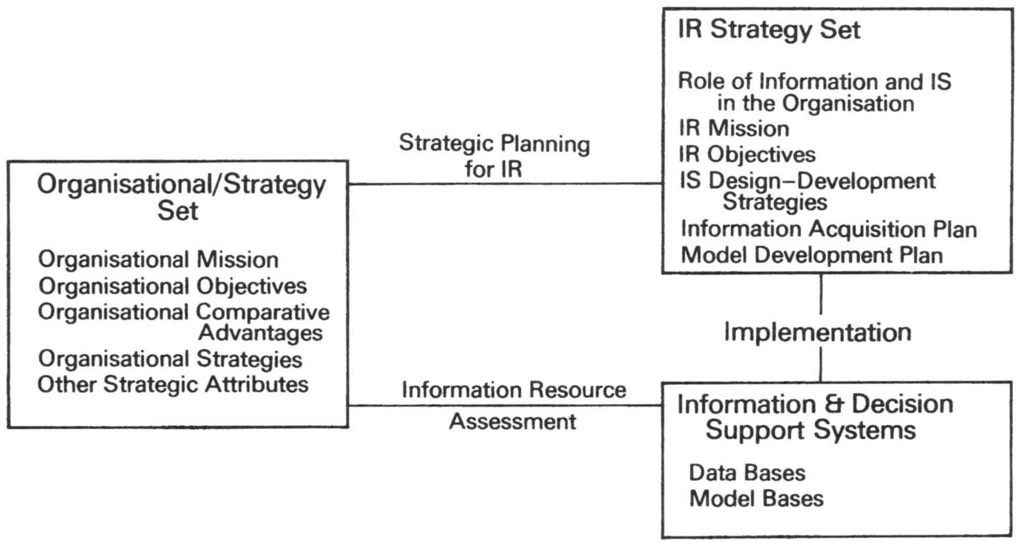

ation systems, design-development strategies, information acquisition strategies, and model development strategies for the decision, forecasting and predictive models that support management's strategic decision-making. Detailed illustrations of many of the elements that make up both of these sets are given by King (1978) in the context of strategic planning for information systems. Here, we deal only with those aspects that are most directly related to information as a strategic resource.

The process of 'SP for IR' that is depicted by the top arrow in Figure 11.1 is based on the premise that there must be a 'match' between the organisation's 'business' strategy and its information strategy. Since information is so important at all levels of modern complex organisations, it is unlikely that organisational objectives will be attained if the organisation's information and information systems are not specifically planned to be congruent with its business plan. Thus, the 'SP and IR' process is one through which business strategy is translated into information-resource strategy.

This is accomplished at a number of levels as indicated in the IR Strategy Set in Figure 11.1. At the highest level is the specification of a role for information and information systems in the organisation. We have already noted the distinction between a service role and a role in which information is viewed as a strategic resource. However, there are a variety of different service roles that may be selected as well. For instance, it may be determined through the 'SP for IR' process that the most appropriate role of information in some organisations is that of providing operational control - i.e. of providing the basis for the control of the operating activities of the organisation. An alternative service role is that of management control - providing information to support the resource allocation choices that must be made (Anthony et al, 1965). Another role is that of strategic management - i.e. supporting the strategic choices of the organisation.

These various service roles as well as the role of information as a strategic resource are available for management consideration. In different organisations, various of the alternative roles may be deemed to be appropriate. However, it is the 'SP for IR' process that provides the opportunity for management to specifically consider alternative roles and to select a role for the IR that is appropriate to the organisation.

Whatever the role selected, the 'SP and IR' process also provides for the selection of other elements that constitute the IR Strategy Set. It is apparent that some changes in organisational strategy will require new supporting information or information systems. If this process for acquiring new information and systems is to be anything other than opportunistic, a systematic process of 'SP for IR' must be conducted.

For instance, if a firm is newly embarking on an acquisition-oriented business strategy, it will require both new data (e.g. concerning possible acquisition candidates) and new knowledge regarding the manipluation of data (e.g. models for screening and evaluating high-potential candidates). These data and relevant knowledge must be planned for in the sense that they must be identified, an objective must be specifically formulated, and a plan must be developed for fulfilling the objective by acquiring both the appropriate information and the models in a cost-effective and timely fashion. Moreover, since such data and models cannot be acquired instantly, there will need to be detailed plans involving the development of sub-sets of the required data, sub-sets of the models, etc., so that the newly acquired data and models can be put to use as they are developed. The alternative - waiting until a large new data base or system is completely installed before any benefits are obtained - has been found to be ineffective.

Other elements of the 'IR Strategy Set' represent choices of how information is to be acquired (e.g. developed internally or purchased), how models for manipulating information are to be developed, etc.

Each of these issues is an element of 'SP for IR'. Each can be resolved only through an organisational planning process such as that which is routinely applied to various business functions (King and Cleland, 1978), but only infrequently applied to information systems (Porter, 1981) and only rarely applied to information resources. However, the mechanisms for conducting such a process are well developed for other organisational contexts and they are readily transferable to the IR domain.

## Information Resource Assessment

The lower arrow in Figure 11.1 represents 'information resource assessment' (IRA) - a process of using information and knowledge to support the development of the organisation's strategic business direction. In effect, it is the mirror image of 'SP for IR' in the sense that it is the process through which information and knowledge are used to identify strategic comparative advantages and to create and evaluate new strategies - i.e. to influence change in the 'Organisational Strategy Set.'

Figure 11.1 shows that this influence does not come directly from the 'IR Strategy Set', but rather from the IS databases and model bases that have been created to implement the 'IR Strategy Set.'

The basic IRA process is one of identifying information that is crucial, or potentially crucial, to the organisation's strategy set. This may be of the nature of 'new' information that has not previously been used to advantage, or it may be information that has been re-evaluated and updated. Such information and knowledge may be put to use in creating information products or in developing new and more effective business strategies, objectives, or organisational missions.

One variety of IRA influences the creation of information that is available to the firm through its IS. For instance, Dunn and Bradstreet have an on-going creative process of 'inventing' new information products and creating new markets based on analyses of their existing data bases (Business Week, 1981).

However, the creation of information products is only one of the ways in which information can be made to be a strategic resource. King and Cleland (1978) have developed a technique of 'strategic data bases' that may be used to illustrate the way in which IRA can be conducted. The basic idea is that much of the data on which the organisation's strategy may be based is often routinely collected and analysed as 'data' rather than as strategic 'information'. The distinction between data and information may appear to be pedantic, but it is a useful one to be made in this instance.

Data are the numbers, letters and other symbols that are used to represent events, activities, entities, etc. (The best known set of organised data may be the telephone directory.) 'Information' is data that have been evaluated for some use or purpose. (For instance, a name and phone number on a message that says that your offer to purchase a house has been accepted is information rather than data.)

Information is clearly required for the effective support of strategic planning and for the making of good decisions in an organisation. Yet, many of the processes that are directed toward decision support utilise and present data rather than information.

Illustrative of this are the strength-weakness assessments that are frequently made by a firm in support of its strategic decision-making and planning. Most concepts of strategic management and planning incorporate strength-weakness assessment as an important determinant of strategy (Abell and Hammond, 1979). According to these concepts, the firm should base its future strategy on its primary strengths and avoid basing strategy, even implicitly, on weaknesses.

To implement this concept, many firms charge staff planners with doing a 'staff study' of strengths and weaknesses. The predictable result of such a study is often a voluminous report that more represents data than it does information.

The same is true in other areas of critical information that are essential to the development of effective business strategy. Environmental opportunities and risks are routinely assessed and reported in the form of voluminous data that are not easy to use in the strategy-making process. Indeed, it may be argued that such reports cannot realistically be directly used in strategy formulation and assessment.

Formal models may be well used in providing such strategic decision support. For instance, models may 'automatically' review companies for their 'acquisition potential' - the degree to which their acquisition would serve to enhance the goals of the firm. However, the effective use of such models requires the input of criteria that can only be generated by the organisation's managers.

These 'acquisition criteria', like strengths and weaknesses, environmental opportunities, and a variety of other strategic information must be developed through organisational processes that are here termed 'IRA'. 'Strategic data bases' (King and Zaltman, 1981) represent one way to implement IRA. They are concise statements of the most significant strategic parameters that will guide the use of the models that are in the IS and their application to the development of strategy. A set of criteria to be used in the evaluation of acquisition candidates is a strategic data base (SDB) if it is developed through an organisational process that ensures that the different points of view of the managers of various functions and product-market groups have been taken into account, that there is a reasonable degree of organisational consensus concerning it, and that it is accepted by the organisation's managers. So too may a concise list of organisational strengths and weaknesses be a strategic data base if it has the same characteristics.

To illustrate this, consider, for example, the traditional process that might be used in an organisation to conduct a strength-weakness assessment. This approach commonly relies on staff analysts, who gather data and prepare documents which are to serve as background information for the support of planning activities and strategic choices. Because the planners and analysts who perform these tasks often have neither the managerial expertise nor the authority to make the significant choices that are involved in any information evaluation process, the typical output of such an exercise is a document which seems to have been prepared on the basis of 'not leaving anything out'.

Such an emphasis on ensuring that nothing relevant is omitted rather than on attempting to distinguish the most strategically relevant information from the mass of less relevant serves only to perpetuate the existing state of affairs regarding the informational support provided to managers at all levels: top executives and planners are deluged with irrelevant information, while at the same time they are unable to find elements of information which are crucial to the identification of comparative advantages and to the determination of strategy (King and Cleland, 1978).

The 'strategic data base' approach to implementing IRA, on the other hand, involves the institutionalisation of on-going processes in which task forces, each of which is made up of managers representing various of the parochial interests within the organisation, are charged with gathering and evaluating the data in strategic areas such as strength-weakness analysis, acquisition criteria, etc. In effect, these task forces use the information resources of the organisation to change and up-date its organisational strategy set. Such 'strategic data bases' as they produce represent information in its most valuable form rather than data since, in this process, large quantities of data have been evaluated and condensed to a form which can be feasibly used in the direct support of strategic decision-making.

The strength-weakness SDB may be used as an illustration. A task force, composed of key managers in each of the major functional and product sub-units of the organisation, is charged with developing a concise concensus list of the most important strengths on which the company (business) should base its future and the most significant weaknesses on which it should avoid having its future become dependent. Thus, a team is given the job of producing the strength-weakness 'answers' and of making the strategic information choices of those strengths and weaknesses on which the business' future will depend.

This team of managers, supported by staff, is charged with arriving at conclusions concerning a specified approximate number (usually from 10 to 15) of the most important strengths and weaknesses which should influence the future of the organisation.

The development of conclusions on the 10 to 15 most important organisational strengths and weaknesses can be, as any experienced manager knows, a difficult task, when it involves managers representing various organisational interests and points of view. Developing a twenty page list of strengths and weaknesses could be accomplished relatively easily, but a list of the 10 to 15 most significant requires substantial analysis, debate and negotiation among the various individuals and interest areas that are involved. This is so both because of the judgements which are needed and the potential organisational impact which such a list will inevitably have as it is used in the development of strategy.

The strength-weakness SDB that may be so developed is clearly a substantial basis for assessing potential comparative advantages and for evaluating proposed strategies. For instance, once such an SDB is in place, proposed strategies can be screened using it as a standard, in a somewhat mechan ical fashion, just as a proposed acquisition candidate might be 'automatically' screened using an 'acquisition criterion' SDB that has been similarly developed. In the case of the strength-weakness SDB, this would be done through the routine application of a set of questions:

(a) Which specific strength of our firm does the proposed strategy build on?
(b) What is the relative importance of each strength to using the proposed strategy in achieving the firm's goal's?
(c) Does the proposed strategy implicitly or explicitly assume the existence of some strength that the firm does not possess?
(d) Is the proposed strategy explicitly or implicitly dependent on <u>any</u> weakness, even though it may be <u>primarily</u> based on strengths?

This illustration of a strength-weakness SDB process illustrates the information resources assessment process of Figure 11.1. It is a routine organisational process that is used to translate the informational resources of the organisation into sources of potential strategic comparative advantage.

It is, in effect, the mirror-image of the 'strategic planning for information resources' process which makes the reverse transformation to ensure that business strategies are supported by appropriate information and knowledge bases.

## SUMMARY

The notion of information as a strategic resource is only recently coming to achieve a degree of reality in organisations. The opportunities for greater achievements will be greatly enhanced by the explosion of technology which is taking place in the offices and work-stations of business firms and other organisations.

As this occurs, it will be necessary to create systematic organisational processes that will enhance the likelihood of making information into a strategic organisational resource. Here, two such processes have been described and illustrated.

'Strategic planning for information resources' is a process that serves to ensure that the organisation's business strategy is supported by its information resource. 'Information resource assessment' is the process that serves to alter the organisation's business strategy on a direct and continuing basis that draws on the information resources.

Clearly, the two processes will not be separate and distinct in every organisation. If a firm has an established data base, the determination of strategy-relevant criteria for screening acquisition candidates may be organised as a part of the IRA process, for example. However, a firm that has now such a data base will find that it must perform the same analytic steps, probably at a less sophisticated level, as a part of its SP for IR process. Thus, each of the two processes complements the other, and it is only through the institution of both generic processes - although not necessarily in the precise form described here - that information will be systematically made to be a strategic organisational resource.

## REFERENCES


Abell, D. F. and Hammond, J.S. (1979) Strategic Marketing Planning, Prentice Hall

Anthony, R. N., Dearden, J. and Vancil, R.F. (1965) Management Control Systems, Richard D. Irwin, Homewood, Ill.

Bell, D. (1973) The Coming of Post Industrial Society, Basic Books, New York, 1973

Branscomb, L. M. (1981) 'The Electronic Library', Journal of Communications, Winter, pp. 143-50

Business Week, (1981) 'How D & B Organizes for a New Product Blitz', November 16, 87-90

Coleman, R. J. and Riley, M.J. (1972) 'The Organizational Impact of MIS', Journal of Systems Management, March

Davis, R. and Lenat, D.B. (1982) Knowledge-Based Systems in Artificial Intelligence, McGraw-Hill, New York

DPMA Educational Foundation (1981) Computer Information Systems Curriculum, pp. 115-26

Drucker, P. M.(1965) The Age of Discontinuity, Harper and Row, New York

Dutta, B. K. and King, W.R. (1980) 'A Competitive Scenario Modeling System', Management Science, 26 (3), 261-273

Grant, J. H. and King, W.R. (1982) The Logic of Strategic Planning, Little Brown, Boston, Mass.

IBM (1981) Business Systems Planning: Information Systems Planning Guide, GE 20-0-527-3, Third Edition, July

Kaiser K. and King, W.R. (1982) 'The Manager-Analyst Interface in System Development', MIS Quarterly, 6 (1), 49-59

Keen, P. G. W. and Scott Morton, M.S. (1979) Decision Support Systems: An Organizational Perspective, Addison Wesley, Reading, Mass.

King, W. R. (1978) 'Strategic Planning for MIS', MIS Quarterly, 2 (1), 23-67

King W. R. and Cleland, D.I. (1977) 'Manager Analyst Interaction in MIS', Business Horizons, 14 (2), 59-68

King, W. R. and Cleland, D. I. (1978) 'A New Method for Strategic Systems Planning', Business Horizons, 18 (4), 55-64

King, W. R. and Zaltman, G. (1981) Marketing Scientific and Technical Information, Westview Press, Boulder, Colorado

King W. R. and Zmud, R. (1981) 'MIS: Policy Planning, Strategic Planning and Operational Planning', Proceedings Second International Conference on Information Systems, Boston, Mass.

Laurie, E. J. (1979) Computers, Automation and Society, Richard D. Irwin, Homewood, Ill.

McClean, E. and Soden, J.V. (1977) Strategic Planning for MIS John Wiley, New York

Nolan, R. L. (1977) 'Managing the Crises in Data Processing', Harvard Business Review, March-April, 115-126

Porter, M. E. (1981) Competitive Strategy, Free Press, New York

USDHEW (1973) Records Computers and the Rights of Citizens Report of the Secretary's Advisory Committee on Automated Personal Data Systems, U.S.Department of Health, Education and Welfare, July

Westin, A. F. and Baker, M.A. (1972) Data Banks in a Free Society, Quadrangle Books, New York

Whisler, T. L. (1970) The Impact of Computers on Organizations, Praeger, New York

# 12. Organisational Networks: The Structural Imperative of the Information Age*

by William E Halal

## INTRODUCTION

A prophetic event occurred in 1983 when Time magazine chose the personal computer as 'Man of the Year' to signal a major step toward the coming Information Age. Suddenly, computers were no longer esoteric devices used by scientists, corporations, and bright kids - they began entering ordinary offices and homes by the millions, irrevocably transforming organisational structures from the machine-like hierarchies of the industrial past into organic networks that are compatible with the flow of knowledge.

The hierarchical pyramid has been the most striking symbol of social structure since ancient times, while later it was perfected to build what Galbraith (1967) called the 'technostructure' of experts who run the 'New Industrial State'. Hierarchy is such a basic Western concept that it appears on the $1 bill as a 'pyramid of life' topped by the eye of God, and most of us automatically believe success can only be reached by climbing to 'the top'. Socialist countries have carried the idea even further because planned economies are managed by a single hierarchical system, as if General Motors were to run the entire U.S.

But recent events indicate that the great pyramids of business, government, and other major institutions are collapsing. The economic crisis of 1980-82 forced firms to lay off blue collar workers and middle managers whose work can now be done by robots and computerised information systems, portending the elimination of the bottom and middle layers of the pyramid (Business Week, 1983a). Droves of brilliant young people like Steve Jobs, the founder of Apple Computer, are shunning big companies to start their own firms. Great empires like AT&T are disaggregating into smaller units, some of the largest corporations are

---

* Adapted from the author's book, The New Capitalism (New York: Wiley, 1986).

threatened with extinction, and even the biggest hierarchy in America - the U.S. Government - is under fire, proving that size alone is no longer an asset but a liability.

So after centuries of faithful obedience to the rule of hierarchy, these giant monoliths are tottering, their lower halves are vanishing, and the remainder is breaking up into small pieces. 'Rigid hierarchical structures have begun to crumble at the best-managed companies,' said Business Week (1983a). In a few years, the great organisational pyramids that once formed the foundation of the Industrial Epoch may seem like ancient, decaying monuments of a vanishing culture that worshipped machines.

This chapter describes how the exploding complexity of the Information Age is transforming hierarchical organisations into flexible networks composed of loosely connected ventures. The large bureaucracies of the 'Old Capitalism' produced concentrations of power that made a fiction of the ideals of individual freedom and market competition. But now the organic principles of creative enterprise are finally coming to flower as progressive corporations restructure modern economies to provide the innovative change needed to pioneer a difficult new frontier.

## COMPLEXITY IN THE INFORMATION AGE

The computer could not have arrived at a better time because it is desperately needed to manage the enormous complexity of a new economic era. A vast frontier is being opened up as information technology spreads like wildfire to fundamentally alter the technological base of modern society. Routine work is being eliminated, thereby shifting attention from the old 'internal' orientation of operating 'core technologies' to an 'external' focus on 'boundary interaction'. The result is to transform organisations into automated systems embedded within a turbulent set of economic, social, and political problems. The most critical task now is to integrate institutions into the larger social system from which they derive their very life.

Within that larger system, a more skilled work force must be managed using new forms of leadership. An ethic of 'less is more' requires better control of environmental pollution and energy usage. Society has become more diverse and now includes working women, a maturing baby-boom, a melange of races, and a large body of older people. Growing interest in self-fulfilment is producing a higher order of personal values and life styles. Future growth will increasingly focus on developing efficient transportation, powerful information systems, better health care, more effective education, and other personal needs that improve the quality of life. Scientific and technological progress is producing revolutionary breakthroughs that will add even further to these difficult changes already underway. Political demands are growing among sophisticated groups like labour, customers, investors, the public and minorities. A burgeoning world economy is heightening competition and escalating resource demands by many orders of magnitude.

All these forces are creating an extremely complex social order that is going to be very difficult to manage harmoniously in the decades ahead. Consider, for example, the following signs suggesting an enormous increase in diversity. It is estimated that there are now more than 700 different models of cars in the U.S., 200 brands of cigarettes, 4,000 magazines, and 9,000 radio stations. A mass mailing firm offers 55,000 different lists to its clients. The computerised U.S. Census is broken down into 250,000 distinct groups of people. Business Week (1983b) observed: 'A nation that once shared homogeneous buying tastes has splintered into many different consumer groups - each with special needs and interests'.

## THE CUTTING EDGE OF INFORMATION TECHNOLOGY

The consequence is that this new domain of economic activity no longer concerns physical tasks involving the manufacture of goods, but the use of sophisticated information systems to manage complex institutional relations. As Stafford Beer (1975) noted, 'The old world was characterized by the need to manage things - the new world is characterized by the need to manage complexity.' Journalist Russell Baker poignantly captured this changing nature of modern work life:

> In the common everyday job, nothing is made anymore. Things are now made by machines ... Consider the typical 12-storey glass building in the typical American city. Nothing is made in this building and nothing is repaired ... Still the building is filled with people who think of themselves as working. At any given moment of the day, perhaps one-third of them will be talking into telephones. Most of these conversations will be about paper, for paper is what occupies nearly everyone in this building. Some jobs in this building require men to fill paper with words. There are persons who type neatly on paper and persons who read the paper and jot notes in the margins. Some persons make copies of paper and other persons deliver paper. There are persons who file paper and persons who unfile paper. Some persons mail paper ... Some persons confer about paper. In the grandest of offices, men approve of some paper and disapprove of other paper. The elevators are filled throughout the day with ... vital men carrying paper to be discussed with the other vital men (Baker, 1970).

In an age when information technology is rapidly making it possible to acquire, process, store, retrieve and disseminate virtually any form of information from communication networks that span the globe, the implications should be obvious. A revolution is imminent in the way organisations work. The central fact of our age is that the cutting edge of science is now developing the technology to harness this flow of information that has become the most crucial commodity in a modern Knowledge Society - just as the assembly line harnessed the power of physical technology to create an Industrial Society. Jean-Jacques Sevan-Schreiber (1980) noted the significance: 'information is destined to hold the place that energy one held in yesterday's industrial society.' Consider some examples of how this new source of power is rapidly becoming the focus of economic activity:

> Apple Computer Company grew from a small garage operation in 1977 to become the first company to join the Fortune 500 in five years. In 1982 it ranked 411th in sales, 201st in profit, and 26th in return on equity.
>
> 10 million computers are being sold annually, in contrast to a short time ago when only a few expensive machines were used by major corporations and research laboratories. Now big organisations often order computers in quantities of thousands.
>
> Computer sales increased from about $10 billion in 1980 to about $30 billion now, and are estimated to reach about $400 billion before the century is out.
>
> 150 computer makers now compete on the U.S. market alone.
>
> Software is becoming the biggest growth area as 3,000 software firms slash prices to compete. The market is growing by more than 30 per cent per year and should reach $30 billion in 1988.
>
> 80% of the public believes that computers will be as common as telephones, television and dishwashers in the near future.
>
> Electronic memories will become the cheapest means of storing information within this decade, thereby emptying out files, libraries, and other collections of musty old paper we have laboriously collected and shuffled through over many years.
>
> Computer stores first opened in Los Angeles in 1977.

Now dozens of them operate in every major city, just as auto dealerships proliferated a few decades ago when industrialisation began. Nation-wide there are now about 10,000 such stores.

Computer publications have skyrocketed to 46 magazines and 2,400 books within the past few years alone.

Computer blue books that list market prices for used computer equipment are now published, just as blue books organised the thriving market for used cars in the industrial era.

Teleconferencing is being used in more than 200 systems now, and is likely to increase dramatically as the technology improves, the costs of travel increase, and the need for long-range communication grows.

The entire information industry is estimated to exceed $1.4 trillion by 1992, becoming the largest segment of the economy.

There persists a fear that this technology will reduce work to its simple, inhuman basics by driving out the skill of the craftsman. But a long-term perspective shows that this is not true generally. The main change has been the level of 'abstraction' in work. In an Agrarian Society the vast majority of people worked at menial task on farms, in an Industrial Era they tended machines, and now in an Information Age they handle knowledge. Some of this new 'knowledge work' is also menial and boring, of course, but routine tasks are precisely what computers are good at, leaving humans free to handle more demanding jobs. About half of young people attend college today, producing for the first time in history a society composed largely of a professional class. 'The central occupational category in the society today is the professional and technical,' points out Daniel Bell (1973). George Beitzel (1983), a Senior Vice President at IBM, estimates, 'By 1989 there will be 60 million office workers comprised of 40 million managers and professionals.'

The long-term trend is fairly clear. Working life was earlier characterised by hard physical labour and repetitive routine however, today most jobs are fraught with difficult interpersonal relations, information overload, and other such stressful, confusing problems that defy our crude institutional mechanisms. These tasks are creating a modern equivalent of 'economic man' who is not primarily occupied with physical concerns but with social and intellectual interests - what could be thought of as a new prototype of 'intellectual man'. 'Where once we stood simply on the edge of the production line,' said Douglas Davis (1973), 'we stand now on the edge of consciousness.'

## COMPUTERS REPLACE AUTOMOBILES

The significance of this change is symbolised by the replacement of the automobile with the computer as the primary tool of modern society. Time (1983) said, 'The enduring American love affair with the automobile is now being transformed into a giddy passion for the personal computer', and Business Week (1983c) proclaimed, 'From the pre-World War I years until the mid-1960s, the automobile was the engine that made the U.S. economy grow. Nowadays, the major stimulant may be the microchip.'

Because the automobile was the principle machine about which the industrial age was organised, its influence on American life has been pervasive, but so ordinary that we scarcely even notice the effects. Auto making once used roughly one-sixth of the labour, capital, and other resources of the U.S. to produce an equivalent portion of the GNP, which is why the decline of this industry alone is a major cause of the economic crisis. Cars have also produced a sprawl of roads and parking areas that cover vast portions of our cities with concrete and asphalt, sprinkled liberally with gas stations, billboards, and shopping centres, and making pollution and traffic congestion a way of life (Cornish, 1977).

Automobiles will continue to be used in the Information Age, of course, but the growth of these "industrial tools" peaked in the 1970s and may continue to decline (Brown, 1984). Where once cars were indulged as an alter ego of Americans, now in an era of limited energy most people simply want a practical means of transportation. As the auto declines, the use of computers is becoming dominant, thereby transforming the entire structure of the economy. In an industrial order that focused on physical objects, the lives of most people were organised about a series of moves to conduct business and personal affairs: from home - to their place of work - to shops - to schools - to hospitals - and so on. In an age of the computer, the information contained within these institutions will instead come to us through powerful new information systems. 'Now, increasingly there will be alternative ways to meet and "share a common experience",' says Peter Drucker (1980). 'The first impact will probably be a sharp drop in business travel.'

As a result, institutions are no longer discrete collections of persons meeting in some physical location, but complex information systems that connect people in myriad economic and social relationships. Alvin Toffler (1980) compared this transition to the earlier shift from an agrarian to an industrial era:

> Watching masses of peasants scything a field three hundred years ago, only a madman would have dreamed that the time would soon come when the fields would be depopulated, when people would crowd into urban factories to earn their daily bread. Today it takes an act of courage to suggest that our biggest factories and office towers may, within our lifetimes, stand half empty, reduced to use as ghostly warehouses or converted into living space.

It should be noted that the vacancy rate in office buildings has been increasing dramatically during the past few years, causing building values and construction to plummet, which may be an ominous sign that such changes are already occurring (Guenther, 1983a, 1983b).

## THE REVOLUTIONARY POWER OF INFORMATION

Obviously, it will take decades for these changes to unfold, and nobody fully understands how they will work out. But the one thing that is certain is that the new social order will be far more complex and turbulent, and that information technology offers the main hope for managing this spiralling growth of rich diversity that would otherwise become uncontrollable disorder. Even now the growing power of computerised information systems is enabling scores of institutions to collect and analyse huge amounts of data on their clients from a strategic perspective. 'The role of top leadership in large American business is shifting - to that of the manager of the information system,' noted consultant Robert Greenleaf (1977).

Furthermore, information is far more powerful than physical technology because it forms the invisible links that bind a society together. Many scholars have pointed out how the revolutionary effects of television, the computer, and telecommunications networks allow humans to interact faster and more widely, they accelerate the rate of technological innovation, extend our range of experience, and amplify our ability to control events. Studies indicate that the bulk of economic progress is not due to capital investment or other physical factors, but the result of better education, technical knowledge, creative innovation, and other forms of information that are now growing exponentially (Bell, 1973).

Adam Osborne (1979), creator of the portable computer, claims the information revolution will radically transform modern economies: 'Of all jobs in the industrial world today, perhaps half will be eliminated during the next twenty-five years ... Entire industries ... have been severely crippled or wiped out by competition from a quarter they never anticipated ... that is the consequence of the revolution'.

Osborne himself became a victim of this revolution later when his own firm failed. And Clive Sinclair, the English entrepreneur who invented the first pocket-sized electronic calculator, offers the stunning forecast: 'The 1990s will differ from the 1970s as profoundly as the 19th century from the 18th' (Osnos, 1983). As the inexorable rise of the Information Age enriches our environment with more accurate information, greater knowledge, increased power, broader choices, and heightened awareness, we all contribute to the forces that drive social evolution in this new direction. An essay that appeared in a small Berkeley underground newspaper captures the profound meaning of this new form of power:

> Communication systems will spread like a raging fire, out of control, beyond prediction, the mirror image of a bursting comet. Every man, every woman will soon be able to be a star in the heavens and will of his own mind, and as free to spread his own message as the limits of the imagination permit. Freed from the technological constrictions of antiquated communication structures, the mass will vanish, the individualistic appear, and a renaissance of the creative spirit will dawn. (Spencer, 1979)

This fundamental change presents a crucial warning that modern economies have entered an era of unusually complex, difficult, constantly changing relationships which cannot be mastered using traditional structures. Present hierarchical institutions are pervaded by a sense of ineptness, a chronic aridity of thought, and a deep emptiness of the spirit that has produced widespread stagnation in productivity, innovation, and commitment, along with grumblings of rebellion and despair. But a quiet trickle of fresh new ideas is flowing from creative entrepreneurs that promises to build into a wave of change to sweep away these obsolete pyramids. The existing organisational infrastructure was built on the old foundations of the assembly line, and now computerised information systems are beginning to create an upheaval in the economic order that will alter the structure, behaviour, and texture of society as a whole. Business Week (1983c) warned:

> Considering the impetus behind the electronics revolution, these early changes may represent only the first tremors of an earthquake.

## CONFEDERATIONS OF ENTREPRENEURS

This exploding complexity of the Information Age produces an unyielding imperative that demands its own structural form, just as the Industrial Age produced an inevitable fit between physical technology and the hierarchical pyramids that governed the past. Alfred Chandler (1962) showed that the task of creating efficient production systems caused business to evolve from single manufacturing plants into vertically integrated organisations that later diversified into huge multidivision enterprises - all arranged in a hierarchical system. These pyramids of centralised power were good for providing rational control of mechanistic tasks, but now a new structural form must provide quick, flexible, strategic responses to adapt to the constant change, rich diversity, and endless novelty of a Post-Industrial Era. The management of this unprecedented level of complexity is the key strategic challenge institutions face today, so it dictates the central requirement for the organisational structures that are evolving. Churchman (1977) expressed it best: 'The spirit of our age is to hit complexity straight on, taking it for what it is.'

Various intellectual fields all indicate the same 'technological imperative'. In management science, scholars agree on the central principle that institutions - like all other organisms - must adapt to a more complex, turbulent environment by developing equally complex, organic structures. In general systems theory, a 'law of requisite variety' holds that the degree of environmental complexity any system faces must be matched by an equivalent degree of complexity in its form of control. And Alvin Toffler (1980) expressed a similar concept in terms of information 'The more diverse the civilization the more information must flow between its constituent parts.'

How will we hope to create this more sophisticated model of organisation? By bringing the principles of free enterprise that govern the external marketplace directly into large organisational structures themselves. Thomas Gilmore (1983) of the Wharton School posed the problem as follows:

> We can no longer control people by authority and bureaucracy. Ways must be found to create real entrepreneurial opportunities for managers who want them within corporate frameworks. I see that as a major challenge for the American economic system.

The structural form that is emerging to provide this entrepreneurial capability is the network, primarily because networks offer a higher level of more sophisticated control by which the swelling turbulence of an Information Age can be managed. 'The network is the institution of our time,' observed Marilyn Ferguson (1980), and John Naisbitt (1982) predicted, 'In the future, institutions will be organized according to a management system based on the networking model.'

Networks are growing all about:

> Business networks are being formed through the growing use of computerised financial and communication systems that provide electronic banking, data storage and retrieval, teleconferencing and other information handling functions.
>
> Personal networks are evolving through linkages of people sharing common interests, associations, and other relationships to the point that a directory of networks is published.
>
> The USA as a whole is being transformed into what Starr Roxanne Hiltz and Murray Turoff (1978) describe as a 'Network Nation': 'In place of a nation or society as a collection of communities, we need to think of it as a complex set of overlapping networks.'
>
> Russia is even feeling these changes according to a Soviet computer scientist: 'The development of communications networks, of data banks and information systems, makes necessary an administration which differs completely from what has gone before - international, non-hierarchical cooperative systems.'

## FIRST STEPS: THE MULTI-DIMENSIONAL MATRIX ARRIVES

Business began the move away from hierarchies and toward networks years ago with the development of a matrix form of organisation. The matrix is defined as a 'multiple command system'. It comprises 'a new species of business organisation' that 'represents a sharp break with traditional forms of business', says Walter Wriston, former Chairman of Citicorp.

As Table 12.1 shows, about two-thirds of 25 firms in a study I conducted (Halal, 1980) were structured along more than one organisational dimension: functional areas, corporate staff units, product divisions, project teams, client or marketing groups, geographic regions, and the like. Strong controversy persists over the matrix, but it is an established fact today because most large organisations find it necessary to operate different types of units that cut across one another. One company in this study, General Electric, summed up the rationale this way:

> We've highlighted matrix organisation (because it's) a bellwether of things to come - all of us are going to have to learn how to utilise organisation to prepare managers to increasingly deal with higher levels of complexity and ambiguity in situations where they have

**Table 12.1: Multiple Hierarchies in Large Corporations**

| | Hierarchical Dimensions of Organisation | | | |
|---|---|---|---|---|
| | Functional Areas of Expertise | Products or Projects | Clients or Markets | Geographic Regions |
| Exxon | * | | | * |
| General Motors | * | * | | |
| Texaco | * | * | | * |
| IBM | | * | | * |
| General Electric | * | * | | |
| Atlantic Richfield | | * | | |
| Dow Chemical | | * | | |
| United Technologies | * | * | * | |
| Boeing | * | * | | |
| Xerox | | * | * | |
| TRW | | * | | |
| Texas Instruments | | * | | |
| Crown-Zellerbach | | * | | |
| Mead | | * | | |
| Hewlett-Packard | | * | | |
| Digital Equipment | * | * | * | * |
| Clarck Equipment | | * | | |
| Rexnord | * | * | | * |
| Bankamerica | | | * | * |
| Citicorp | | | * | * |
| Mariott | | * | | * |
| Comsat | * | * | | |
| Walt Disney | | * | | |
| Hoffman-LaRoche | * | * | | |

Source: Halal, W.E. (1980) Strategic Planning in Major US Corporations, General Motors Report

> to get results from people and components not under their direct control - where so many complex, conflicting interests must be balanced. (Davis and Lawrence, 1978)

## THE PARADOX OF ACHIEVING CONTROL THROUGH FREEDOM

But there are many approaches to matrix organisation. Early applications were 'centralised grids' in which two command systems simultaneously controlled operating units, producing not greater flexibility but great rigidity by compounding problems through two overlapping bureaucratic hierarchies. Texas Instruments, for example, was recently forced to free its profit centres from the stifling effects of a 2-dimensional grid controlled by 'strategic' and 'operating' executives. One TI operating manager complained:

> You cannot be an entrepreneur and make great things happen while doing review after review after review They've created a paperwork mill that makes it absolutely impossible to respond to anything that moves quickly. (Business Week, 1982b; 1983d)

This centralised grid type of matrix fails to provide the flexibility that is so badly needed because it exemplifies the worst feature of the old 'rational', or 'mechanistic', model of management. By having two hierarchies rather than one, the grid highlights conflicting demands that form a perennial dilemma facing all institutions: the need to provide freedom for fostering innovation, while maintaining adequate control to safeguard against disorder. Some executives abdicate their responsibility and permit anarchy and poor performance to go unchecked, but the more typical response is a confining, even dictatorial, form of control that strangles the very life out of institutions. Robert Levison, an operating executive at a major company, described eloquently the effects on managers:

> As a businessman I am sick and tired of the waste - not only the waste of opportunities and money, but the more tragic waste of the people who are managers - that our present highly centralized forms of management create ... big companies have become almost socialistic in their policies and practices ... the division manager is summoned to corporate headquarters every so often for an 'in depth review'. Typically, you have 25 corporate executives in the room with you, staff nitpickers who never had to meet a payroll ... These people sit and listen to you expound about your operation like drama critics called in to review a tottering Broadway production ... The payoff? Humiliated division

> managers, who learn once more that their job is to execute orders, not to make decisions ... by the time the whole damn thing got cooked through, salted, spiced and chopped up, we had nothing much left but a hodge-podge of numbers, and the task now was to juggle the numbers and make them come out the way the experts thought they ought to come out ... management people throughout the United States (should) rise up in rebellion. (Levison, 1983).

The underlying cause seems to be that the old concept of hierarchical control is so entrenched in our society, most executives feel a strong obligation to ensure subordinates behave in an 'orderly' manner. But, as the difficulty of coping with a complex organisation and escalating turbulence in the environment increases, this threatening disorder is dealt with by redoubled efforts to impose more detailed hierarchical controls, creating an impossible situation in which the typical executive tries vainly to gain a Godlike omniscience in knowing 'each sparrow that falls'. 'Part of the macho self-image of some CEOs is the conviction that a good manager must know in detail the results of divisions and units,' writes Thomas Naylor, an economics professor.

Not only is this 'mechanistic' approach overwhelming, but it dooms the organisation to mediocrity as well because all 'unapproved' behaviour becomes suspect, leading to a sterility of thought that is anathema to innovation. One of the most debilitating features of institutional life today is that most large organisations suppress creative disorder and dissent, causing executives to be surrounded by 'yes men' while those with new ideas and critical views are regarded as malcontents and whistle blowers. Peter Drucker (1976) summed up the problem with one of his bits of wisdom: 'So much of what we call management consists in making it difficult for people to work.' Peters and Waterman describe the underlying beliefs of this old philosophy which produces rigid complexity, time-consuming committees, deadening analyses, and endless approvals from higher authority:

> Big is better ... make sure everything is carefully and formally coordinated ... the manager's job is decision making ... analyze everything ... produce fat planning volumes ... get rid of the disturbers of the peace ... control everything ... keep things tidy ... specify the organization structure in great detail ... write long job descriptions. (Peters and Waterman, 1982)

This approach may have delighted 'organisation men' who saw the management process as an end in itself, but in an age crying out for entrepreneurial action these elegant but creaky old immobile structures are as outmoded as the tailfins on a '57 Chrysler. A centralised control system at Xerox was so stifling that operating managers could not modify design details (like the size of a light bulb in a copier) without complicated approvals; 'What should have taken two weeks to a month took two years,' one lamented. Ford was labouring under 15 levels of management - while Toyota used 6. A manager described the typical response: 'If we had to go through channels, we would never get anything done.' At Levi Strauss a groaning organisational behemoth became so unwieldy that one manager admitted: 'We had enough staff and organisation to run General Motors'. James Affleck, the CEO of American Cyanamid Co., cautioned executives:

> We will have to recognise that no chief executive or management team can or should attempt to manage the activities of thousands, or hundreds of thousands, of individuals under their nominal control eight hours a day. That cannot be done any more than their thoughts can be managed. (Affleck, 1978)

The apparent paradox of achieving both control and freedom has always troubled leaders, but creative executives understand that the key to its resolution is to combine tight control of performance with freedom of operation - what Peters and Waterman (1982) call 'simultaneous loose-tight properties'. The central principle is that both control and freedom are enhanced by allowing individuals and units to select assignments to be accomplished on a contractual basis. They are then held accountable for agreed upon goals, while also being free to achieve results as they see fit. 'The basic orientation of the entire organisation must be psychologically attuned to results,' said an executive at Dow Corning, (Goggins, 1973). Controls need not be strictly technical or financial, but could also rely on creating a strong organisational culture which employs the 'spirit' of the institution to guide behaviour.

A wealth of research evidence shows people are very capable of defining their own roles, selecting units to work in, and choosing their co-workers, thereby producing 'bottom-up' structures that offer far better productivity, flexibility, and innovative adaptation to complex environments than 'top-down' structures - what Karl Weick calls 'self-designed systems'. Operating units then become self-managing organisations which are easier to control. Another result is to instill a sense of commitment that is vital for good organisational performance - to create what Russell Ackoff calls 'purposeful systems'. Peter Vaill, who has pioneered in the study of high-performing systems, stated: 'The definition and clarification of purposes is a prominent feature of every high performing system I have ever investigated.' Peters and Waterman (1982) found the most creative projects were usually hidden away in some small illicit 'skunk works' run by a few eccentric but highly motivated geniuses. (Van Zelst, 1952; Galbraith and Nathanson, 1978; Weick, 1977; Ackoff and Emery, 1972; Vaill, 1982)

By maintaining central control over results but decentralising operations, the paradox of control versus freedom is resolved to enhance both goals. In fact, a superior form of control is achieved, not at the expense of freedom, but through freedom, by allowing large numbers of self-managed enterprises to nibble away at complex problems. Richard Cornuelle (1975), a former executive at the National Association of Manufacturers, described this philosophy as 'Demanaging America' - 'In this way the process is self-managing. It works without authority, and it works sensibly, creating order out of potential chaos.'

Although the concept may appear to be dramatically different, in fact it simply represents an extension of the trend that began decades ago when growing corporations found it necessary to decentralise into semi-autonomous product divisions.

Major forces are now relentlessly restructuring big corporations in this direction. Foreign competition is producing great pressures to eliminate unneeded middle managers and permit greater freedom for innovation, while the development of powerful new information systems is encouraging a more effective form of decentralised control. Corporations like Firestone, Crown-Zellerbach, Chrysler, Brunswick and Xerox have cut their middle management ranks by as much as 40 per cent. Many of these firms have eliminated levels in the middle of the hierarchy so that product division managers report directly to the CEO. Some establish a new rule of thumb limiting the hierarchy to no more than 6 levels between the CEO and any employee. One executive described the changes this way: 'We made the layers because we couldn't move information fast enough. If information becomes available instantaneously, then you have to ask why you need all those layers.' Business Week's special issue on 'A New Era For Management' summed up the changes underway:

> As more top managers see that much of the information once gathered by middle managers can be obtained faster, less expensively, and more thoroughly by computers, they have begun to view many middle managers as 'redundant' ... They look on the very fiefdoms they have created as vast cost centres ... Where once they eagerly added to staffs as symbols of their power, today they enviously eye Japanese competitors who all along realised that less meant more ... Corporate structure is changing to let data flow from shop floor to executive suite without

> the editing, monitoring, and second-guessing that had been the middle manager's function...corporate pyramids are flattened, with fewer levels. (Business Week, 1983a)

These reorganisations are not temporary, nor are they minor adjustments. They reflect the beginning of an historic restructuring of large institutions that was anticipated long ago by management scholars like Herbert Simon who foresaw the automation of middle-management, Warren Bennis who proposed the use of organic organisations, and executives like Peter Townsend who rejuvenated Avis by reducing its encrusted Bureaucracy (Simon, 1960; Bennis, 1966; Townsend, 1978).

## BEYOND THE GRID: DECENTRALISED NETWORKS

The concept of control through freedom shows that the primitive matrix of a centralised grid seems to be an intermediate stage between the traditional hierarchy and a full-fledged network. Freedom is the critical element that transforms the matrix from a more constraining bureaurracy into a flexible system. In its mature form, the matrix is decentralised to allow units and individuals to move through the system freely, taking on responsibilities as they choose and drawing on the organisation's capital, facilities, personnel and information to accomplish their task. The responsibility of executives is to define the framework that forms this system, set up a basis of accountability and incentives, and encourage this 'internal market' to allocate resources spontaneously rather than through administrative fiat. Additionally, the advanced matrix may incorporate three or even four dimensions, which increases the variety of units and the degrees of freedom. Digital Equipment and Dow Corning are structured as 4-dimensional matrices, and these firms are known for their innovative managerial systems. An executive at Dow Corning described his organisation this way:

> The single most pressing problem that faces any industrial organization is how to cope with change. The multidimensional organization is designed to combat that problem...We perceive our organization to be a dynamic one, and to date, our experience indicates that we do indeed have the ability to manage change rather than be managed by it. (Goggins, 1973)

Figure 12.1 illustrates schematically a mature matrix network for three dimensions including product, functional, and geographical command structures. The productive heart of the system is the small business units spun off by product divisions as innovative ventures. These ventures operate as profit centres, developing and distributing new products and

**Figure 12.1: Network Formed by a 3-Dimensional Decentralised Matrix**

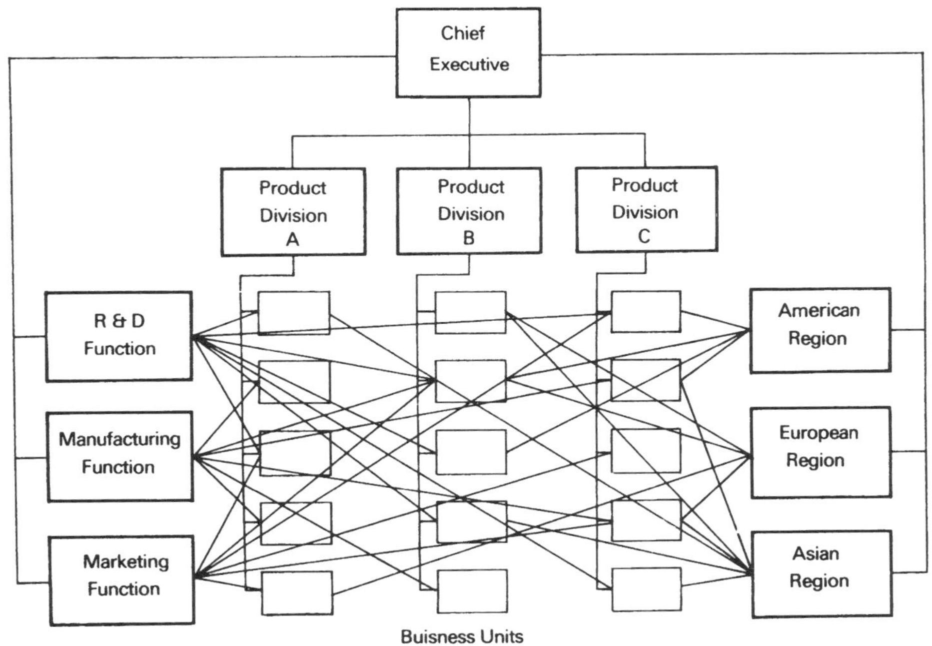

services. Functional units typically recruit, train, and release specialists to work on products and geographic units. They are usually cost centres, but may also sell their advice and assistance to other units using internal transfer prices to become profit centres. Geographic areas may also be profit centres, buying products from product divisions and distributing them to clients in their region, thereby providing the closer, more integrated service that single product divisions cannot. As various units interact in this internal market system, the changing flow of lateral relations constitutes the fluid, organic quality that is uniquely advantageous about a network. From this view, the organisation is no longer seen as a one or two dimensional hierarchy, but as a web of tensions pulling in different directions that are all essential. Numerous examples indicate that this philosophy of decentralisation is catching on:

> Hewlett-Packard holds employees accountable for project results but gives them wide operating latitude. The first has created a 'striking new managerial style - with a uniquely American entrepreneurial spirit'. As one executive described it, 'The financial controls are very tight - what is loose is how (people) choose to meet those goals.'
>
> Tandem Computer has developed an entrepreneurial environment that is easy-going on methods but tough on results. 'Most companies are overmanaged,' said an executive. 'We give (people) a lot of responsibility and tell them where we want them to go. The 1 percent who abuse the freedom we fire. It's that simple.'
>
> Interlake sold its failing steel plants to a new management team that permitted plant managers local control over all major decisions. The newly organised firm, Newport Steel Corporation, sparked a renaissance of entrepreneurial behaviour and commitment that quickly produced a striking turnaround.
>
> TRW has achieved success using a philosophy of management autonomy. A vice president explains, 'We don't legislate anything out of corporate headquarters', while a division manager says, 'It's my responsibility to find ways to grow this business - not the president.'
>
> Xerox has decentralised control of its 24 strategic business units to grant operating managers power to select the products and technologies they feel are most promising, speeding up the process of getting a product to the market from years to months.

> GE has decentralised to allow strategic business units to do their own planning; it has doubled the level of expenditure not requiring authorisation, and extended its incentive system to cover 5,000 managers. The CEO, John Welch, expressed his philosophy this way: 'If you pick the right people and give them an opportunity to spread their wings - and put compensation as a carrier behind it - you (almost) don't have to manage them.'
>
> Eagle-Pitcher claims, 'Decentralization is a virtual religion with us.' The company provides capital, but allows operating managers complete control over budgets, profits, capital investments, marketing, product development and salaries.
>
> Curtice-Burns has a central staff of only 12 people because it allows its seven divisions to operate autonomously. The Chairman says of the risks entailed by his approach, 'We, as managers, have to have failures to learn.'
>
> Business Week, (1983a) summed up the result:
>
> Companies are discarding their organizational charts and simplifying their chains of command. This gives chief executives more flexibility, keener and quicker assessment of performance, clearer and faster lines of action, and a quick grasp of the information needed to run their companies... they are frantically trying to push (decisions) down to those who are closest to the marketplace, giving more autonomy to plant managers, sales people, and engineers...creating environments in which compensation depends on performance and freedom to improve performance provides the psychic reward.

Even these moves toward decentralisation seem likely to pale in comparison to what may come soon as the growth of computerised information systems 'short-circuits' the traditional hierarchy. The inexorable use of manufacturing robots, combined with distributed networks using microcomputers on each desk, all hooked up to teleconferencing systems, should produce an unstructured, changing form of interaction to revolutionise the way institutions work. Consider the following:

> Microcomputers are predicted to become the organising focus of the work habits of 65 per cent of professional workers by 1990.
>
> Fortune 500 Companies are almost all implementing systems that provide computerised data files,

teleconferencing, electronic mail, and other capabilities.

Texas Instruments has installed an information network that links 50 plants in 19 countries in a corporate-wide network that sends 100,000 messages a day at an average cost of 8 cents in less than 10 seconds each.

Bank of America executives in different cities have been holding regular teleconference meetings since 1968, and Aetna has done the same since 1981.

Atlantic Richfield has installed a $17 million teleconferencing system that connects its Los Angeles headquarters with offices around the nation. The company expects to save $10 million per year in travel expenses while providing faster communications.

Ford Motor Company recently held a video conference showing new car models to 18,000 dealers and sales people at 38 sites.

VideoNet in California and various hotel chains represent a new breed of ventures that are now establishing teleconferencing capabilities for commercial use.

As these trends continue, a new electronic freedom to work throughout large organisations should soon become reality. Murray Turoff, the developer of one of the first computerised conferencing systems, outlined the potential for this new medium, 'The beauty of (an electronic information system) is that it does not impose to any great degree a social structure but lets people develop their own.' At Bell Research Laboratories, a trial of computerised conferencing shifted communications among managers from a traditional pattern of funnelling contacts through headquarters to direct lateral contacts among local offices. The former chairman of AT&T, John DeButts, said, 'The Bell System's main aim in seeking to apply the computer to our operations is not efficiency; it is freedom.' Terrence Deal and Allen Kennedy predict that these systems will produce 'an "atomized organization" in which individuals will be connected by the information network and a common culture rather than the organizational chart'.

## THE ENTREPRENEURIAL BOOM

The decentralised network is more than just a 'flexible structure', but an 'entrepreneurial system' that uses its flexibility to encourage the spontaneous formation of innovative ventures. The unavoidable reality is that mergers will continue to concentrate economic power into oligopolies of a few global corporations dominating each industry world-wide, thereby posing an unavoidable challenge of finding a way to overcome the debilitating threat of bureaucracy as organisations grow ever larger. The solution is evolving now as decentralised organic networks spawn multitudes of small, semi-autonomous, self-managed, 'internal' enterprises. Peters and Waterman (1982) found that excellent companies are good at 'chucking' - breaking a complex system into self-contained units or problems that are manageable in size. Here are some examples:

> IBM used a self-contained, autonomous 'independent business unit' (IBU) form to develop its successful personal computer, and the same concept is being applied to 15 other new ventures.
>
> Apple developed its revolutionary Macintosh computer using an 'A team' strategy that emulates the original 'garage' operation which launched the company: a small handpicked group allowed almost complete freedom to work alone within the corporation.
>
> Hewlett-Packard spins off new divisions when they exceed 1500 people to sustain the sense of small, autonomous units. 'If we're going to improve productivity,' argues an executive, 'workers have got to care about their company.'
>
> Texas Instruments has created 9,000 short-lived problem-solving teams to improve various aspects of their operations, and is decentralising into small autonomous profit-centres.
>
> GE scattered production of aircraft engines from a former centralised plant into 8 'satellite' plants.
>
> 3M Company's 52,000 employees are divided into 39 divisions with units that average 270 people to produce a total of 50,000 products. A vice president said, 'We make a conscious effort to keep our units as small as possible because we think it helps keep them flexible and vital. One consistent request we get from our people is that they be allowed to run a business of their own.'
>
> Dana Corporation created the 'store manager' concept to give 90 factory managers almost complete autonomy for all aspects of their operations.

Proctor & Gamble uses the brand manager role to encourage entrepreneurial control of each product in their line.

Crown-Zellerbach has integrated all functions (credit, labour, marketing and sales) into its 16 container plants, producing an increase in productivity and decreasing costs.

Kollmorgan, a hi-tech company of 4,500 employees, consists of 13 divisions that are further decentralised into autonomous product teams. The company strives to create a 'spirit of freedom, equality, mutual trust and respect', which has been so successful that sales have doubled every three and a half years.

Convergent Technologies creates a 'strike force' to take on new ventures as a 'company-within-a-company'.

Nucor Corporation proves the same concept works with steel-making. The company built 7 mini-mills using teams of 20-30 employees who install each plant and then hire additional workers. 30 small 'bonus groups' are also used to take on short-lived projects for bonuses that may double their base pay.

This trend toward small-scale enterprise is destined to increase because the soft technologies that will dominate the future do not require concentrations of capital and economies of scale that characterised the Industrial Era. Providing services, the development of software, R&D, information handling, and other forms of soft growth lend themselves to small ventures. As some of the above examples show, even manufacturing plants can become smaller, more efficient 'focused factories' that minimise bureaucracy because automation permits economies of scale as low as a few hundred units. Average size of new plants decreased from 644 employees in 1970 to 210 in 1980. For instance, the new 'mini-steel mills' have enjoyed such strong growth that their share of domestic steel production has increased to almost 20 per cent. New 'mini-photo labs' that operate locally to provide 1 hour colour film service are springing up by the thousands to capture a growing share of the market from giants like Kodak. Beer is being made increasingly in 'microbreweries' that can produce small runs of more expensive brands for special market niches. Small scale farming is also becoming common among farm entrepreneurs who grow speciality crops for direct sale to customers.

The growth opportunities in this new domain of the Information Age are virtually limitless, so a rising number of entrepreneurial ventures is underway that is simply the beginning of a huge boom of hi-tech innovation that will sweep through modern economies for decades. In 1950, the total number of new ventures was 93,000 per year, while it has now increased to more than 600,000 per year. During this same time, roughly half of the Fortune 500 firms disappeared through mergers or failures. A splurge of investment in venture capital has taken place recently as 900 new companies raised $13 billion in stock equity during 1983 alone, which is nine times greater than in 1982 and more than the entire period since 1972. A GE executive believes, 'We are at the tip of the iceberg in the exploitation and application of technology' and a researcher at the Battelle Institute says, 'We see a sort of resurgence in getting technology into products across the whole economy.'

Big corporations are starting to respond to this boom not only to take advantage of a good thing, but simply to combat the threat these new ventures pose. Goliath IBM was forced to move quickly to regain its dominance in computers after the David of Apple Computer took the lead in the exploding future of personal computers. Other large corporations like GE, TRW, Exxon, GM and Xerox are frantically searching for ways to establish a claim on the exciting new businesses that are popping up like spring flowers, using licensing deals, capital investment, and joint ventures. GE alone is investigating $100 million in 30 startup companies that look promising.

But these are attempts to cash in on the success of independent entrepreneurs, whereas the real challenge facing big corporations is to make their own organisations hospitable for innovation. When Exxon bought its way into the computer business, its heavy hand stifled the creativity of that young enterprise. Xerox drove away its promising Diablo Systems and Schugart Associates divisions because of highly centralised controls. A former Intel manager who left to start out on his own, recalls, 'If I wanted to do a new project at Intel, I had to visit all those committees.' James Brian Quinn at MIT observes:

> Many corporations fail to tolerate the creative fanatic who has been the driving force behind most major innovations ... he is obnoxious, impatient, egotistic and perhaps a bit irrational in organizational terms.

On the other hand, these young entrepreneurs actually need the company as much as it needs them. Starting a new business is fraught with risk, filled with agonising doubt, and overwhelming in its demands on individuals who go it alone. People like Steve Jobs who founded Apple are the few who have survived the ordeal of the entrepreneur. For every Steve Jobs there are at least two or three other creative and dedicated people who fail and are left financially and emotionally bankrupt. There are scores more who are simply afraid to take such enormous risk. Once again, the mythical ideal is far removed from the harsh reality. Americans worship the entrepreneur as a valiant hero, but this glorifies the thinly disguised fact that the Herculean challenge of starting a business is so severe that the vast majority of creative talent in our society goes unused.

Exciting new possibilities are occurring, however, as corporations and creative individuals learn to form an alliance that will accommodate one another. Firms are developing an entrepreneurial environment in which talented people can work their fresh ideas into successful new ventures. Business Week reports: 'Large companies increasingly are recognising the startup as a valuable resource, and they are (making) internal changes designed to instill entrepreneurial values in their own companies'. A GE vice-president said, 'Some people are stifled in a corporate environment. We want to get them into one where they can be more creative.' And the CEO of Intel described how to avoid losing good talent: 'Our best defense is to keep this an exciting place to work and to move things to the market as rapidly as we can.' To really put some teeth into these intentions, companies like TRW are offering stock equity and other incentives that give a piece of the action to engineers, technicians and even secretaries for helping a startup get off the ground. William Miller, President of SRI, believes, 'This may be a permanent change in the way we do business.'

Conversely, small entrepreneurs are learning that big corporations are useful for providing venture capital, risk assuming capacity, access to technology and facilities, and colleagues to collaborate with. A manager who started a new venture at Convergent Technologies credited a major part of his success to the fact that 'We had a healthy company behind us, with the financial resources to help things happen.' Senior managers acted as 'kind of an informal board of directors'.

The consequence is to redefine the very nature of big business. Rather than the traditional concept of a bureaucratic hierarchy of decision-makers, large organisations are rapidly becoming what Norman Macrae, an editor at The Economist called 'confederations of entrepreneurs'. Executives at GE expressed the new philosophy this way:

> Our philosophy is to encourage talented managers to act as entrepreneurs expert in their businesses, markets and communities with direction and support from the corporate headquarters ... We're trying to reshape GE in the minds of its employees as a band of small businesses ... to take the strength of a large company and act with the agility of a small company. (Landro, 1982)

If corporations can foster this new mode of internal enterprise, the culture of business should shift away from the hierarchical fetish for controls, rational analysis, and paperwork toward that single ingredient that marks the successful entrepreneur - action. Discipline and other traditional qualities remain essential, of course, but organisational excellence is distinguished by fluid environments that offer opportunities to experiment, to take risks, to try out new ideas.

## THE INTRAPRENEUR

The role of organisational members in a network is similar to the professional model adhered to traditionally by self-employed physicians, engineers and attorneys. Employees are free to move within this organic field, contracting for various responsibilities to create their professional 'practice'. Norman Macrae foresees these trends eventually permitting even clerical tasks to be contracted for by self-managed units that may compete with one another within the organisation - the age of the intrapreneur. Macrae views the goal 'to give ordinary people more scope for becoming tycoons'. Jay Forrester envisions these future working relations this way:

> In the new organisation, an individual would not be assigned to a superior. Instead he would negotiate, as a free individual, a continually changing structure of relationships. (Forrester, 1975)

A large 'intrapreneur movement' is occurring in Sweden, other parts of Europe, and the U.S. as consultants like Gifford Pinchot III promote the idea. The focus now is on implementation, and with fleshing out the concept by defining 'intracapital' and other management practices that form the internal equivalent of an external market. There is such strong interest in the possibility of transforming bureaucracies into innovative systems that The Economist called intrapreneurship 'a major social invention'. Following are a few creative examples:

> 3M Company allows personnel to chose their assignments, and anyone with an idea for a new venture is free to shop around at various divisions to obtain venture capital and support. The result has been described this way: '(The company) is so intent on innovation that its essential atmosphere seems not like that of a large corporation but rather a loose network of laboratories and cubbyholes populated by feverish inventors and dauntless entrepreneurs who let their imaginations fly'.

Arthur D. Little is an international research and consulting firm that has been managed as an organic network for many years. The autonomy of self-managed teams of professionals at ADL is so keen that the old superior-subordinate relationship is reversed and the main responsibility of management is to support its employees. A company document states: 'Most high-ranking administrators consider their roles to be that of facilitating the work of the professional staff.'

Levi Strauss put up $3 million in venture capital in 1982 to fund six projects, one of which, 'Two-Horse Jeans', has been the firm's 'single most profitable product'. The available funding has been increased now to $4 million.

Control Data has started 80 small ventures in the past few years.

McCormick & Co has developed a bidding system that allows employees to compete for better jobs.

Advanced Technology is a new firm built completely on the principle of fostering entrepreneurial ventures among all its employees. The company 'reorganises as it grows' organically, and after five years it now employs more than 1,000 employees that produce almost $100 million in sales.

One healthy outcome is to legitimate internal competition within organisations. There is a terrible fear among those of bureaucratic heart that people or units may act in ways that are not compatible with one another - which is a bit strange in a society that professes the free enterprise ethic. Interesting cultural studies show that the degree of individualism a nation exhibits is strongly related to its wealth-producing capacity, as conservatives have always argued. The U.S. is rated as one of the most individualistic cultures, yet we have severely restricted the freedom of employees in large organisations, thereby failing to use this cultural trait very effectively.

Many successful corporations like IBM, HP, 3M, TI and others make an express policy of encouraging internal competition for the same reason it is fostered in the economy as a whole - in a world of unmanageable complexity, competition allows the best solutions to emerge. Proctor & Gamble has a policy that encourages 'a free for all among brands with no holds barred' because 'creative conflict - is the only way to keep from becoming too clumsy.' IBM favours parallel project development until a competing performance review - a 'shootout' - is held to determine which approach is to be further developed.

This freedom is also fostered by a number of variations on the traditional 9-5, 5-day-a-week job, such as the use of flexitime schedules, part-time jobs, job sharing and other such arrangements that enhance employee freedom. It is estimated that half of German workers use some variation of flexitime, as well as roughly 20 per cent of all Europeans. In Switzerland 95 per cent of workers favour the concept. In the U.S., temporary help is growing at 20 per cent per year and now includes 4 million workers, while the total number of Americans using various forms of flexible scheduling is about 30 per cent of the work force.

The most exotic impetus is coming from the growing use of computers and teleconferencing systems that allow white collar workers to conduct their work virtually anywhere, rather than in the confines of the office - creating a new breed of 'teleworkers' to operate what Alvin Toffler (1980) calls 'electronic cottage' industries. About 5 million Americans work out of their homes now, most of whom are 'telecommuters' employed by 35 companies experimenting with the idea, mainly because productivity gains can reach 50 per cent. A researcher at the University of Southern California estimates that 10 million people will be telecommuting by 1990, and Toffler (1980) claims half of the population could do so now. Those involved in the field offer some startling visions:

> Home based businesses are growing and they are going to expand terrifically - Over the next 10-20 years, most people in all levels of business will work at home at least two or three days in a week. - The way we work in this society is going to be transformed. The 9-5 era is over.

As these new freedoms unavoidably break down the old 'industrial' concept of work, an even greater variety of new working arrangements should emerge that we can only guess at. One strong possibility is to relinquish the quaint old idea that people should devote their allegiance to one single organisation. Professionals are increasingly taking on assignments for different institutions, further expanding the intrapreneur model to actually become true entrepreneurs who cultivate a professional practice that cuts across not just, departments, but entire organisations. Xerox Ltd. in England encourages middle managers to go on an 'outside consultant' basis in which they are free to work out of their homes for other firms as well. The result could not only benefit individuals, it could prove a boom to institutions by providing access to a far greater range of talent than they could employ on a full-time, permanent basis, and increasing flexibility in the work force during times of expansion and contraction.

## INTERORGANISATIONAL NETWORKS: THE GLOBAL SUPRASYSTEM

Linkages between organisations are expanding to form inter-organisational networks that connect organisations to one another. The most elementary examples are between organisations in the same field, such as trade associations, real estate brokers jointly listing property, and other traditional types. A modern example is the Briarpatch Network, consisting of almost 200 small firms that have formed a loosely connected cooperative in the San Francisco area. Another common form of cross-institutional network is the Japanese tradition of Zaibatsu in which a variety of firms join together for their mutual benefit, roughly equivalent to the American conglomerate. Small firms also cluster as satellites to a large 'host' manufacturer, which is common for major corporations and their suppliers and distributors in industries like auto manufacturing and aerospace. These arrangements are going to increase dramatically because information technology permits the proliferation of small scale ventures, such as the 'mom and pop' hi-tech cottage industries that are springing up as software and small part suppliers, forming a network of feeders to large host companies.

The more unusual of these arrangements are hybrid associations, such as the partnerships that all American auto makers have formed recently with their counterparts abroad. While GM, Ford and Chrysler compete against Toyota, Fiat, Renault and other foreign auto firms, they are also cooperating with these same adversaries in making and selling auto parts and entire cars for one another. This same trend is flourishing in hi-tech fields where a dozen or so joint ventures and research consortiums have been consummated. Even IBM and its new rival AT&T are beginning to share some computer products. Thus, the post-industrial economy is rapidly growing into new structural forms that exceed bizarre fantasies one could have dreamed of just a few years ago.

This intermeshing growth of interorganisational networks is making it difficult to tell where one organisation stops and another begins. There are estimated to be some 1,300,000 corporations in the U.S. today, 90,000 schools and universities, 330,000 churches, 17,000 miscellaneous associations, and myriad numbers of other institutions all interacting with one another to weave a rich tapestry of social structure. These links were always in place, of course, because the need was there. Now they are being facilitated as information systems increasingly connect organisations into working relationships that constitute the organic structure of the economy and society itself. The entire real estate industry, for example, is merging into a single national market operated by information exchanges that list all property in the U.S. Academics are studying the growth of this new phenomenon, which has been identified as 'interorganisational relations', 'coalitional structures', 'transorganisational systems', and related terms. Social scientists specialising in this field summed up the implications:

> Patterns of linkage and dominance between large-scale organisations are basic features of social organisation in (advanced) societies. Progress in research on interorganisational relations will very likely pave the way for analytically linking the study of organisations with the study of total societies.

At the world level, international organisations like the Law of the Sea Conference, political blocs like the Common Market, multination scientific research programmes, and other such collaborative efforts among nations are growing exponentially. Jessica Lipnack and Jeff Stamps, who have pioneered the study of networks, report the number of international organisations increased from 1,000 in 1950 to 4,000 in 1970, to 20,000 by 1982. Interinstitutional networks are rapidly coalescing into a central nervous system for the planet, with nation states, transnational corporations, and other major organisations acting as nodes in this global network. As Teilhard de Chardin and many others have speculated long ago, the conclusion should be a tightly knit constellation of human organisation covering the entire globe which interacts as a single unified organism, exhibiting unprecedented levels of higher intelligence which can only be dimly perceived but which are certain to transcend any presently known powers. Marshall McLuhan foresaw this prospect at the dawn of the Information Age: 'It is the principal aspect of the electric age that it establishes a global network that has much of the character of our central nervous system.' And Alvin Toffler updated the vision:

> What appears to be emerging is neither a corporation-dominated future nor a global government but a far more complex system similar to the matrix organisations we saw springing up in certain industries. Rather than one or a few pyramidal global bureaucracies, we are weaving nets of matrices that mesh different kinds of organisations with common interests. - In short, we are moving toward a world system composed of units densely interrelated like the neurons in a brain rather than organised like the departments of a bureaucracy.

(Toffler, 1980)

## FROM PYRAMIDS TO LIVING SYSTEMS

Naturally, this brave new world of computer based organisational networks has its drawbacks. Many people do not like the idea of working with complex, impersonal information systems, and others abhor being isolated in the home as a place of work. Some managers are nonplussed at the notion of controlling employees who work away from the office. 'We're trained to supervise people who are sitting there and who look like they're working,' said one worried manager. These problems may be alleviated as teleconferencing becomes commonly available to provide some sense of personal contact. Also, nobody advocates replacing normal human contacts with exotic information technologies, but simply to augment face-to-face relationships.

Many organisations cannot rely on an organic structure and will remain committed to the traditional 'command and control' approach. Large, highly precise projects like military operations and space launches unavoidably involve the close coordination of thousands of people in split-second timing. It is hard to envision a military commander asking his men if they would like to 'take that hill' when and how they see fit. But as IBM reminds us in its ads, information is power, and this power can be used in a variety of ways to create decentralised networks or to improve centralised control. So there will be a rich growth of different structural forms that suit the unique needs of differing institutions. If we were to think of mechanistic versus organic structures as a continuum ranging from 0-10, most bureaucratic organisations today would be at about two or three on this scale, while the adaptive ones would be located at about seven or eight. These are differences of degree, so even the most organic institutions will retain a basic hierarchy as a rudimentary skeleton supporting the networks that form their living tissues.

One of the most controversial aspects of organic systems is that multiple reporting relationships smear up the tidy lines of authority in which each subordinate reports to only one boss - the traditional injunction of scientific management insisting on 'unity of command'. The individual working in a network typically reports to leaders of several projects, so there is a common fear that such compound working relations provoke unmanageable conflict because they violate an ageless belief going back to the Bible: 'No man can serve two masters.' However, multiple allegiances are increasingly a fact of life. The danger arises when these various interests are denied to form hidden conflicts, rather than being addressed openly in a productive manner. William Ouchi (1981) reports that in Japanese companies, 'Every employee, from top to bottom, is simultaneously a member of as many as eight or a dozen work groups, each with a different task.' Digital Equipment is a successful company that encourages such freedom and self-responsibility that one executive remarked: 'Damn few people know who they work for.' Studies show that people working on several jobs of their own choosing perform far better than those on a single assignment, they develop wider knowledge, improve interdepartmental coordination, and develop a commitment to succeed.

Persons raised on the chain-of-command concept are also concerned that such freedom will result in losing organisational control. The key to understanding networks is that they offer a different form of control that is more subtle. In place of today's unrealistic responsibility for knowing 'each sparrow that falls', network executives focus on influencing only a few strategic factors that really count: the design of systems that measure performance, resolution of strategic issues, development of new technologies and skills, resolving conflict within the system, and providing help and inspiration to operating managers.

Another major drawback is that organic structures are going to be messier than the clean, tidy controls of bureaucracy, and this disorder may become widespread as networks proliferate. To an extent this is an unavoidable price we must pay for the creative productivity of free enterprise, but it is also important to see that such problems can be best understood as useful indicators of organisational performance which were formerly hidden by the use of authority. In general, the behaviour of networks can always be grasped in terms of its equivalent in free markets. Is a supervisor unable to staff his unit with voluntary transfers? In a market this would signal that working conditions are unattractive. Are some units suffering chronic losses? Again, the marketplace would allow them to fail because they are not providing a valuable function. Do wide differences in personal income exist? These disparities may disturb a sense of equity, but they encourage good performance and avoid the need to fire people for poor work. Thus, what may appear to be disorder in a network is actually vital information to be heeded.

Davis and Lawrence (1978) acknowledge all these problems, but they also feel the advantages are more compelling:

> The matrix seems to have spread despite itself and its pathologies: what was necessary was made desirable ... For generations, managers have lived with the happy fiction of dotted lines ... As executives develop greater confidence with the matrix form, they bring the dotted line relationship out of the closet, and grant it legitimacy ... in the future matrix organisations will

become almost commonplace and managers will speak less of the difficulties and pathologies of the matrix than of its advantages and benefits.

## A HORIZONTAL OUTLET TO CHALLENGE THE BABY-BOOM

The biggest problem we will face increasingly in organisational networks, however, stems from the very advantages they offer. Freedom is a difficult thing for most of us to handle, and many find the challenge of defining their own working roles an overwhelming burden. The responsibility of balancing a variety of conflicting assignments, managing multiple working relationships, facing the uncertainty of an ambiguous future, finding the will to be self-reliant, and other such problems facing the intrapreneur are not for everyone. Many will prefer the safe haven of a secure traditional job working for one boss who tells you what to do.

But these problems have always faced people who carve out their own niche in life, and the proportion of such persons is growing dramatically now. Young people tend to be bored with the narrow specialisation of jobs in a bureaucracy, which is why one third of them are switching careers. There is also a reluctance to define one's worth along the crude scale of a hierarchy, where by definition most of us are left competing at lower levels for some meagre measure of identity and meaning. A study of graduate business students showed an almost unanimous attraction to the idea of acting as intrapreneurs within a flexible organisation because it would permit the freedom to use their best talents at work, and the concept was regarded as a key solution to the revitalisation of modern economies (Helm, 1982).

Networks also offer a powerful solution to the frustration over limited job prospects. The sheer numbers of these young people threaten to overwhelm the diminishing opportunities for advancement now that middle management ranks are being automated, so they are feeling trapped in limited promotion paths. 'Hierarchy is their enemy,' claims Yale business professor Rosabeth Moss Kanter. One young manager feels 'Blocked - completely, totally, and utterly. The only way around it is out.' By redefining institutions as networks offering entrepreneurial roles, this stifled energy of the baby-boom can be channelled into horizontal avenues rather than fighting their way up the hierarchy.

And although there is a surplus of employees presently, later in a decade or so the trough of the 'baby-bust' that follows the baby boom will reverse this situation to create an acute labour shortage, so institutions will have to compete for personnel by striving to become attractie places of employment. Peter Drucker summed up the need to define new alternatives:

> The one and only way to provide satisfaction and achievement for these young managers and executives is to make jobs bigger, more challenging, more demanding and more autonomous. (Drucker, 1983)

## THE UNION OF MYTH AND REALITY

One of the greatest advantages of networks is that granting employees working freedom would alleviate the debilitating coercion that cripples most institutions today. Forcing people to work for a particular superior at assignments they do not choose is a crude carry-over from an earlier age that has massive dysfunctional consequences. The belief that power imparts control is increasingly seen as an illusion that only leads to stifling bureaucracies. In fact, the arbitrary use of formal power invariably drives the true behaviour of subordinates underground, insulating managers from the subtle realities of organisational life such that they really lose control. Studies show that the ubiquitous 'grapevine' is far stronger in institutions where free communication is suppressed, whereas in an organic system the grapevine is allowed to surface and become absorbed with the formal communication system as a legitimate, useful function (Chhuan, 1976).

This situation persists because the ideal of a competitive labour market is largely another of our cherished myths that obscures a harsh reality. Employees cannot usually move to other organisations because they would lose their seniority rights, pension benefits, and other rewards that often lock people into their present jobs, and most people typically lack information about other opportunities that are available. Internal transfers are often prevented to serve the convenience of managers. These factors cause all but the most intrepid and resourceful individuals to become virtual slaves of their employers rather than free agents. The Los Angeles Times reported the not uncommon problem of being consigned to work for a 'crazy boss': 'The unhappy fact remains that many people today work for abusive domineering and erratic bosses' (Grant and Timnick, 1980).

Eliminating this coercive use of authority would turn bureaucracies into enterprises by wiping out the messy cabals that are rife in organisations. There is a hot undercurrent of office politics smouldering beneath the surface of most typical conflict-ridden organisations today that occasionally erupts into an explosive battle or scandal. This is likely to become an even greater problem as the increasing diversity of the work force throws persons of different sexes, races, ages and values together, making it almost impossible to preselect a compatible work team. How will we manage such inhospitable differences when people have such trouble getting along with one another under the best of circumstances? The magnitude of the problem was best expressed by Robert Shrank, an academic who has studied working life by holding ordinary jobs:

> Humans seem to have an almost limitless ability to solve mechanical problems and at the same time show an enormous inability to understand how to live with each other. (Shrank, 1978)

These harsh realities could be greatly reduced by recognising that those who can't get along should simply be free to go their own way by voluntarily selecting some other assignment to disengage from a difficult situation gracefully. Allowing people to choose their work roles will then permit these heretofore hidden differences to emerge into constructive forces that are part and parcel of the strength of free markets but which have been submerged in bureaucracies. The net result should be to allow a playful but tough form of entrepreneurial management to emerge out of the illicit informal organisation that has to bootleg and connive to accomplish anything. Here is how Peters and Waterman describe this rich, informal creativity in excellent companies:

> In company after company, we found ten-person skunk works that were regularly more innovative than fully equipped R&D and engineering groups with casts of hundreds. We found example after example of internal competition, of various teams working on the same thing, of product-line duplication and overlap, of people experimenting and pointing with pride to their useful mistakes. We found myriads of tiny, quick-hit task forces ... We observed less standardization of procedure and a concomitant greater willingness to 'let them do it any way they want if it makes sense and works'. (Peters and Waterman, 1982)

Networks offer the promise of permitting the informal organisation to surface where it can become a source of energy and talent for the formal system, instead of an unacceptable deviation to be suppressed. The result would constitute the union of myth and reality that were separated by authoritarian bureaucracies, which can only make organisations more free, more human, and more productive.

## THE METASTRATEGY OF LIVING SYSTEMS

As the exploding complexity of the Information Age compels old hierarchial pyramids to move toward this more fluid new species of networks, institutions should develop the organic features that mark all living systems whether natural organisms or social organisms. Actually, excellent organisations have always behaved this way, so we are simply getting closer to the truth that others have seen:

> William Ouchi, author of Theory Z: 'My ideal of a completely efficient and perfectly integrated organisation is one that has no organizational chart, no divisions, no visible structure at all. In a sense, a basketball team that plays well fits this description, although on a small scale. The problem facing a basketball team is huge in its complexity, and the speed with which problems occur is great. Yet an effective team solves these problems with no formal reporting relationships and a minimum of specialisation of positions and tasks.' (Ouchi, 1981).

> John Sears, manager of Reagan's 1980 presidential campaign: 'By the time you get to the election, the campaign has a life of its own; it's a living, breathing thing that you no longer can control. The candidate and a few of his close advisers sit atop this creation, holding on for dear life as it plunges toward Election Day.' (Sears, 1980)

> Lewis Lapham, a journalist: 'If we could imagine the biological processes of civilization being held together by systems of trade and credit and thought, certainly as fragile and as beautiful as the ecological systems that bind together the chains of life in a pond or estuary, then...maybe we could conceive of structures infinitely more creative and diverse.' (Lapham, 1983)

From a strategic view, this living quality provides a powerful metastrategy that transcends specific strategic decisions. Organic networks create instead a strategic system that produces an unending stream of adaptive strategic changes, making them uniquely suited to the complexity of a new era. Virginia Hine, the founder of the network concept, claims:

> A network is built for change, beautifully adapted to change and the transformation of an established unchanging structure. I suspect that's why it's becoming the paradigm of the New Age. (Hine, 1981)

This 'network metastrategy' recognises that modern organisations cannot be understood or managed using the older perspective of structure as a relatively fixed and enduring arrangement, but as a pattern that emerges out of the constantly evolving, self-directed behaviour of people. A network can be thought of as a 'metastructure' - it is a living system of changing structures, rather than a structure itself. Within this fluid organisational framework, individuals and units comprise the self-arranging modular components or cells that interlock in an infinite variety of unpredictable ways - much as a set of modular toys (Leggo or the old tinker toys) - to meet changing institutional needs. Business Week described how the CEO of TRW, Ruben Mettler, is creating a new corporate strategy that exemplifies this model of the firm as an organic network:

> Mettler ... has already discovered that merely mandating policy is ineffective. So his goal is to reshape TRW's culture, pushing line managers, themselves, to look for innovative ways of improving their business, either alone or cooperatively ... (he is) setting up formal committees to encourage cross-fertilization of ideas ... a cadre of independent entrepreneurs ... new information networks ... and new financial reporting methods and productivity and quality programmes to force managers ... to search relentlessly for ways to rejuvenate mature businesses ... established networks for communicating with line and staff managers ... and developing an index of the company's technological capabilities along with a data base that allows professionals working on some 250 independent R&D projects to share knowledge. (Business Week, 1982a)

Such systems offer a unique form of power as the self-directed actions of individuals and units constantly evolve in an open-ended way, producing an uncanny ability to adapt to environmental complexity. Nobody need predict the future or direct the organisation; it feels its way along like a giant superorganism with a life all its own. In a future that should see more change than we can imagine, the advantages are enormous.

## NETWORK LEADERSHIP

The role of corporate executives should change markedly in these new institutions. Managing a traditional hierarchial pyramid was similar to operating other 'mechanisms' in an Industrial Age - rather like running an automobile or a turret lathe. The operator has to make critical decisions to keep the machine running smoothly, to insure an adequate supply of energy and parts, and to perform repairs during breakdowns. In terms of managing an organisation, this would translate into making all important business decisions, hiring people and buying raw material, resolving conflicts and crises, etc. But in an Information Age of organic networks there is no such machine - just a fluid tangle of individuals and units going their own way in a larger web of societal connections. Harlan Cleveland captured the essence of networks a decade ago:

> The organizations that get things done will no longer be hierarchical pyramids with most of the real control at the top. They will be systems - interlaced webs of tensions in which control is loose, power diffused, and centres of decision plural. (Cleveland, 1972)

This model of organisations raises difficult new questions. Without the old hierarchical structure of logically related units, what really is an institution? If it becomes simply a collection of autonomous units, what distinguishes it from the marketplace at large? What gives a network its identity, and makes it more than the sum of its individual parts? In short, what is the executive really managing?

Such questions are bound to stir a lot of anguish over the next decade or so as we grope with the transition to a New Capitalism. But I think there are two main strengths that have to be nourished carefully by executives because they constitute the fundamental identity of modern institutions. The first is the unique store of technology, information, skills, and other 'hard' resources that are shared by members of the network. For instance, conglomerates are fighting for survival because this common body of technical skills is weak. Consequently, they realise meagre benefits from their acquisitions that often do not justify the added costs and difficulty of maintaining a larger and more complex institution. Studies show that diversified companies do not perform better economically. An interesting legal case is underway in which Trans World Corporation is being sued by stockholders who want the firm to divest its ownership in Trans World Airlines, Hilton Hotels, Century 21 Real Estate, and other unrelated businesses because they believe these disparate subsidiaries have actually reduced their net worth.

Executives of the future should enhance the commonality of these technical skills and encourage collaboration among units to add to this critical resource. This ability to create synergy is the unique power of the new information technologies - they multiply value by sharing information, and this knowledge generating function lies at the heart of the Information Age. Successful firms today comprise applications of 'social technology' that are managed like research laboratories or universities in order to create valuable new knowledge. So the corporation of the future can be best thought of as not simply a production system, nor as a social system, but as a knowledge generating information system. Those that can accomplish this task will outperform others in the competitive world marketplace.

For instance, McGraw-Hill has acquired a diverse range of capabilities in publishing, information services, and electronic systems. To exploit this diversity, the strategy of the CEO, Joseph Dionne, is to use task forces, incentive systems, training, and liaison personnel to encourage cooperation among various units to form an 'intellectual community' that 'adds value' to make the 'whole more than the sum of its parts'. A key element of this strategy is the development of a computerised 'information turbine' that would comprise a central data base, fed by all units and drawn on to serve various clients, to drive the entire corporation.

The other major leadership focus is the set of beliefs, values, culture, and other 'soft' qualities that make any institution a community. There is a virtual revolution in thought underway that finally acknowledges the crucial importance of these more subtle aspects of management which can be observed in some firms with strong corporate cultures. Their leaders provide the motive force that ultimately keeps any institution together, distinguishes it from others, and drives it to success. Peters and Waterman (1982) found:

> Virtually all of the better performing companies we looked at ... had a well-defined set of beliefs ... rich tapestries of anecdote, myth and fairy tale ... the stronger the culture and the more it was directed toward the marketplace, the less need was there for policy manuals, organization charts, or detailed procedures and rules.

Successful executives avoid the temptation to get immersed in the intricacies of day-to-day operations in order to concentrate on these 'spiritual' needs that only they can provide. They inspire by offering a vision of the future, they are skilful at communicating these shared beliefs, they know how to encourage others to realise their own talents and how to subtly move large organisations. Many people do not share the values espoused by leaders like President Reagan and Prime Minister Thatcher, for instance, but almost all will acknowledge that their great strength lies in precisely this ability to transcend operational matters to focus on these charismatic aspects of leadership that are extremely crucial and powerful. Their weakness, however, lies in using a traditional hierarchical approach to impose their decisions, rather than creating more flexible forms of government that may allow the people of their nations to resolve their extraordinarily complex new problems themselves.

These new leadership responsibilities are time-consuming and they can only be attended to if there is some assurance that more routine operational matters are under control. That is precisely where the great power of information technology should liberate the modern executive to redefine his/her role in these more sophisticated terms. The powerful new robotics, computerised management networks, and other such information systems are rapidly integrating factory, office, and field operations into an automated enterprise. Managers report the change this way:

> The computerised system has eliminated 95 percent of my emergencies - I know what we need and when. Now I spend my time planning, not reacting - Before you had a vice president in an ivory tower sending out directions. Now the factory manager can make many decisions unilaterally. Managers now have more time to participate in planning and forecasting, and more time to manage people. (Business Week, 1983a)

With this new ability to control technical matters more easily, executives are becoming free to relinquish their former concern for operational problems to address the two focal points of network leadership described above. They are designing a flexible organisation that fosters innovative problem-solving, and then using their personal influence to create a tightly-knit intellectual community. Michael Maccoby's study of changing leadership styles showed that modern managers exhibit more 'flexibility about people and organisational structure, and a willingness to share power'. Thus, rather than acting as a traditional 'boss' or 'decision maker', leaders are becoming more like a coach, teacher, and catalyst, assisting their confederation of fellow entrepreneurs to assume leadership themselves for creating healthy new growth in the organic network they manage jointly. So an exciting new situation is evolving in which there is no limit on the number of people exercising shared leadership. Harlan Cleveland expressed it well:

> For a generation it has been conventionally wise to predict that more complex technologies would make for more centralization of leadership. My impression is the opposite: complexity of organization systems is diffusing the opportunity to lead and multiplying the requirement for leaders. (Cleveland, 1972)

This same metastrategy also applies to the problems currently being faced by national leaders in managing the economic macrosystem. Free enterprise economies are themselves network systems, albeit they are often overly rigid, leaderless networks lacking in useful market information and other needs that are vital to network performance, which is largely why they are in a state of crisis. The solution to these problems is not to hope that sheer laissez-faire conditions wil l suffice, nor is an interventionist 'industrial policy' needed. The key is to redesign modern economies so they behave as more effective free market systems, which is to say better networks. So the concepts presented here apply to all levels of political economy that are being transformed by the approaching Information Age: a supervisor managing an organic team of subordinates, a large organisation managing a confederation of entrepreneurs, or a nation managing a free enterprise economy.

## THE FLOWERING OF ENTERPRISE

Although this image of organic institutions has often inspired people, it has been seldom realised until the crisis in economics and the explosive growth of information technology finally forced this ideal into reality. As Prigonine and other theorists of change have pointed out, all systems remain stable for long periods until a vast increase in complexity creates such disorder that they suddenly make an evolutionary leap in a very quick, discontinuous structural transformation. After two or three decades of slowly building momentum, the transition to a new era seems to have just recently reached a critical mass where the economic system is rearranging itself into a new structural state within a few years. Now the major corporations that comprise the nexus in a complex institutional infrastructure are breaking out of the bureaucracy that has paralysed modern economies in an organisational gridlock, releasing deep reservoirs of energy that have been long suppressed. This transformation is still in its infancy, and it is impossible to predict where it will lead. But what is clear is that these changes are occurring, and they are coming spontaneously from the actions of myriad organisations at the grassroots level where revolutions originate.

Not only is this transformation occurring in corporations, it is also taking place in other institutions. Communities, universities, hospitals, churches, and other organisations are breaking up their pyramidal structures to form organic networks of collaborative working relationships. The Catholic Church revised its code of canon law in 1983 to redefine the church from a traditional hierarchical society governed by the clergy into a community of believers endowed with rights and obligations. Universities and hospitals increasingly are organised along the line of a matrix with disciplines cutting across programme offices for conducting research, degrees that are offered, and the other activities. John Naisbitt observes:

> Centralized structures are crumbling all across America - the people of this country are rebuilding America from the bottom up into a stronger, more balanced, more diverse society.(Naisbitt, 1982)

The same trend is also taking place in other Western nations. England is encouraging new venture formation as their staid old financial markets are deregulated to permit very ungentlemanly competition. The socialist government in France is moving toward free enterprise concepts to rejuvenate their stagnating economy. And even the Japanese tradition of lifetime loyalty to one employer is breaking down now as talented professionals switch jobs.

As this imperative of the Information Age unfolds, institutions should increasingly foster an unstructured form of interaction among internal ventures that pass resources, employees, and information freely across the organisational hierarchy and its permeable external boundaries. The resulting economic conditions - numerous small competing enterprises, freedom of entry and exit into contracts, and, above all, the widespread availability of more acurate market information - constitute the requirements that economists have defined for the operation of 'perfect markets'. Large institutions are thereby becoming part of the open marketplace, bringing the advantages we have always attributed to the free enterprise system directly into the internal operation of organisations themselves: flexibility for adaptive change, easier management of complexity, entrepreneurial freedom for innovation, and other advantages for coping with a turbulent environment.

Thus, the widespread development of organisational networks seems likely to raise to life the classical laws of economic theory formulated long ago. Rather than simply being unrealistic textbook ideals, these elegant, precise principles may begin to closely approximate actual economic behaviour as the organic decisions of near-perfect markets replace the elitist solutions of bureaucratic corporations and governments that produced blunt, crude forms of control fraught with the risk of limited vision and human rebellion. The beauty of free enterprise is that it slowly but perpetually draws on the collective ingenuity of countless individuals to evolve the most brilliant new possibilities that could never have been dreamed by any one group, and it does so while preserving personal freedom. As organisational networks become woven together, this more organic economic system will liberate creative individuals, reconcile the conflict between freedom and control, unify the formal myths of institutional life with the richer reality of the informal organisation, and take advantage of both the power of large economic concentrations as well as the innovation that only occurs in small ventures. Politically and geographically, it will link together major institutions in the private and public sectors to form international systems of collaboration that unify the earth into a coherent whole.

This structural transformation should realise the original vision which Adam Smith and others saw only vaguely at the start of the Industrial Revolution. Before this century ends, I suspect that modern economies are likely to become alive with the growth of infinite numbers of small, innovative, constantly changing enterprises offering an endless variety of sophisticated goods and services. This transition will require many years of disruptive change, and there will always be a need to retain some traditional controls. But over the long term the relentless growth of information technology should cause the free enterprise system as a whole to bloom into full flower as a vastly more productive and liberating foundation for the New Capitalism.

## REFERENCES

Ackoff, R.L. and Emery, F.E. (1972) On Purposeful Systems, Aldine-Atherton, Chicago

Affleck, J.G. (1978) 'The Constructive Orchestration of Chaos', Management for the Future, 3

Baker, R. (1970) 'What Did You Do Today', New York Times, June 9

Beer, S. (1975) Platform for Change, Wiley, New York

Beitzel, G. (1983) Presentation to a Committee of the US Senate

Bell, D. (1973) The Coming of Post-Industrial Society, Basic Books, New York

Bennis, W. (1966) Beyond Bureaucracy, McGraw-Hill, New York

Brown, L. (1984) 'The Automobile's Future', The Futurist, June

Business Week (1982a) 'TRW leds a Revolution in Managing Technology', November 15

Business Week (1982b) 'An About Face in TI's Culture',

Business Week (1983a) 'A New Era for Management', April 25,

Business Week (1983b) November 29, 96

Business Week (1983c) 'The Tinkerer Who Turned on Detroit', April 25

Business Week (1983d) 'Texas Instruments Cleans Up Its Act',

Chandler, A. (1962) Strategy and Structure, MIT Press, Cambridge, Mass.

Chhuan, P. (1976) 'A Study of Grapevine Communications Within Organizations', An Unpublished Paper, The American University

Churchman, C.W. (1977) 'A Philosophy for Complexity', in Linstone, H. A. and Simmonds, W. H. C. (eds.), Futures Research: New Directions, Addison-Wesley, Reading, Mass.

Cleveland, H. (1972) The Future Executives, Harper & Row, New York

Cornish, E. (1977) The Study of the Future, World Future Society, Washington, D.C.

Cornuelle, R. (1975) De-engaging America, Random House, New York, p. 87

Davis, D. (1973) 'The Soft Sell', Newsweek, July 23

Davis, S.M. and Lawrence, R.R. (1978) 'Problems of Matrix Organizations', Harvard Business Review, May-June

Drucker, P. (1976) 'The Wisdom of Peter Drucker', MBA, October

Drucker, P. (1980) 'Managing the Information Explosion', The Wall Street Journal, April 10

Drucker, P. (1983) 'Squeezing the Firm's Midriff Bulge' The Wall Street Journal, March 25

Ferguson, M. (1980) The Aquarian Conspiracy, J P Tarcher, Los Angeles

Forrester, J. W. (1975) 'A New Corporate Design', Industrial Management Review, July, 824

Galbraith, J. K. (1967) The New Industrial State, Signet, New York

Galbraith, J. and Nathanson, D. (1978) Strategy Formulation, West Publishing, St Paul, Minn. 56-7

Gilmore, T. (1983) Business Week, April 25, 61

Goggins, W. (1973) 'How the Multidimensional Structure Works at Dow Corning', Harvard Business Review, January-February, p.142

Grant, L. and Timnick, L. (1980) 'A Nightmare: Working for a 'Crazy' Boss', The Wall Street Journal, September 19

Greenleaf, R. (1977) Servant Leadership, Paulist Press, New York

Guenther, R. (1983a) 'Office Building Values Fall', The Wall Street Journal, March 16

Guenther, R. (1983b) 'Office Glut', The Wall Street Journal, October 7

Halal, W. E. (1980) Strategic Planning in Major U.S. Corporations, General Motors Report

Helm, S. (1982) 'A Review of Intrapreneurialism' (Unpublished paper), George Washington University

Hiltz, S. R. and Turoff, M. (1978) The Network Nation, Addison-Wesley, Reading, Mass.

Hine, V. (1981) 'Networks Empower Social Change', Leading Edge Bulletin, July, 20

Landro, L. (1982) 'Electric Switch', The Wall Street Journal, July 12

Lapham, L. (1983) '..and a Feeling of Hope', Washington Post, January, 1

Levison, R. (1983) The Decentralized Company, Amacom, New York, preface, 20-1

Naisbitt, J. (1982) Megatrends, Warner Books, New York

Osborne, A. (1979) Running Wild: The Next Industrial Revolution, Osbourne/McGraw-Hill, Berkeley, Calif.

Osnos, A. (1983) 'Hi-Tech Wizard Sees Brave New World in '90s', The Washington Post, March 6

Ouchi, W. (1981) Theory Z, p.90

Peters, T. J. and Waterman, R. H. (1982) In Search of Excellence, Harper and Row, New York, 42-4, 113

Sears, (1980) 'A Matter of Timing', Washington Post, October 9

Servan-Schreiber, J. (1980) The World Challenge, Simon and Schuster, New York

Shrank, K. (1978) Ten Thousand Working Days, MIT Press, Cambridge, Mass.

Simon, H. (1960) 'The Corporation: Will It Be Managed by Machines?', in Anshen, M. and Bach, G. L. (eds.) Management and Corporations 1985, McGraw-Hill, New York

Spencer, W. (1979) Berkeley Independent Gazette, October 31

Time (1983) 'A New World Dawns', January 3

Toffler, A. (1980) The Third Wave, Bantam, New York

Townsend, P. (1978) Up the Organization, Fawcett, New York

Vaill, P. (1982) 'The Purposing of High Performing Systems', Organizational Dynamics, Autumn

Van Zelst, R. (1952) 'Sociometrically Selected Work Teams Increase Production', Personnel Psychology, Autumn, Vol.5, No.3

Weick, K.E. (1977) 'Organization Design: Organization as Self-Designing Systems' Organizational Dynamics, Autumn

# 13. Formulating Information Technology Strategies

by Michael Earl

## STRATEGIC ADVANTAGE

It is increasingly asserted that information technology (IT) is becoming a strategic resource. The convergence of data processing, communications and automation technologies, the reducing cost trends in computing and the advances in software provide business with new strategic options in a political and economic context which both needs technological innovation and is encouraging it - a context of global competition, economic uncertainty and industry deregulation. As evidence we see IT being exploited for strategic advantage as firms make spectacular competitive thrusts on the back of information systems, as sector boundaries are eroded and fused by the joint application of computing and telecommunications, as smokestack industries invest for survival in advanced manufacturing technologies and as new firms are created by making a software- and hardware-based business of information. A stream of persuasive articles has emerged to make these points (Parsons, 1983; McFarlan, 1984; Benjamin et al, 1984; Porter and Millar, 1986) and the concept of information as a strategic resource is further developed by King in this volume.

We can generalise that IT can be applied for strategic advantage in at least four different ways:

- to gain competitive advantage

- to improve productivity and performance

- to enable new ways of managing and organising

- to develop new businesses

The first class is exemplified by such well known examples as American Hospital Supply's market share success which was won by customer and supplier linkages through computer-based inventory and ordering systems. Likewise, Merrill Lynch's acclaimed inventory and ordering systems or their applauded use of computing and communications to offer its integrated financial services package, the Cash Management Account, or Nottingham Building Society's thrust into homebanking with its Homelink facility. Exploitation of IT by the automobile industry in both manufacturing and distribution typifies the second class (as discussed by Ingram in Chapter 10), whilst a specific example perhaps is afforded by United Airlines' use of teleconferencing when planning and controlling its flight operations. New ways of managing and organising are illustrated by Rank Xerox's experiments with executive home-working or DEC's use of expert systems to change the operations, management and functioning of its engineering personnel. 'Businesses of information' would be typified by Reuters' commercial development of its vast information processing capability or information retrieval and analyses services such as Lockheed's Dialog facility and the distributor/franchise operations it has spawned.

A management consequence of this new era is that IT and information systems (IS) should no longer be seen as just a support activity serving management's planning and control needs and automating business operations. They also should be harnessed to support the firm's strategy (Scott Morton and Rockart, 1984; Parsons, 1983) and be exploited as a potential strategic weapon (McFarlan, 1984; Porter and Millar, 1986; Wiseman, 1985) and even be considered as inseparable from strategy in general (Kantrow, 1980). These new perspectives have led to renewed demands to plan the use of IT and IS strategically (Earl, 1984; Lucas and Turner, 1982) but perhaps with a stronger eye on strategic advantage than earlier workers such as King (1978) and McLean and Soden (1977) called for. To the former rationales of ensuring top management direction, defining a hardware path and systems framework, forecasting resource requirements, allocating scarce resources effectively and controlling information processing are now added the needs to exploit the strategic opportunities afforded by IT and to align IT with business strategies.

Formulation of IT strategies thus would seem to be a key concern and task for senior managements as well as IT executives. Surveys by Earl (1985) and Dickson et al (1984) tend to confirm this. Furthermore IT strategy formulation may be one means of bridging the 'strategic gap' emphasised by several writers, namely the difficulty that many executives have in both understanding how IT can contribute to business strategy and recognising opportunities to exploit IT. This paper, derived from active and on-going research in UK and US organisations, seeks to provide some frameworks for IT strategy formulation - frameworks which offer practical guidance, emphasise the differences in strategic context of different firms and recognise the complexity of managing IT strategically in practice. Hopefully it adds to the prescription of my paper in the previous volume of this series that in the information age firms should formulate IT strategies.

## STRATEGIC FRAMEWORKS

Early work in IT strategy formulation has often produced frameworks for analysis. They are labelled awareness, opportunity and positioning frameworks. Awareness frameworks seek to educate on the strategic possibilities and impacts of IT, opportunity frameworks provide a means of identifying strategic opportunities offered by IT and positioning frameworks help a firm establish the strategic importance of IT and the management implications. These different frameworks, their purposes, limitations and potential are examined in detail elsewhere (Earl, 1985). One, however, which has aimed to help management identify opportunities, but which is perhaps more useful as a pedagogic, awareness device, is that of Benjamin et al (1984) reproduced in Figure 13.1 with some of the example case studies referenced earlier, shown within.

**Figure 13.1: Strategic Opportunities Matrix**

| | Competitive Market Place | Internal Operations |
|---|---|---|
| Significant Structural Change | Merrill Lynch | DEC |
| Traditional Products and Processes | American Hospital Supply | United Airlines |

Source: Benjamin et al, (1984)

Conflating the two parameters underpinning the axes of their matrix, the Benjamin et al paper suggested two questions that senior executives should ask: (a) can IT be used to make a significant structural change in the way we are doing business in order to gain competitive advantage; and (b) should we exploit IT to improve our approach to the market place or to improve internal operations? As we shall see later awareness and opportunity frameworks for analysis do have an important but partial role in IT strategy formulation. More detailed, micro and operational approaches, however, are required to spot specific opportunities, Porter and Millar's (1986) value chain analysis perhaps being one of the more promising techniques - not least in that it is derivative of Porter's (1985) recent work on competitive advantage.

McFarlan et al (1983) have produced perhaps the most well known positioning framework (Figure 13.2), in which the past and future strategic impact of IS and IT are assessed to produce four metaphors to describe the requirements of information management.

**Figure 13.2: Strategic Grid**

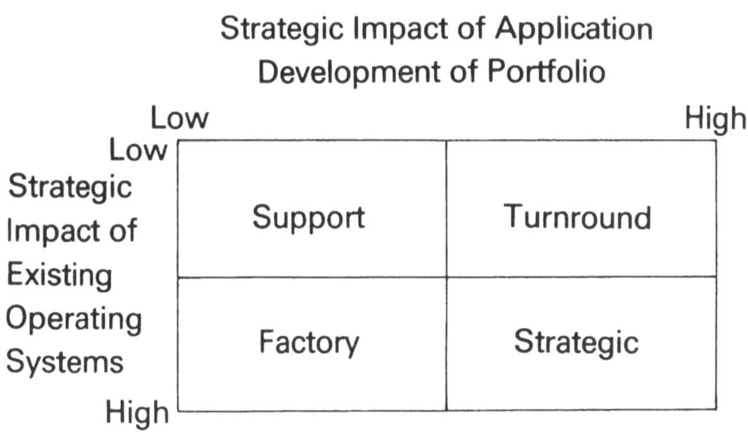


Source: McFarlan et al, 1983

Many of the stunning examples of IT being applied for strategic advantage have arisen in companies and sectors which might be described as 'turnaround' or 'strategic' - but not all. IT does have the potential to be a strategic tool or weapon even in 'support' or 'factory' contexts. For example, expert systems are being used for offensive competitive strategy in 'support' situations and niches of advanced information technology may create new business opportunities in seemingly 'factory' situations. Furthermore as we become an information society, or an information economy, and particularly as firms and sectors reach out into other firms and sectors through IT, any organisation can find itself faced with strategic opportunities or threats through the actions of others. (I have described elsewhere (1984) the forces being exerted on my own academic institution.) Thus my own more descriptive positioning framework in Table 13.1 may be more generally appropriate for those concerned with strategic advantage.

**Table 13.1: Strategic Positioning of IT**

| Strategic Use of IT | Characteristic |
|---|---|
| IT is the means of delivering goods and services in the sector | Computer-based transaction systems underpin business operations |
| Business strategies increasingly depend on IT for their implementation | Business and functional strategies require a major automation, information, communications capability and are made possible by these technologies |
| IT potentially provides new strategic opportunities | Specific applications of technologies are exploited for developing the business and changing ways of managing |

This picture suggests there are three ways in which IT can be seen as a strategic resource. The three statements can be formulated as questions and if a firm, division or strategic business unit scores positive on any of them, we can posit that IT strategies should be formulated. As we shall see later, the mode of strategy formulation may vary according to the firm's positioning in this framework.

## IT STRATEGY FORMULATION

As executives search for IT strategy formulation methodologies which provide a substantive and ongoing procedure for both directing the application of IT and gaining strategic advantage from it, a common confusion can be found. This exists partly because of the loose terminology of planning and strategy in discourse and the literature, partly because organisations are still learning how to plan IT and partly because senior management tends to be concerned about both technology policy issues and business needs and about information resources and controlling them. The delineation in Figure 13.3 between ends and means or between applications and delivery has proved to be valuable in clarifying concepts and practice in formulating IT strategies.

**Figure 13.3: Information Systems Strategies Delineated**

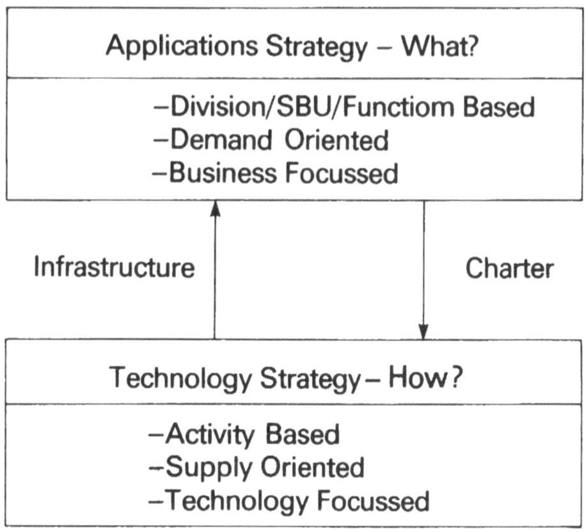

In business it is not unusual to find general managers with inadequate experience and qualifications addressing the technology strategy and IS executives, who cannot know all about business needs, trying to drive the applications strategy. It is common to find steering comittees quite confused about which of these levels of strategy is their concern. Of course the two levels are not entirely separable - application needs suggest the charter for the IS function and the technology posture provides the infrastructure which underpins applications. Indeed Lucas and Turner (1982) contend that 'effective control of information processing' (much of which can be achieved through technology strategy) 'is a necessary prerequisite to the integration of technology with strategy' (applications strategy).

The remainder of this paper focuses on formulating the applications strategy - on aligning the application of IT with business strategy and on seeking strategic opportunities for the exploitation of IT. However, whilst these are goals that most organisations would wish to pursue, my own research suggests that there are at least three different ways of proceeding - three distinctive modes of formulating IT strategies (Table 13.2). They relate to the positioning framework in Table 13.1, and emphasise the interdependence between the two levels of strategy depicted in Figure 13.3. The infrastructure-led mode is typified by some banks.

**Table 13.2: Strategy Modes and Methods**

| IT STRATEGY MODE | EMPHASIS IN STRATEGY FORMULATION |
|---|---|
| Infrastructure-led | Bottom-up/Leg 2 |
| Business-led | Top-down/Leg 1 |
| Mixed | Inside-out/Leg 3 |

They depend on IT to drive their delivery and transaction systems - a failed computer network brings down the bank's operations, an inefficient one raises its operating costs and an inflexible one constrains its product development. Consequently banks have had to invest in IT infrastructure, lay down the foundations for the future, be guided by technological executives on what posture to adopt at what pace, and plan resources in some ignorance of future business needs. This technology-driven mode has been reported as being implicitly criticised by some workers, with the observation that senior bank executives are now beginning to consider market opportunities and business needs in their IT planning (Touche Ross, 1985). However without building an infrastructure, the banks were limited strategically and in many cases a technological view had to be taken despite the financial and economic uncertainty they faced and the lack of top management vision, understanding and priority often prevailing.

The automobile sector provides a good example of the business-led mode. For British Leyland, their corporate strategy for survival and regeneration identified that investment in IT for manufacturing, distribution and marketing was essential. However IT plans and investment proposals were derivative, if integral, elements of the business strategy. Ford's moves into computer-aided engineering and computer-aided design equally appear to be business-inspired. In contrast, General Motors' (computing) mission for, and management of, IT increasingly seems to reflect an infrastructure-led approach, only loosely connected to business needs, which some observers judge to be somewhat risky. In some senses, unlike banking and financial services, the scope, direction and justification of IT in automobile manufacturing is more certain, analysable and manageable. A business-led approach thus is more feasible.

In many manufacturing and service businesses, aggregate IT spend may never be a large percentage of sales, but in specific areas it may offer potential for product development, new management methods, organisational change or even new business creation. The challenge here is to identify, facilitate and resource such opportunities. Exploitation here should be in line with current business needs or future strategic direction but often infrastructure is a key enabler - hardware capability, software aids, database facilities and specialist support are required to both prompt and deliver strategically clever applications of IT. A mixed approach is needed and often seems to be premised on, and promoted by, a corporate desire and policy to exploit IT for strategic advantage.

The multiple methodology for IT strategy formulation described in the next section can be tailored to fit the above three strategy modes.

## A MULTIPLE METHODOLOGY

Organisations' felt need to plan IS together with the more recent desires to align IS development with business plans and exploit IT strategically have spawned several methodologies for strategy formulation and prompted some evaluative research. Early work borrowed from long range planning, proposing approaches such as PPBS and arguing the benefits of top-down versus bottom-up philosophies (McFarlan, Nolan and

Norton, 1973). Later work proposed general frameworks to discover business strategy and interpret it into IS needs (King, 1978) or to analyse internal and external environments, strengths and weaknesses and business objectives to formulate IS goals (McLean and Soden, 1977). More recently, more structured techniques have been developed both by academics and consultants, one example being the 'critical success factors' approach (Bullen and Rockart, 1984) which seeks to logically derive business goals, critical success factors needed to achieve the goals and IS requirements needed to support or deliver the critical success factors. At the same time computer manufacturers have continued to develop or enhance their planning tools, an example being IBM's 'Business Systems Planning'.

Evaluative work has sought to discover when, how and whether these methods work, for example Shank et al's (1985) appraisal of 'critical success factors' and McLean's (1983) comparison of this method with Business Systems Planning. Useful guidelines are beginning to emerge, but in general the conclusions seem to be that most techniques work in the appropriate context, with skilled analysts and in a supportive environment. Sullivan (1985), however, recently has argued for a contingency approach where he proposes that different methods suit different contexts, the key determinants being how diffused are the organisation and its technology and how infused (how well developed and important) are the applications. Pyburn (1983) too derived a situational approach when he suggested three different approaches to IS strategic planning dependent on factors such as business environment, technological context, management style and organisational structure.

My own work suggests a more complex approach is needed. The resultant framework however does have a contingent implication. A multiple methodology is proposed because in practice a firm's management is seeking a way forward bearing three questions in mind: (a) what are our business needs; (b) what are the technology opportunities; (c) what is our capability and current position? Figure 13.4 depicts this multiple approach. No one methodology is likely to satisfy these three concerns or always be the preferred approach.

The desire and need for formal attempt to match IS investment with business needs is met by leg one of the model. It proposes the identification of business plans and goals, followed by deduction of IS/IT needs using an analytical approach with a formal methodology and requiring inputs from a coalition of line, general and IS managers. Essentially 'top-down' it 'puts the business into IS'. Commonly business plans and goals are not formally available or are ill-defined and rarely will be expressed in terms easily translated into IS/IT needs. Thus a formal methodology is required to both elicit business strategy and derive

**Figure 13.4: IT Strategic Planning: A Multiple Methodology**

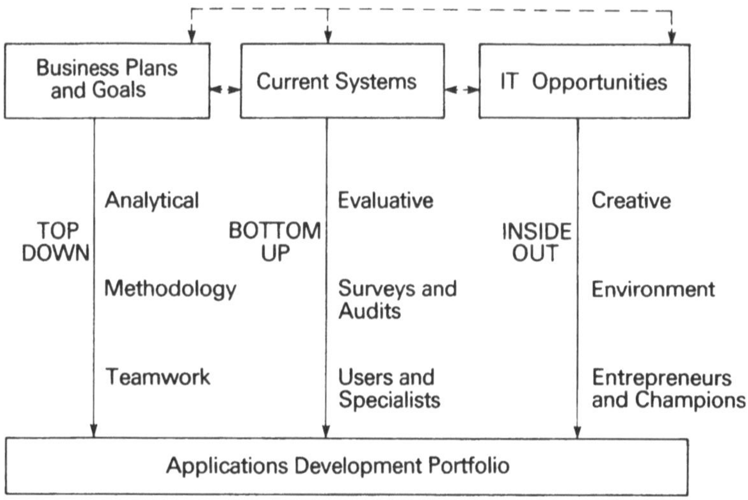


IS needs. The properties required are that it is easily understood and used by line and general managers, it can cope with varying robustness of business strategy, it does not consume too much time or resource, it can be repeated as circumstances inevitably change and, as a result of these needs and because it could not achieve anything else, it points to directional IS needs and not detailed specifications. The 'critical success factors' approach seems to possess some of these qualities (Bullen and Rockart, 1984) and from my own experience is particularly valuable when prior strategy analyses have been done, but also provides a workmanlike solution where strategic understanding is low. Figure 13.4 displays a partial and slightly generalised example of one application of the method.

Leg three of the model presents a quite different proposition. The research evidence is beginning to suggest that opportunities for innovative use of IT are neither identified nor prosecuted by the formal and structured approach suggested by leg one. Indeed one recent study (Runge, 1985) found that conditions for exploitation of telecommunications-based systems for competitive advantage more closely resembled the patterns characteristic of industrial innovation. Investigations into some of the exemplar cases quoted earlier in the paper have emphasised that often focused and intensive one-off studies preceded the decision to make a strategic strike through IT. In other cases, opportunities to apply IT to exploit competitive forces seem to be identified by entrepreneurial managers operating at the boundaries of the business who see how to build on existing systems to reach out to customers and suppliers. Internal application of IT for strategic advantage is often promoted and prosecuted by 'brightsparks' who have been given hardware and software tools with which to experiment and have been given the necessary technical support and education. In many cases these new strategic developments have been backed by a product champion who worked around the formal procedures inherent in the IS administration of large organisation, (Runge, 1985). Thus the requirement here is for a creative emphasis fostered by an innovative environment where special studies can be resourced, organisational processes are not defeated by systems and structures, and IT aids and support are provided. This environment must be populated by entrepreneurs, product champions and brightsparks placed in appropriate locations. Leg three therefore can be thought of as an 'inside-out' approach.

Leg two is more bottom-up. Most organisations, when they begin or renew their attempts to plan IT strategically, need to understand and evaluate their current IT investment. This is for several reasons. It may be important to demonstrate the quality and coverage of IS hitherto in order to gain, retain or work for credibility. Top management is not often informed about the current IS position of the business. IT strategies are rarely developed from a greenfield site but have to recognise the strengths and weaknesses of the current applications portfolio. Then examination of current systems may suggest some could either already be better exploited for strategic advantage or be built upon to yield significant added value. Thus an evaluative approach is required, typically satisfied by commissioning an audit or survey of current systems. Several techniques exist; the necessary elements are examination of both business value (preferably by the users) and technical quality (preferably by the specialists) of each major system, considering not only the existing performance but also the system's potential. It also may be useful to appraise the capability of the organisation to develop further, considering such factors as user awareness, management support, IS administration and technological experience - as implied by Gibson and Nolan's (1974) model of the stages of EDP growth.

This three-legged multiple methodology recognises that alignment of IT strategy with business needs is essential, that innovation and ideation is more a process of fermentation and opportunism than of structured analysis and that many significant developments and much of what is feasible grow incrementally out of today's inherited position. Furthermore, a three-pronged approach is required to cope with ever-changing external demands, variability of internal capability, the stage of an organisation's IT historiography and the pace and breadth of technological change. From time to time, however, and from business to business the emphasis will change. A contingent overlay of time and situation is proposed in the next section.

## Planning to Plan

A multiple methodology may seem to contradict the notion of different modes of IT strategic planning proposed in Figure 13.3. However each mode represents an emphasis and each of the three legs of the multiple methodology can be foregrounded or backgrounded according to the relevant mode (Table 13.2). For instance the most concrete guidance available in an infrastructure-led mode is to learn from the present systems base. Thus the bottom-up leg is very influential, but modified by a vision of business needs identified by leg one and by a desire to create a facilitative technological context in which the key actors of leg three can prosper. In a business-led mode, the organisation needs to invest heavily in leg one but not be deaf to indicators derived from leg two or to ideas emanating from leg three. In a mixed mode, all three legs are important but strategic opportunities are more likely to emerge by adopting loose IT policies, creating a soft as much as hard technological infrastructure and paying close attention to organisational and management development, that is designing explicitly for leg three.

In practice, however, all this takes time. Organisations seem to learn very gradually how to plan IT strategically. Part of the required learning is that no one technique will work. Another lesson to be recognised is that the early benefits of IT strategic planning are <u>process</u> not product gains. Table 13.3 documents the five dominant expected and realised benefits reported by a sample of large organisations who were in the early stages of formulating IT strategies. Educational, commitment and involvement benefits seem to be the principal outcomes - benefits which are not insignificant given the history of IS in most organisations.

In many organisations, however, a related lesson emerges. Close alignment of IT plans with business strategy takes time. Often to gain credibility, to enlist the support of all relevant managers and to be able to provide an IS base on which business strategies can depend, the <u>evaluative</u>, bottom-up approach of leg two is dominant in the first two years. As managerial and organisational confidence and competence

Table 13.3: Benefits of IT Planning

| Expected Benefits | Realised Benefits |
|---|---|
| Improved top managment support | Improved top management support |
| Improved user involvement | Improved resource forecasting |
| Improved resource forecasting | Improved business planning |
| Improved business planning | Improved user communication |
| Understanding the organisation/business | Understanding the organisation/business |

grow, strategic direction and innovation - as represented by legs one and three - begin to appear. It is some time, perhaps four to five years, before good alignment of business strategies and IT plans is achieved. By then, expectations may be over-ambitious, technologies have advanced further and conditions have changed so that it becomes important to recognise that all three legs of the multiple methodology are required with perhaps different emphases one year with another.

This evolution is idealised into a stage model in Figure 13.5. It is important to recognise and understand the dynamics behind the model; then organisations can decide how to plan and position themselves in the progression. The biggest danger in IT strategy formulation is that managements expect too much too soon and then give up out of impatience and inexperience.

## CONCLUSION

Formulating IT strategies is the major concern for many IS executives today as well as for their senior managements. The need may be obvious but discovering an appropriate method is more difficult. Furthermore strategy formulation methodologies are only one element required for meaningful strategic management of IT (see Earl, 1985). Nevertheless an appreciation that a multiple methodology is more likely to work, that the emphasis or mode should fit the strategic context, that balance of methods will change over time and that the early benefits are more likely to be soft rather than hard, should help organisations pursue strategic advantage through IT in a practical manner, with realistic expectations.

**Figure 13.5: A Critical Success Factors Approach**

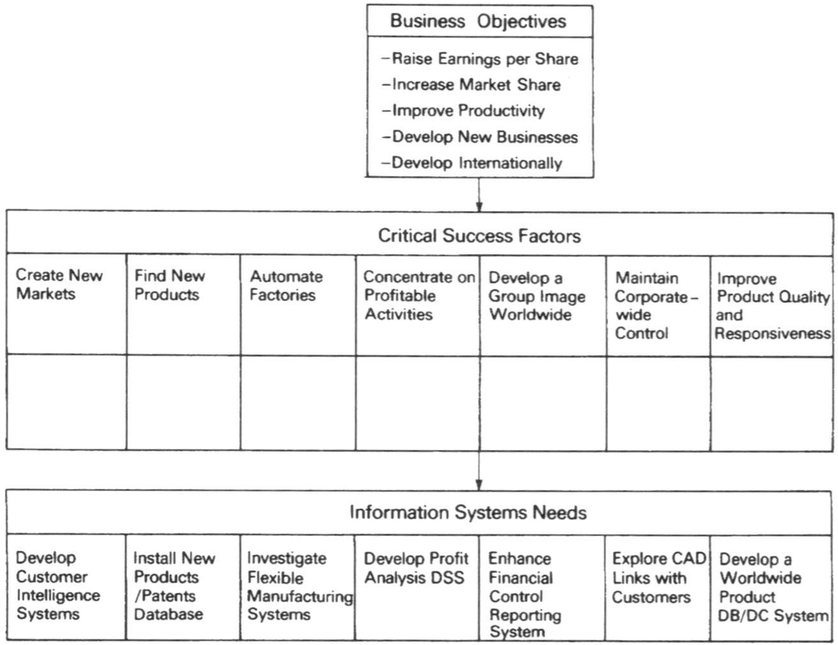

## REFERENCES

Benjamin, R.I., Rockart, J.F., Scott Morton, M.S. and Wyman, J. (1984) 'Information Technology: A Strategic Opportunity', Sloan Management Review, Spring, pp. 3-10

Bullen, C.V. and Rockart, J.F. (1984) 'A Primer on Critical Success Factors', CISR Working Paper No. 69, Sloan School of Management, MIT, June

Computing (1985) 'A Driving Force in the Technical Race', Computing, 25 June, pp. 7-8

Dickson, G.W., Leitheiser, R.L. and Wetherbe, J.C. (1984) 'Key Information Systems Issues for the 1980s', MIS Quarterly, September, pp. 135-159

Earl, M.J. (1984) 'Emerging Trends in the Management of New Information Technologies', in Piercy, N. (ed.) The Management Implications of New Information Technologies, Croom Helm/ Nichols, Beckenham

Earl, M.J. (1985) 'Information Systems Strategy Formulation', in Boland R.J. (Jnr.) and Hirscheim, R. (eds.) Critical Issues in Information Systems Research, J. Wiley

Gibson, C.F. and Nolan, R.L. (1974) 'Managing the Four Stages of EDP Growth', Harvard Business Reivew, January/February, pp. 76-88

Kantrow, A.M. (1980) 'The Strategy-Technology Connection,' Harvard Business Review, July-August, pp. 6-21

King, W.R. (1978) 'Strategic Planning for MIS', MIS Quarterly, March, pp. 27-37

Lucas, H.C. and Turner, J.A. (1982) 'A Corporate Strategy for the Control of Information Processing', Sloan Management Review, Spring, pp. 25-36

McFarlan (1984) 'Information Technology Changes the Way You Compete', Harvard Business Review, May/June, pp. 98-103

McFarlan, F.W., McKenney, J.L. and Pyburn, P. (1983) 'The Information Archipelago - Plotting a Course', Harvard Business Review, January/February, pp. 145-156

McFarlan, F.W., Nolan, R.L. and Norton, D.P. (1973) Information Systems Administration, Holt, Reinhart and Winston

McLean, E.R. (1983) 'Strategic Planning for MIS: An Update', Information Systems Working Paper, *4-83, Graduate School of Management, UCLA

McLean, E.R. and Soden, J.V. (1977) Strategic Planning for MIS, J Wiley

Parsons, G.L. (1983) 'Information Technology: A New Competitive Weapon', Sloan Management Review, Fall, pp. 3-14

Porter, M.E. (1985) Competitive Advantage, Free Press

Porter, M.E. and Millar, V.E. (1986) 'How Information Gives you Competitive Advantage', Harvard Business Review, July/August, pp. 149-160

Pyburn, P.J. (1983) 'Linking the MIS Plan with Corporate Strategy: An Exploratory Study', MIS Quarterly, June, pp. 1-14

Runge, D. (1985) 'Using Telecommunications for Competitive Advantage', unpublished DPhil thesis, Oxford University

Scott Morton, M.S. and Rockart, J.F. (1984) 'Implications of Changes in Information Technology for Corporate Strategy', Interfaces, 14, i, January/February, pp. 84-95

Shank, M.E., Boynton, A.C. and Zmud, R.W. (1985) 'Critical Success Factor Analysis as a Methodology for MIS Planning', MIS Quarterly, June, pp. 121-129

Sullivan, C.H. Jnr (1985) 'Systems Planning in the Information Age', Sloan Management Review, Winter, pp. 3-12

Touche Ross International (1985) The Impact of Technology on Banking, Touche Ross International

Wiseman, C. (1985) Strategy and Computers, Dow Jones-Irwin

## AUTHOR INDEX

## SUBJECT INDEX